Learn Node.js by Building 6 Projects

Build six practical and instructive Node.js projects

Eduonix Learning Solutions

Packt

BIRMINGHAM - MUMBAI

Learn Node.js by Building 6 Projects

Acquisition Editor: Dominic Shakeshaft
Project Editor: Kishor Rit
Content Development Editor: Monika Sangwan
Technical Editor: Gaurav Gavas
Copy Editor: Tom Jacob
Indexer: Mariammal Chettiyar
Production Coordinator: Shantanu N. Zagade

First published: March 2018

Production reference: 1300318

Published by Packt Publishing Ltd.
Livery Place
35 Livery Street
Birmingham
B3 2PB, UK.

ISBN 978-1-78829-363-1

www.packtpub.com

Contributors

About the author

Eduonix Learning Solutions creates and distributes high-quality technology training content. Our team of industry professionals have been training manpower for more than a decade. We aim to teach technology the way it is used in industry and professional world. We have professional team of trainers for technologies ranging from Mobility, Web to Enterprise and Database and Server Administration.

Packt is searching for authors like you

If you're interested in becoming an author for Packt, please visit `authors.packtpub.com` and apply today. We have worked with thousands of developers and tech professionals, just like you, to help them share their insight with the global tech community. You can make a general application, apply for a specific hot topic that we are recruiting an author for, or submit your own idea.

Table of Contents

Preface

Welcome to *Learn Node.js by building 6 Projects*.

Node.js is an open-source, cross-platform runtime environment for developing server-side web applications. Node.js is built on the Google Chrome V8 JavaScript engine, which makes it very fast. It is event-driven and uses a non-blocking I/O model. This makes it asynchronous, and one of the biggest advantages for using asynchronous operations is that you can maximize the usage of a single CPU as well as memory.

The simple answer to what Node.js is it's JavaScript on the server. Usually, JavaScript is executed on the client in the browser, but Node.js allows it to be on the server. In this book, we'll be creating 6 different web applications using Node.js along with many other technologies, mostly are Node modules. We'll be using `npm`, which is node package modules. It allows us to extend the functionality beyond the core Node system.

For this book, you should know HTML and CSS, and you should have a basic understanding of JavaScript. You should also a basic understanding of programming fundamentals, so things like variables, arrays, conditionals, loops, all that good stuff. If you know that, then that's really going to help you out. Knowing HTTP requests and RESTful interface is not required but will definitely help you out if you do have an idea of what some of that stuff is.Who this book is for

If you are a web developer or a student who wants to learn about Node.js in a hands-on manner, this book will be perfect for you. A basic understanding of HTML, JavaScript, and some front-end programming experience is required.

What this book covers

`Chapter 1`, *A Simple Web Server*, will be very basic project. We're going to take the sample code from the Node.js website and expand on that.

`Chapter 2`, *A Basic Express Website*, will be a basic Express website where we'll introduce the Express server.

`Chapter 3`, *The User Login System*, will be a user login system using Passport.

`Chapter 4`, *The Node Blog System*, will explain how to create a blog system using Node.

`Chapter 5`, *ChatIO*, will help you create a community events application using Drywall.

`Chapter 6`, *E-Learning Systems*, will help you create a simple e-learning portal.

To get the most out of this book

You need to have Node.js. We'll explore the other tools along the course of this book.

Download the example code files

You can download the example code files for this book from your account at `www.packtpub.com`. If you purchased this book elsewhere, you can visit `www.packtpub.com/support` and register to have the files emailed directly to you.

You can download the code files by following these steps:

1. Log in or register at `www.packtpub.com`.
2. Select the **SUPPORT** tab.
3. Click on **Code Downloads & Errata**.
4. Enter the name of the book in the **Search** box and follow the onscreen instructions.

Once the file is downloaded, please make sure that you unzip or extract the folder using the latest version of:

- WinRAR/7-Zip for Windows
- Zipeg/iZip/UnRarX for Mac
- 7-Zip/PeaZip for Linux

The code bundle for the book is also hosted on GitHub at `https://github.com/PacktPublishing/Learn-Node.js-by-Building-6-Projects`. We also have other code bundles from our rich catalog of books and videos available at `https://github.com/PacktPublishing/`. Check them out!

Download the color images

We also provide a PDF file that has color images of the screenshots/diagrams used in this book. You can download it here: `http://www.packtpub.com/sites/default/files/downloads/LearnNodejsbyBuilding6Projects_ColorImages.pdf`.

Conventions used

There are a number of text conventions used throughout this book.

`CodeInText`: Indicates code words in text, database table names, folder names, filenames, file extensions, pathnames, dummy URLs, user input, and Twitter handles. Here is an example: "Mount the downloaded `WebStorm-10*.dmg` disk image file as another disk in your system."

A block of code is set as follows:

```
const http = require('http');
const url = require('url');
const path = require('path');
const fs = require('fs');
```

When we wish to draw your attention to a particular part of a code block, the relevant lines or items are set in bold:

```
http.createServer(function(req, res) {
  var uri = url.parse(req.url).pathname;
  var fileName = path.join(process.cwd(), unescape(uri));
  console.log('Loading'+uri);
  var stats;
});
```

Any command-line input or output is written as follows:

```
$ mkdir css
$ cd css
```

Bold: Indicates a new term, an important word, or words that you see onscreen. For example, words in menus or dialog boxes appear in the text like this. Here is an example: "Select **System info** from the **Administration** panel."

Warnings or important notes appear like this.

Tips and tricks appear like this.

Get in touch

Feedback from our readers is always welcome.

General feedback: Email `feedback@packtpub.com` and mention the book title in the subject of your message. If you have questions about any aspect of this book, please email us at `questions@packtpub.com`.

Errata: Although we have taken every care to ensure the accuracy of our content, mistakes do happen. If you have found a mistake in this book, we would be grateful if you would report this to us. Please visit `www.packtpub.com/submit-errata`, selecting your book, clicking on the Errata Submission Form link, and entering the details.

Piracy: If you come across any illegal copies of our works in any form on the Internet, we would be grateful if you would provide us with the location address or website name. Please contact us at `copyright@packtpub.com` with a link to the material.

If you are interested in becoming an author: If there is a topic that you have expertise in and you are interested in either writing or contributing to a book, please visit `authors.packtpub.com`.

Reviews

Please leave a review. Once you have read and used this book, why not leave a review on the site that you purchased it from? Potential readers can then see and use your unbiased opinion to make purchase decisions, we at Packt can understand what you think about our products, and our authors can see your feedback on their book. Thank you!

For more information about Packt, please visit `packtpub.com`.

1
A Simple Web Server

Hello and welcome to your first project. In this project, we will be building a very simple application or website using Node.js. I wanted to keep it very minimal just to show you exactly how it works. We will build a web server right from scratch with no special third-party modules, such as Express. We'll first go to `nodejs.org` and click on the **About** page; it gives us this really simple web server that basically just spits out *Hello World*. We will build an actual HTML server that will serve HTML web pages. We also will implement Twitter Bootstrap to make it look good. Now when I click on **About**, it takes us to `about.html`; similarly, **Services** takes us to `services.html`. Of course, you can keep adding pages to it.

In this chapter, we will learn:

- Installing Node.js
- Introduction to NPM and a basic HTTP server
- Serving HTML pages
- A basic website

Installing Node.js

We will set up our environment for our first project. We will install Node.js. We will also install a tool called **Git Bash**, which is a command-line tool for Windows that gives us a couple of other features that the standard Command Prompt window doesn't have (this is in no way required; you can use the standard Windows Command Prompt or Terminal in Linux or macOS or whatever you'd like to use).

1. To download Node.js, go to `nodejs.org` and click on the latest stable version:

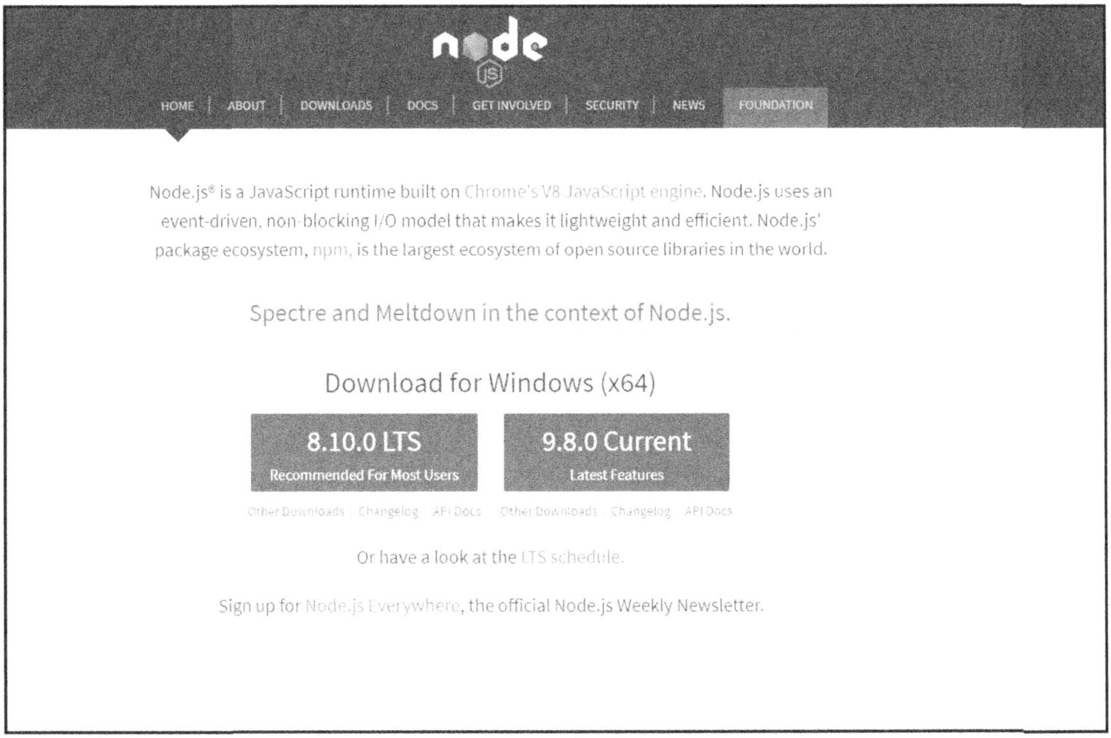

2. After downloading the latest version, we will open that up and run it. It's just like any other Windows installer. Click on **Next**, accept the agreements and the default folder as the `Program Files` folder:

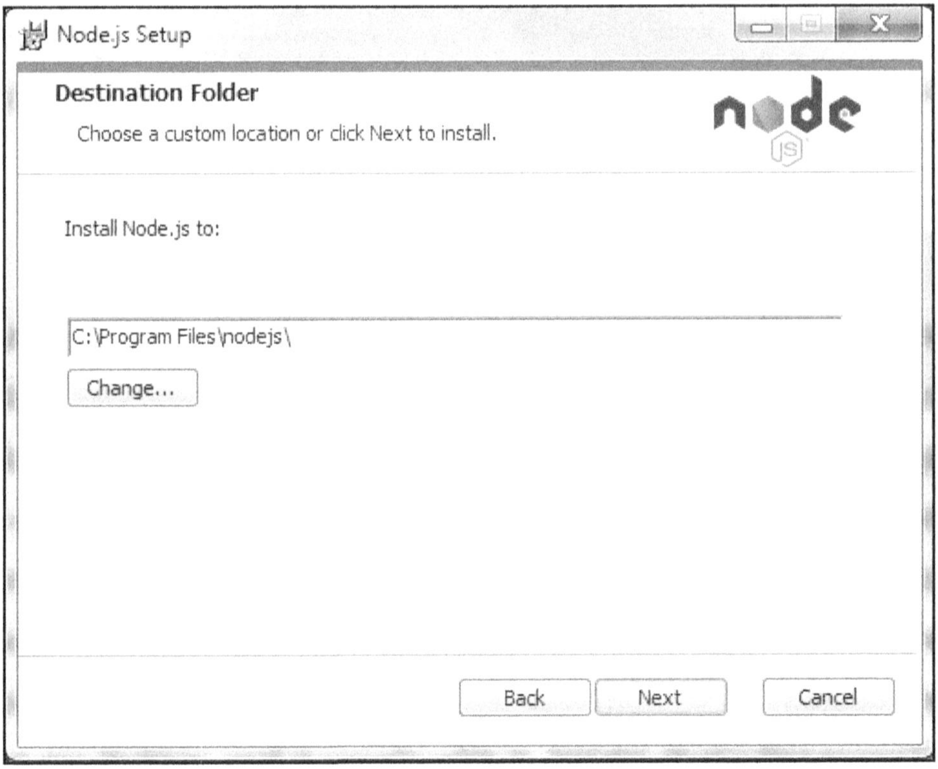

3. We will select **Add to PATH** to access Node and npm from the command line, from anywhere and click on **Next**:

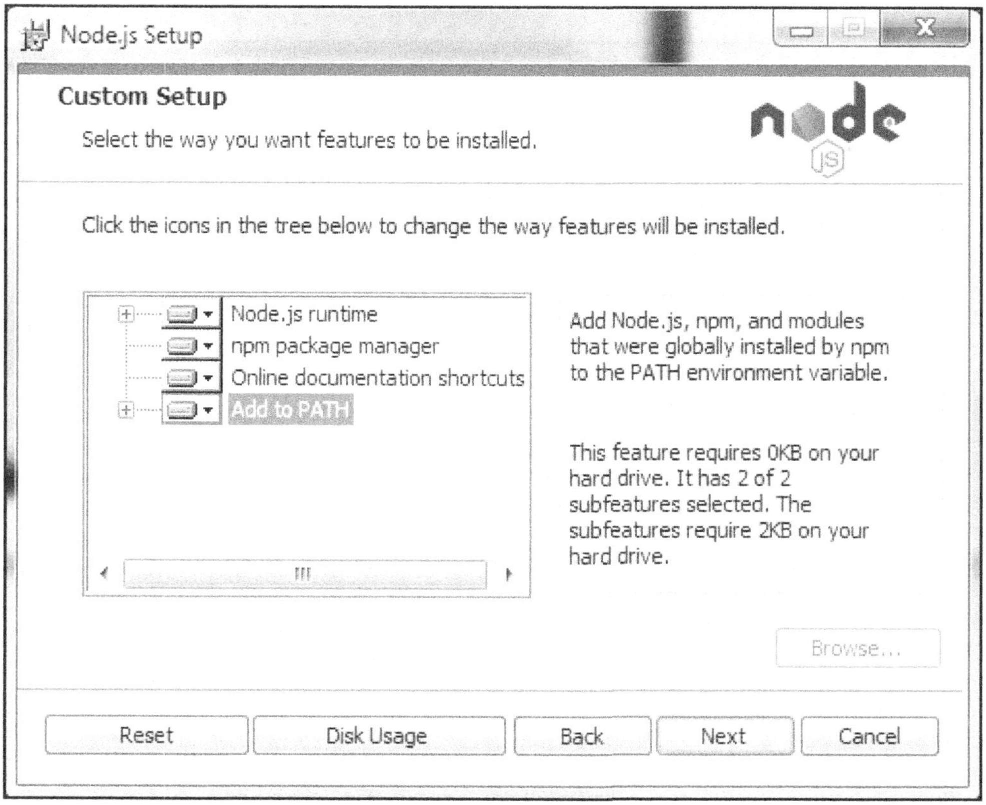

4. We'll then install the Node.js setup. We now have Node on our system.

Installing the Git Bash tool

The next thing is the Git Bash tool. For this, let's go to `git-scm.com` and proceed with the following steps:

1. Let's click on **Download 2.16.2 for Windows** and download that file:

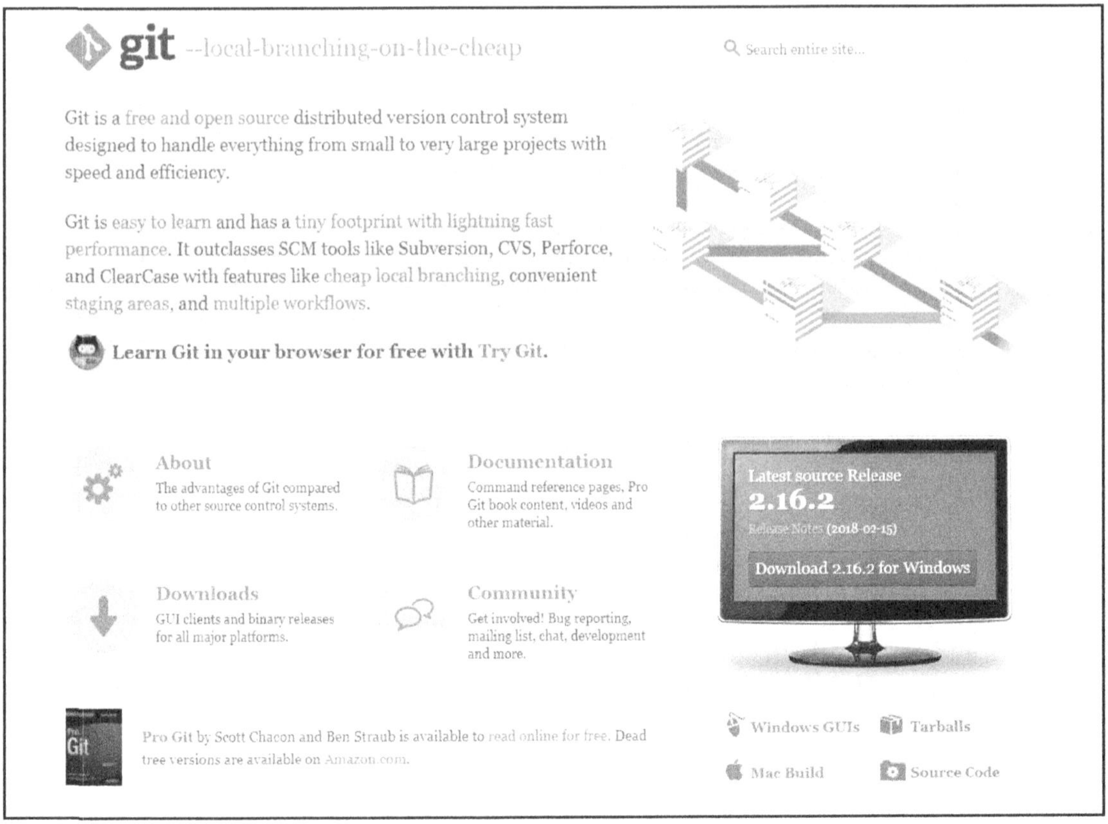

Since this is all set, let's run it. Again this is just a simple Windows installer.

2. We will put the `Program Files` folder and leave the default values as they are. I actually will choose the last option; this will allow us to use some extra Unix tools from Windows Command Prompt:

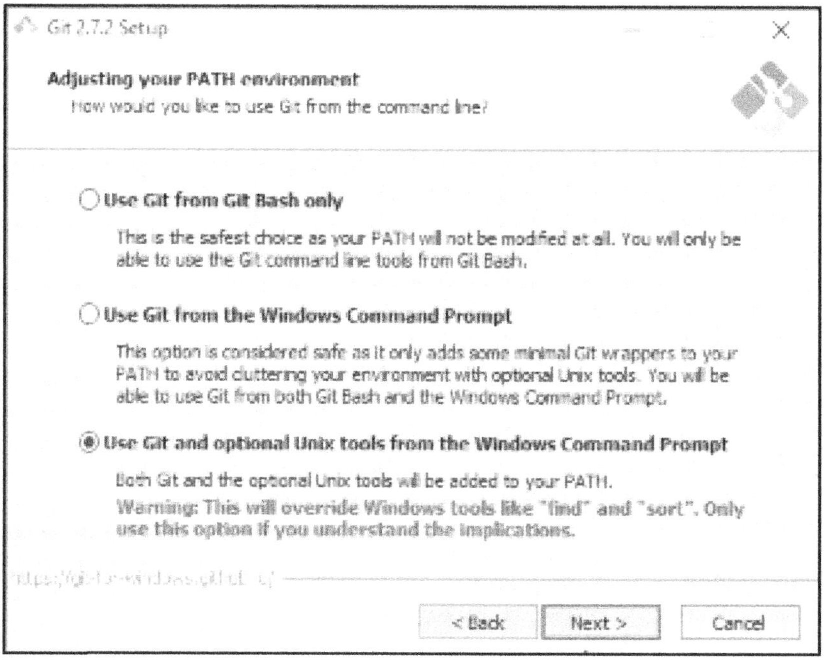

3. We'll select the **Checkout Windows-style, commit Unix-style like endings** checkout and leave the rest of the options as default. This is all set, so click on **Finish**, and we should have Git on our desktop. We'll just search for it using `Git Bash`. Let's go to the actual shortcut and check this.

We'll bring it down into our taskbar so that we can now access it from there. Let's look at another cool thing that this does; if we want to create a folder called `Projects` in our `C:` drive, and if we want to open the command line in this folder, all we have to do is to right-click and click on **Git Bash** from the context menus we get. This will open up the command line for us in that folder! Also, we can use commands such as `ls` and other Unix-based commands.

Now, just to make sure that Node was installed, we can enter `node -v`, which will tell us our version number; also let's try `npm -v` to check:

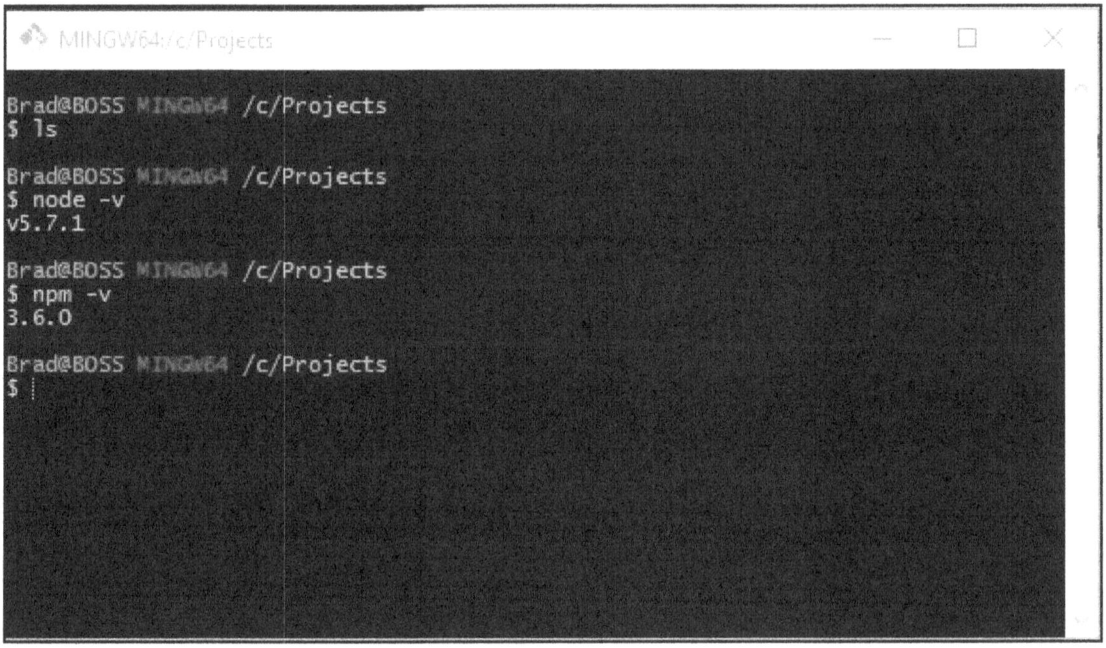

We'll get into `npm` later; it stands for node package modules, and it's basically just a package manager so that we can add and remove plugins or modules to and from our application. This will be it for now. In the next section, we'll look into `npm` more and also look at a basic HTTP server using Node.js.

Introduction to NPM and a basic HTTP server

Now that we have Node.js installed on our system, we will take a look at some very simple code, and we'll also will talk a little bit about `npm` and what that is.

First of all, let's go to the `nodejs.org` website and click on the **About** link:

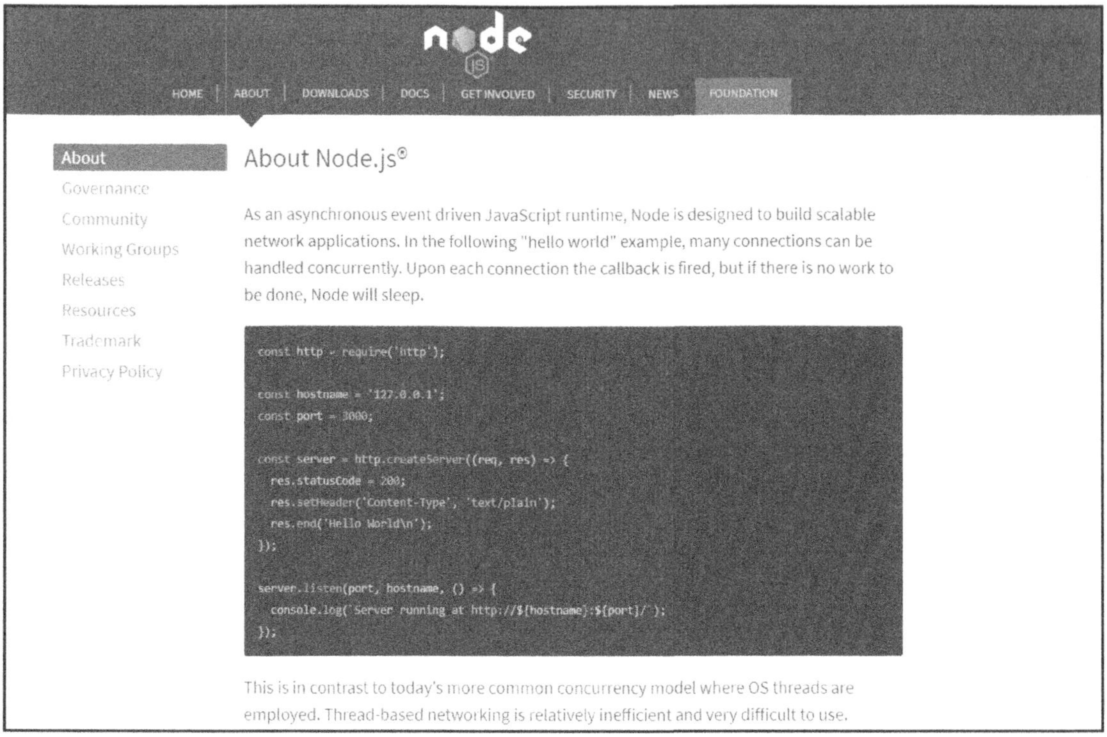

We will see a really simple example of an extremely simple web server that basically will just serve up some text for us.

Next, let's take a look at the code:

1. The first line that we have is `const http`; here, we're just defining a variable called `http`, and we're defining this variable as a constant because it not will change.
2. We're then setting the variable to `require('http')` to include the `http` module. Whenever you see `require`, remember that it's either including a module or another file.
3. Next, we have the `hostname` and `port` constants (our `hostname` will be our `localhost`), and then, `port` is `1337`.

4. We'll take that `http` module and use the `createServer` method or the `createServer` function; this takes in a request (`req`) and response (`res`) parameter. Also, we'll use the `writeHead` method of the response and give it a status of `200`, which means that everything is okay and we're also setting the `Content-Type` to `text/plain`. Then, we will end the response and print `Hello World` in the browser. Then we have to enter `.listen` and pass the `port` and `hostname` name. Once this happens, we can use `console.log`, letting the user know that the server is running.

So, this piece of code is extremely simple and we'll actually run it and see how it works. Before we do this, I just want to go over to `npmjs.com` and show you this website:

This is basically a repository for all of the Node package modules. You have modules that are extremely simple all the way up to a module such as Express, which is an entire HTTP server and framework (which we'll get into later on). You can install these modules from your command line if you have Node installed; you also have `npm`, which we'll get into a little later.

We'll go to the `C:` drive. I have a folder called `Projects`, and I will create another folder in there, called `simpleserver`. This will be our application folder. Now all of our Node applications need to have a file called `package.json`, which is a JSON file that holds a lot of different information such as the application name and description; we have to list all the dependency modules that we want to use. We could create that manually, but we can also use the command line. So I will use my Git Bash tool and just go right into the Git Bash folder.

To create this file, we'll run the `npm init` command, which will initialize a series of questions. For the app name, whatever is in parentheses is the default, since this is fine, we'll keep it; version 1.0.0 is good. For description, we'll just say `Very simple server`; for entry point, you could call this what you want; I like to call it `server.js`. We don't need any of these; for author, you can put your own name. It will verify this stuff and then, we'll press *Enter*.

Now, you can see that we have the `package.json` file. Let's open up this file and take a look at it. I'm using Sublime Text, but of course, you can use whatever editor you want. You can see that we have all that information, such as `name` and `version`, all of that:

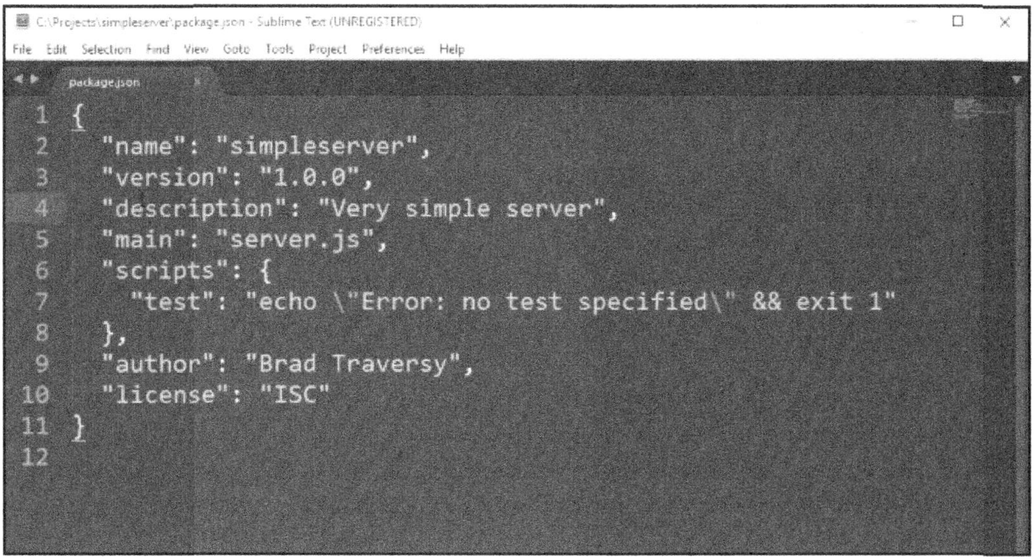

Now if we were using something such as Express or some other kind of Node module, we'd have to put that in our dependencies here; however, we'll get into that a little later.

Since we have our `package.json` file, let's now create the `server.js` file and we will open up that up; I'll just make Sublime my default application, real quick. Now, we'll go to that `About` page and just copy the following block of code:

```
const http = require('http');

const hostname = '127.0.0.1';
const port = 3000;

const server = http.createServer((req, res) => {
  res.statusCode = 200;
  res.setHeader('Content-Type', 'text/plain');
  res.end('Hello World\n');
});

server.listen(port, hostname, () => {
  console.log(`Server running at http://${hostname}:${port}/`);
});
```

We'll just paste this code in the `server.js` file, save it, and go back into our command line. We'll type `node` and then the name of the file; you can type either `server` or `server.js`:

```
node server.js
```

You can see that the command is running:

```
Brad@BOSS MINGW64 /c/Projects/simpleserver
$ node server.js
Server running at http://127.0.0.1:1337/
```

We get **Server is running at http://127.0.0.1:1337/**. Let's check this in the browser. We can enter the `localhost:1337` address. We'll get **Hello World**. So this is, in fact, a Node application that we're running.

Now, a lot of times, you'll see that instead of writing `node server`, you'll see `npm start`; so, if I do that, remember that it does the same thing. You can either use `node` and then the filename, the base server filename, or `npm start`.

So there you go! It is a very simple application, but doesn't do much. In the next section, we'll discuss how we can actually serve HTML files instead of just serving some text like this.

Serving HTML pages

Now we have a very simple web server that's just printing out some text. We'll now bring it up a notch and actually serve HTML pages, which is something that's closer to a real-life situation. So, right now, let's just get rid of the code from from the `hostname` constant; we'll keep the `http` module because we still need it. We also need a couple of other things and a couple of other modules; so we'll also enter `const url`. I will set this to `require('url')`. Since we also need the path module, we'll enter `const path = require('path')`. Then, we also need the filesystem module, so we will enter `const fs` and set it to `require('fs')`:

```
const http = require('http');
const url = require('url');
const path = require('path');
const fs = require('fs');
```

We'll bring in these modules. Now, we will set the type of files that we want to be able to serve. So, we will use a constant, say `const mimeTypes`, and this will be set to an object. We'll say `html`, so this will be `text/html`; we'll use `jpeg`, which will be `image/jpeg`; also, for `jpg`, we'll say `image/jpg` followed by `image/png` for `png`. We want to be able to serve JavaScript files, so `js`, which will be `text/javascript`, and finally, `css`, which will be `text/css`:

```
const mimeTypes = {
  "html": "text/html",
  "jpeg": "image/jpeg",
  "jpg": "image/jpg",
  "png": "image/png"
  "js": "text/javascript",
  "css": "text/css"
};
```

Next, we'll use the `createServer` function that we used before, so we'll enter `http.createServer`. Then, inside this, we will have `function`, which will take in a request and response, and in here, we will set a variable called `uri`—we will use the `url` module for this; we'll also enter `url.parse`.

Next, we will pass in req.url and add .pathname. Now we want a variable for fileName, so we'll say fileName and then use the path module—path.join. We will then enter process.cwd, which is a function; then, another parameter, which will be uri. However, we want to put the other parameter in an unescape function. Let's now enter console.log. I will enter Loading, and then we will concatenate the uri. We will then create a variable called stats:

```
http.createServer(function(req, res) {
  var uri = url.parse(req.url).pathname;
  var fileName = path.join(process.cwd(), unescape(uri));
  console.log('Loading'+uri);
  var stats;
});
```

Now, we'll check for the file that is entered. For instance, let's go to the browser, and inside the address bar, let's enter localhost:1337/page.html. We need to make sure that the page.html is actually there. So we will go right under the stats variable and do a try catch block. We'll enter try and catch and pass in an e.

Here, we want to take that stats variable and set that to fs, which is the filesystem module, and then we want lstatSync and we can just pass in fileName. Now in the catch block, we will add a code that we want to send a 404 error if this doesn't work. So we'll say res.writeHead, and then the status we want is 404; I will send along Content-type. So Content-type actually has to be in quotes, and that will be text/plain. Then, we will enter res.write; I'll just put in some text here, such as 404 Not Found. Then we will say res.end and then, return:

```
try{
  stats = fs.lstatSync(fileName);
} catch(e) {
  res.writeHead(404, {'Content-type': 'text/plain'});
  res.write('404 Not Found\n');
  res.end();
  return;
}
```

So if it doesn't find the file we'll just send a 404. Then, down below, we'll say if(stats.isFile()); so if there is a file, then let's set a variable called mimeType to mimeTypes[], which is our array. In there, we will say path.extname(fileName) and .split.

We will split it at the dot (`.`) because we're getting the extension of the file. We'll see whether it's `.html` or `.jpeg`, or whatever it may be. This is what `extname` does. We want to split it at the dot and then say `.reverse`. We want the first one in the array, so that will be `0`. We'll end this with a semicolon. So, we'll get `mimeType`, and then we want a response of `200`, which means everything's good. So we'll say `res.writeHead`, which will be status `200`. We then want `Content-type`, and then we can simply put in the `mimeType` variable. We'll then create a variable for the file stream, so we'll say `var fileStream`. Let's set this to the filesystem module, and we'll need a function called `createReadStream`. We will now pass in `fileName`. We'll then enter `fileStream.pipe` and then pass in the response:

```
if(stats.isFile()){
  var mimeType = mimeType[path.extname(fileName).split(".").reverse()[0]];
  res.writeHead(200, {'Content-type': mimeType});

  var fileStream = fs.createReadStream(fileName);
  fileStream.pipe(res);
}
```

Now, we'll not have to do all this stuff here in other projects because we'll use something that does all this on its own; something like Express, which is a framework that also has an underlying HTTP server. This is just an example to show you what goes on under the hood of an HTTP server. So if any of this is a little confusing don't worry about it; chances are that you won't have to do this.

Here, we were checking to see whether it was a file or if it was a directory. If it was a file, then it will go ahead and serve that file. Now, down below, we will say `else if` because we want to check to see whether it's a directory. So we'll say `stats.isDirectory`. If it is a directory, then let's say `res.writeHead` and pass in a `302` error, and then, `Location` for redirection. So `Location` will be `index.html`. If there's no `fileName`, it will automatically load `index.html` and then we'll just say `res.end`.

Finally, we'll have an `else` block, and if it's not a file or a directory, we will send a `500` error because obviously it's not there. So let's say `res.writeHead`; this will be a `500` error, so I'll send `Content-type`, which will be `text/plain`. We will enter `res.write('500 Internal Error')`; we all love these! Then we'll put a line break, `\n`. That's it! At the end, we will enter `.listen` and listen on port `1337`:

```
if(stats.isFile()){
  var mimeType = mimeType[path.extname(fileName).split(".").reverse()[0]];
  res.writeHead(200, {'Content-type': mimeType});

  var fileStream = fs.createReadStream(fileName);
  fileStream.pipe(res);
```

```
} else if(stats.isDirectory()){
  res.writeHead(302, {
  'Location': 'index.html'
  });
  res.end();
} else {
  res.writeHead(500, {'Content-type':'text/plain'});
  res.write('500 Internal Error\n');
  res.end();
}
}).listen(1337);
```

So this is a web server. This will serve HTML pages as long as images and whatever else we have as the `mimeTypes` array or object. Let's save it and restart the server. To do this, let's go to our command line and do a *Ctrl* + *C* to stop it. Then, let's enter `npm start` and see what happens. Remember that we don't have any files to load.

Inside the browser, we'll get a **404 Not Found** because we're looking for `index.html`. So let's create an `index.html` file. We'll open this up with the Sublime Text editor and just put in some tags there. In `body`, we'll just put in an `h1` tag to make sure that it parses HTML correctly:

```
<!DOCTYPE html>
<html>
<head>
  <title>Test Page</title>
</head>
<body>
  <h1>Testing</h1>
</body>
</html>
```

Let's save this and reload. We'll get **Testing**, and now it's reading our HTML page. Let's say we create another file, `page.html`, and open it up. I will copy the code from the `index.html` file and paste it inside the `page.html` file. I'll say `Testing Page 2` and save it. Now, if we change this to `page.html`, it will load up.

A basic website

Now we'll just make the website look a little better and create a very simple website using our server. You can see in the command line here as we'll run it; visiting pages will tell us what pages are loading:

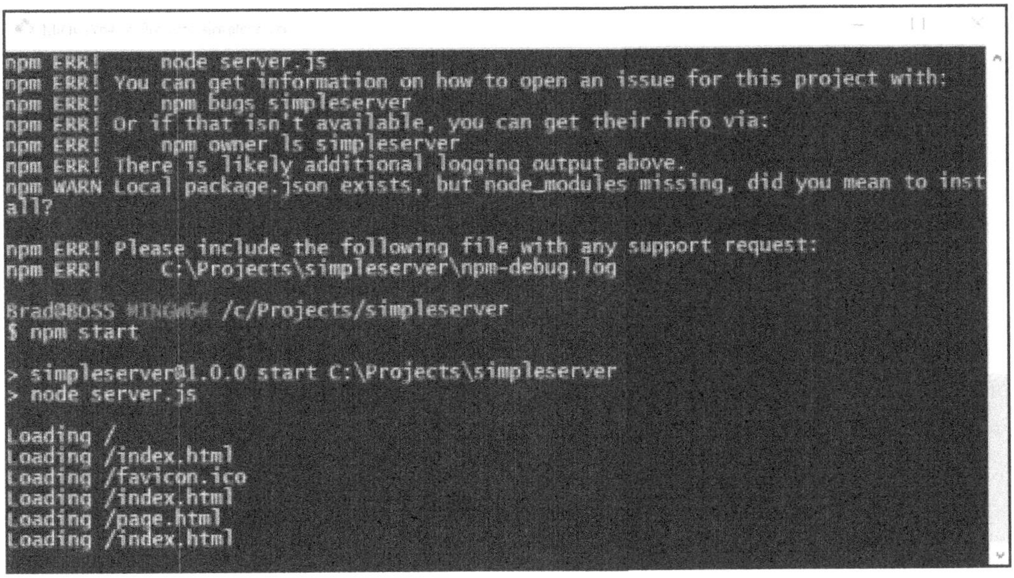

We will now rename the `page.html` file; we'll call it `about.html`. Then we'll create another one and call this one `services.html`. Now if we wanted to use something like Bootstrap, we can do that.

A basic website using Bootstrap

Let's go to `getbootstrap.com` and then to **Examples**. We will be using Bootstrap quite a bit through this section:

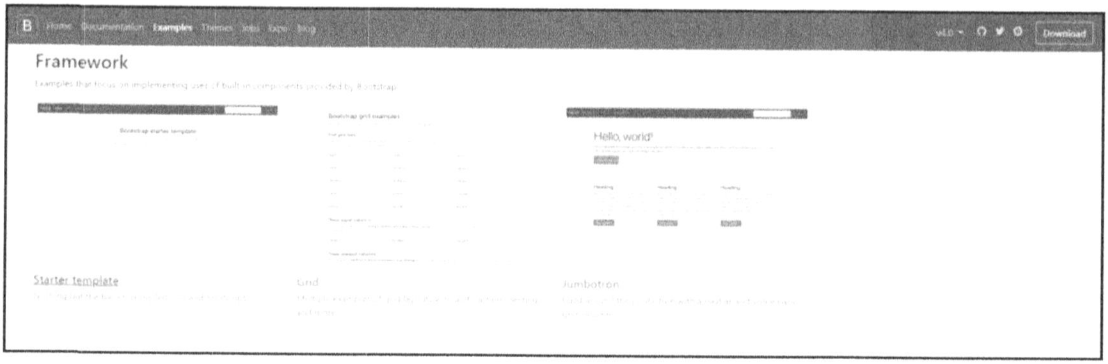

Here, this is just a sample Bootstrap template. I'll grab the code from `navbar` down to the `container` div. We'll put the code in `body` of `index.html`. We have our `Home` page and the link to it will be `index.html`, the link to the `About` page will be `about.html`, and for `Contacts` it will be `services.html`. We'll change `Contacts` to `Services`:

```
<ul class = "nav navbar-nav">
  <li class = "active"><a href="index.html">Home</a>
  </li>
  <li><a href = "about.html">About</a></li>
  <li><a href = "services.html">Services</a></li>
</ul>
```

Then, down below, we will get rid of the `starter-template` div and put in a `div` tag with the class of `row`. Let's enter `h1` and then, `Welcome`. Next, we'll just put a paragraph and say `This is the welcome page`; we'll change the title to `Welcome`. We will need to include Bootstrap, so we'll download it. We'll then take the `CSS` folder from the downloaded Bootstrap files and put it into our file structure. We will create a folder called `css`, bring `bootstrap.css` inside the folder we created, and then, inside `head`, we'll enter `link`; this will go to `css/bootstrap.css`:

```
<head>
  <title>Welcome</title>
  <link rel="stylesheet" href="/css/bootstrap.css">
</head>
```

Inside the browser, let's go back to our `index.html`. We will get rid of the class `navbar-fixed-top` and save, to push the navbar down:

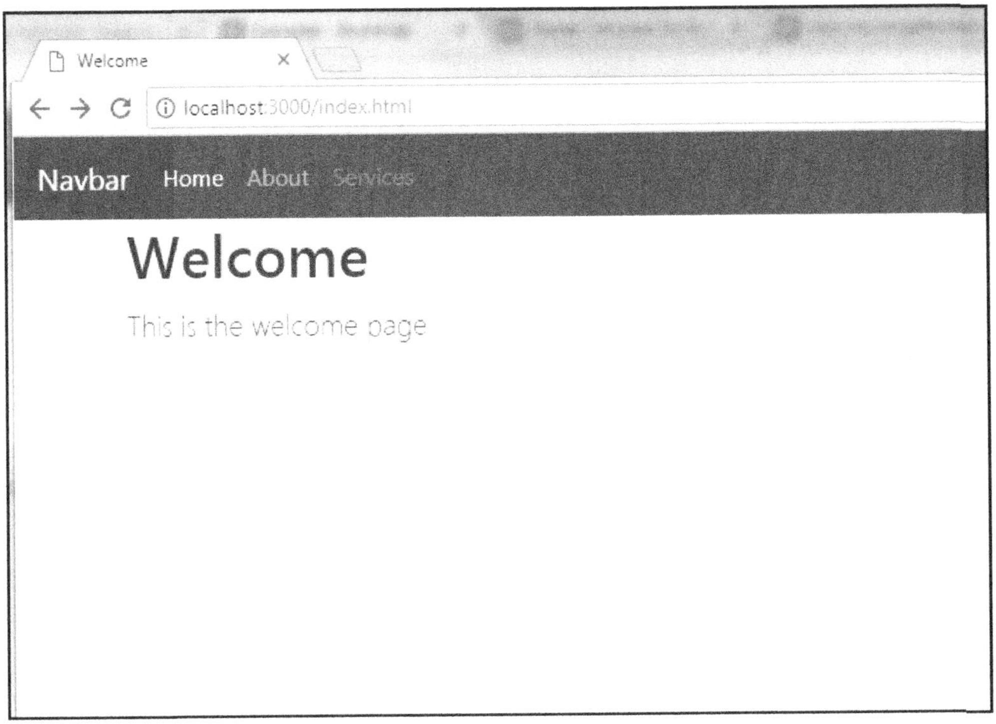

This is our `Home` page.

When we go to the `About` page, we can see that it's loading up just text; however, we want it to be formatted like the `index` page. So we will have to just grab everything that we have inside `nav` and put that in the `About` page; except that we will just change a couple of things. For example, for the class of the `li` tag, `class="active"`, we'll cut that class out and put it in `li` of the `About` page; we'll also change the `h1` heading. For the project name, we'll just say `MyWebsite`. We'll put this for the `Home` page too.

We will copy everything again and put it into the `services.html` page. We'll just change the class of `li` to `class="active"` and put it on the `services` link. So, we'll save that, reload, and go to the `About` page. Since I did not include the CSS, the head, and all that stuff, let's just put them in there. Now having a site like this, where you actually have to include everything on every single page such as the navbar is not really a nice way to build a website, especially if you will be using something like Node.js. This is just giving you an example of building a web server.

Summary

In the first chapter, we started with installing Node.js and the Git Bash tool. We also learned the basic HTTP server along with an introduction to NPM. We then moved to understand serving the HTML pages followed by designing a basic website.

In the next chapter, we'll actually be using Express, which is a framework and it makes it so easy that we don't have to repeat ourselves like this. I still have a project, but I didn't save it, so we won't have to include the `navbar` and all that stuff; we'll be able to create routes and do a bunch of other stuff really. We'll get into stuff that's a little more advanced; this project was basically just to introduce you to Node.js.

2
A Basic Express Website

In this project we are going to learn to build a web application using Node.js and Express. We will begin with exploring Express right from the installation steps. Along with Express, we will then move to understand pages routes and views. After understanding the basics, we will move to layouts of the website. Using this we will create our website!

In this chapter, we will learn:

- Understanding Express
- Pages routes and views
- Adding Layouts
- Nodemailer contact form

Understanding Express

Express is a full web framework and also a web server. We'll build a very, very simple site for computer repair and we'll focus on routing, parsing data using the Pug template engine, and also using a module called Nodemailer, which gives us a contact form:

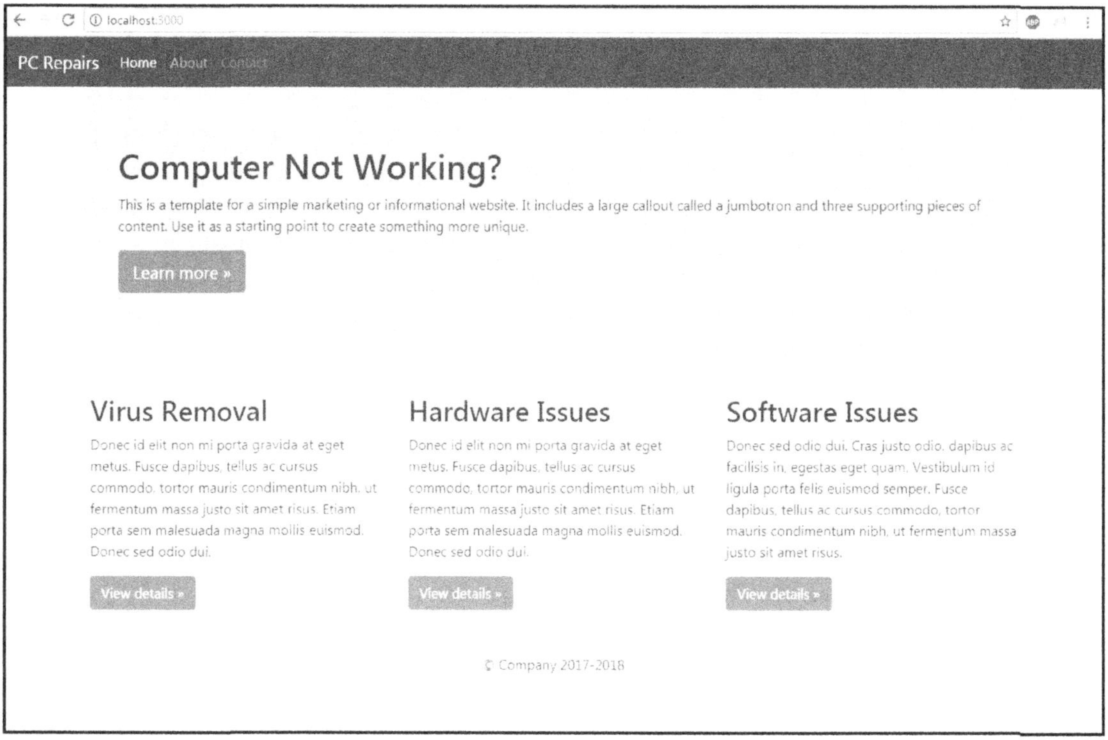

So this is the `Home` page, and then we have an `About` page and also a `Contact` form that works using Nodemailer:

It is a very simple application but it's a nice introductory to Express, which we'll be using throughout the book. So lets get started!

Installing Express

In this project we're going to be building a website using the Express framework. Express is a Node.js module that gives us a full framework, it gives us a routing system and an HTTP server.

To install it, it's really simple we just need to say `npm install express` although we're going to add the `-g` flag because we want to install it globally so that we can access it from anywhere. From the frontend this website is going to be very, very simple, it'll just have a `Home` page, an `About` page, and we'll also use a module called Nodemailer that will allow us to create a `Contact` form. On the backend we'll be using Node.js with Express, and we'll be using Express in quite a few projects in this book. We'll also use Pug, which is a template engine that works really well with Express.

So let's get started. Now I'll open up the `Projects` folder, and create a new folder called `express_website`. I'll then open up my Git Bash tool in too there and, of course, you can use Windows Command Prompt, macOS, or Linux whatever you'd like:

1. The first thing I'll do is install Express globally so we want to say `npm install -g express`:

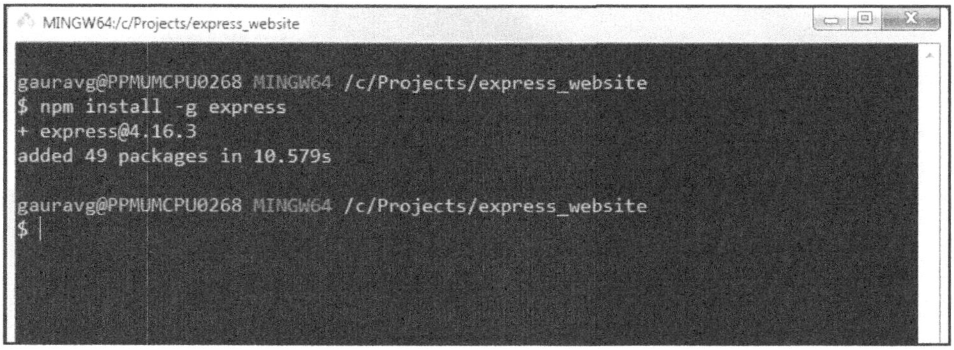

2. Once that's done we'll create a new text file and call it `app.js`.

   We'll also need our `package.json` file, we can do that with `npm init`. Now, we'll just answer these questions. You can put `Simple website` as the description, entry point as `app.js`, and put your own name as the author:

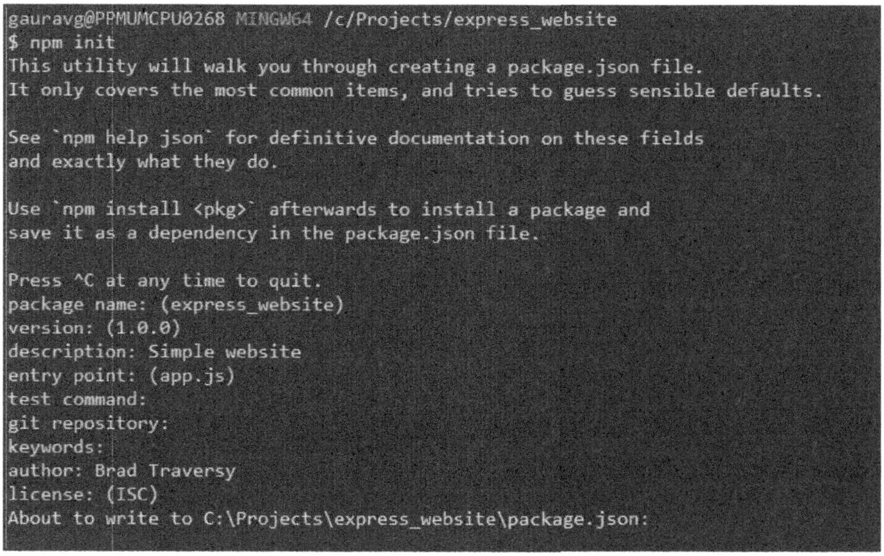

Alright, so that created a `package.json` file.

3. So let's open that up. This time in this project, we'll need a few dependencies including Express. So let's put a comma after `"license": "ISC"`, and we'll say `dependencies`:

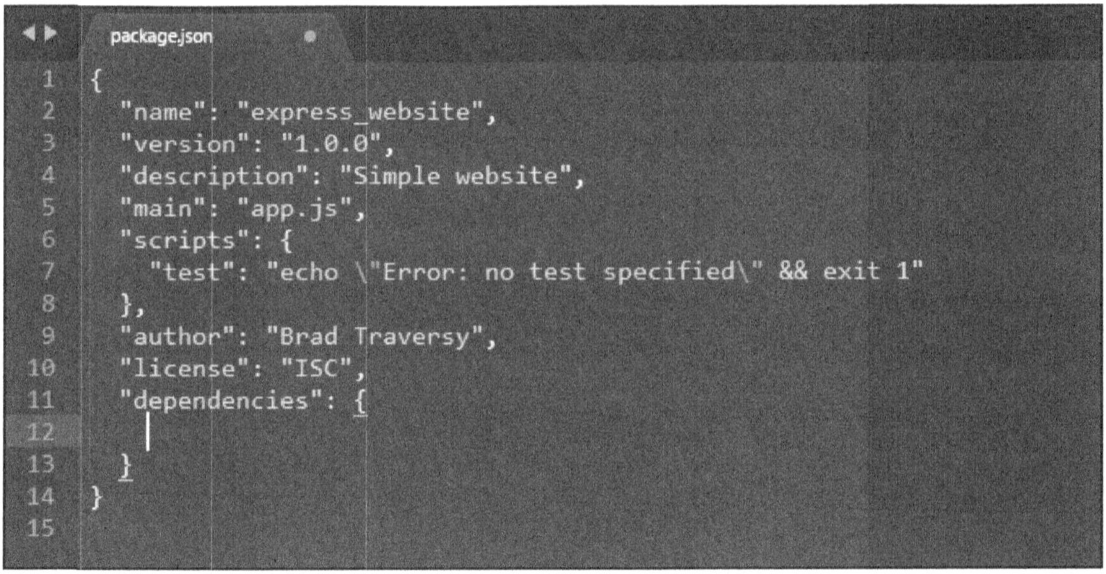

```
package.json
{
  "name": "express_website",
  "version": "1.0.0",
  "description": "Simple website",
  "main": "app.js",
  "scripts": {
    "test": "echo \"Error: no test specified\" && exit 1"
  },
  "author": "Brad Traversy",
  "license": "ISC",
  "dependencies": {

  }
}
```

4. We'll need `body-parser` that will help us parse different types of data including form data. Now if we don't know the latest version or the version we want, we can use an asterisk (`*`) and that'll just say we want the latest version. We also want `express`, we want `pug`, and also `nodemailer`. I'm pretty sure that's it, but if we need more later we can just add them:

```
"dependencies": {
  "body-parser": "*",
  "express": "*",
  "pug": "*",
  "nodemailer": "*"
}
```

5. Let's go ahead and save this, and now we'll go back to our command line and type `npm install`:

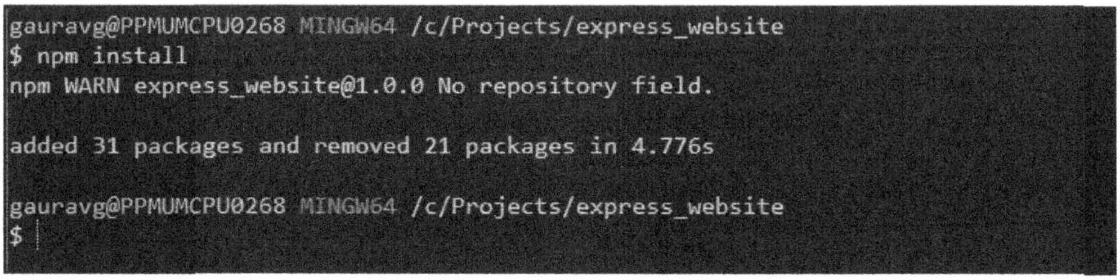

This will get all that stuff installed so now lets go and look at the folder.

6. We now have a `node_modules` folder, and that has a bunch of stuff in it including the dependencies that we listed:

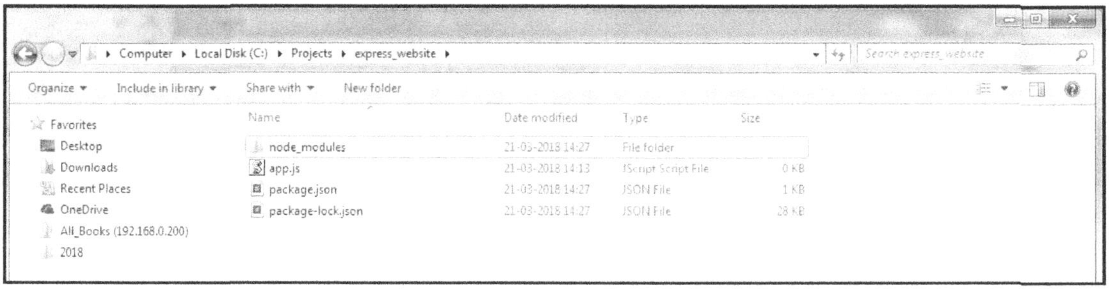

So there is `body-parser` and it should have `pug` right below.

So we don't have to touch anything in there, very rarely do you have to touch anything in the `node_modules` folder. So let's open up the `app.js` file.

Exploring the app.js file

There are a few things we need to do in the `app.js` file. We need to include some stuff so we need `express` and that's going to equal `require('express')`. We'll get the `path` module. Now the reason that we didn't have to list `path` in our dependencies is because `path` is a root module that we don't have to do that with. We'll also need `bodyParser` and `nodemailer`:

```
var express = require('express');
var path = require('path');
```

```
var bodyParser = require('body-parser');
var nodemailer = require('nodemailer');
```

Now let's initialize our app:

1. We'll say `var app = express` and set our `bodyParser` middleware. So we will use `app.use` and this will be `bodyParser.json`.
2. We want to be able to parse `json` if we want, and then we want `app.use(bodyParser.urlencoded)`. We then just want an object with some options, so we add `extended` to it and we'll set that to `false`:

    ```
    var app = express();

    app.use(bodyParser.json());
    app.use(bodyParser.urlencoded({extended: false}));
    ```

3. Let's go down to the bottom, and we'll write `app.listen` and pass in a port, say `3000`. We'll then just use `console.log` and enter `Server is running on port 3000`:

    ```
    app.listen(3000);
    console.log('Server is running on port 3000');
    ```

4. If we go to the command line, we can now type `node app`, and because `app.js` is the name of the file, we get `Server is running on port 3000`:

5. Let's go to `localhost` port `3000`. You can see that now we get the error `Cannot GET /`:

The reason for this is that we haven't created a route for `/`, which is the `Home` page. So that's not going to work in the browser. Let us go ahead and create a route.

6. We'll write `app.get` and then inside it, the route is going to be just `/`, which will call a `function`. This function will get a request and response object followed by `console.log('Hello World')`:

```
app.get('/', function(req, res){
  console.log('Hello World');
});
```

7. Now if I save this, restart the server, and if we visit this page again, you can see that nothing's changed on the client side:

On the other hand, on the server side we get `Hello World` because this file is running on the server:

8. If we want to send it to the client, we could say `res.send('Hello World')`:

```
app.get('/', function(req, res){
  res.send('Hello World');
});
```

9. We'll restart `node app` and now we get `Hello World` on the client side or the browser:

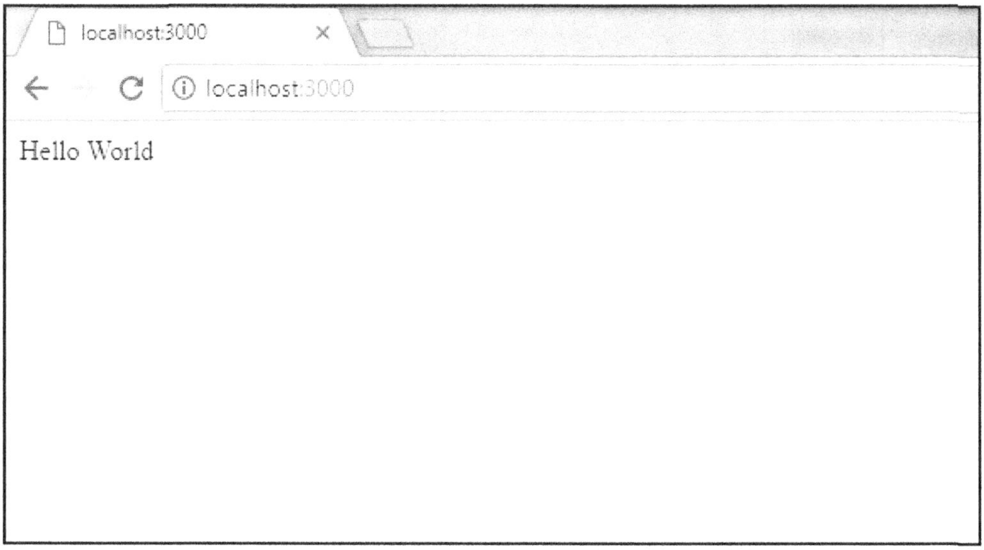

Now obviously that's not what we want to do; I mean we could even put HTML in here if we were to say `h1`, so we can even pass HTML:

```
app.get('/', function(req, res){
  res.send('<h1>Hello World</h1>');
});
```

But we won't put all of our HTML inside a function. Instead, what we'll do use Pug to load a template or a view:

Alright, so in the next section, we're going to configure Pug and we'll be able to add some mock-up to our application and some other routes as well.

Pages routes and views

In the previous section we installed Express and we set up our basic `app.js` file and our `package.json` file. So we have one route above going to the `Home` page and all we're doing is just sending out some text inside an `h1` tag.

We now want to load some Pug views for different routes in our application. But before we do that, we need to actually set up a couple of things.

Setting up View

Let's go to `app.js` and let's type in `app.set`. We need to tell Pug which folder the template files will be in, so we use `views`. Then as the second parameter, we'll use `path.join` and in there, we will put `__dirname` as the first parameter and the second parameter will be the folder name, `views`:

```
app.set('views', path.join(__dirname, 'views'));
```

We also need to set the `view engine`, so I'll use `app.set('view engine')` and then the second parameter will be `pug`. Alright, now instead of typing in `res.send`, we'll type in `res.render` and we'll render the `index` view:

```
app.set('view engine', 'pug');

app.use(bodyParser.json());
app.use(bodyParser.urlencoded({extended: false}));

app.get('/', function(req, res){
  res.render('index');
});
```

We'll save this, go back to our folder, and create a new folder called `views`. In there, we'll create a document; we'll call this `index.pug`. We'll open that up and all we'll put in is an `h3` tag and we'll say `Hello World`:

```
h3 Hello World
```

Save that, we'll restart the server, and now you can see that if we do a *Ctrl* + *U* and look at the source code, it's an `h3`; so we know that it's coming from here:

Now as for the Pug syntax, it really works on indents instead of tags, and I can actually show you the Pug website, I'll give you some examples real quick.

Back to basics

Let's look at **Basics**:

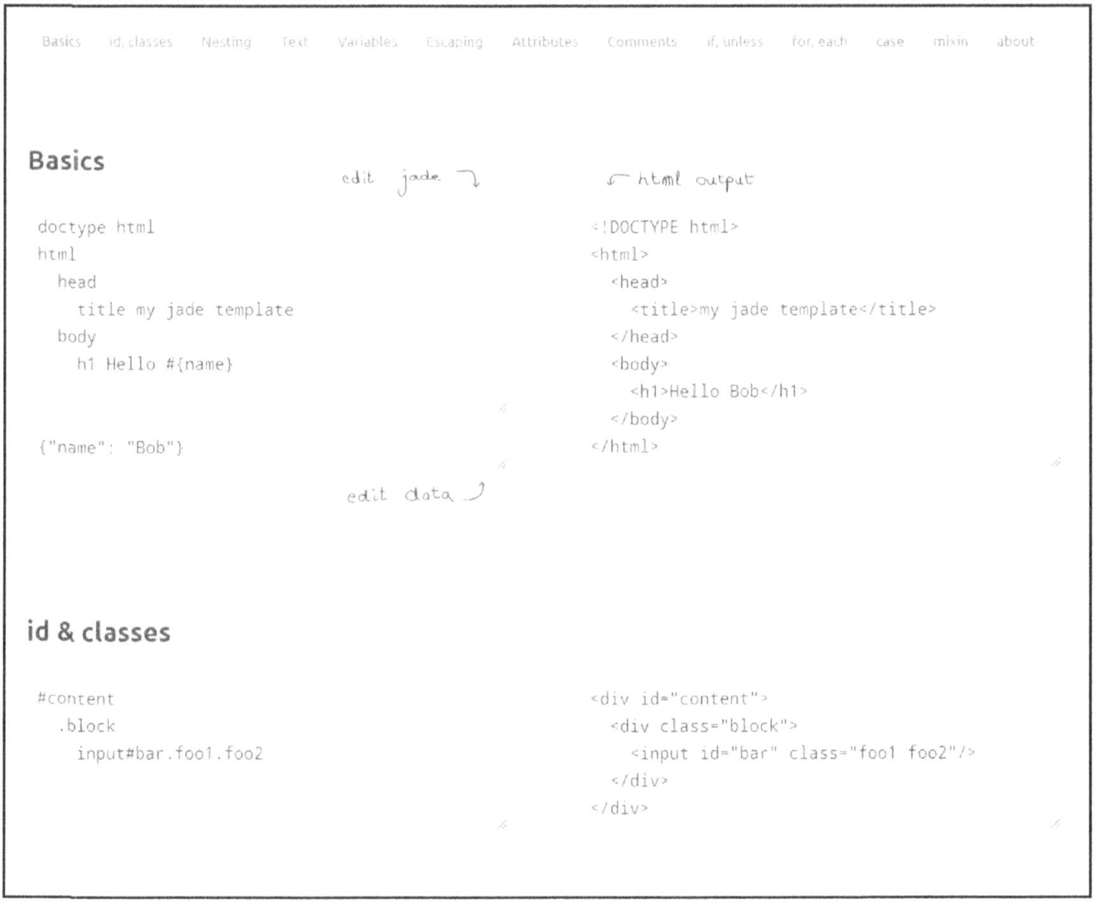

Over here is just your standard HTML. So we have a `DOCTYPE` and HTML tags `head` and `body`. If we look at the Jade version of this we're setting up our `doctype html`, notice that we don't have any greater than and less than symbols for our tag, and there are no ending tags either.

Alright, it works on indents. So under `doctype`, we have `html` and as you can see those are on the same level, so there's no indent. The `head`, however, is inside `html`, so what we need to do is put an indent here. Now your indents can be either spaces or tabs but they have to be consistent; you can't have both.

`title` is inside `head`, so it's going to have an indent. `body` is on the same level as `head`, so we'll go back one level on indent. Then the `h1` is inside the body, so we'll indent it inside `body`.

id and classes

So that's how it works and if we look at `id` & `classes`, so we have a `div` with the `id` of content, inside that we have block and then inside that we have an `input` with the `id` of `bar`. And you can see here that we're just indenting each time:

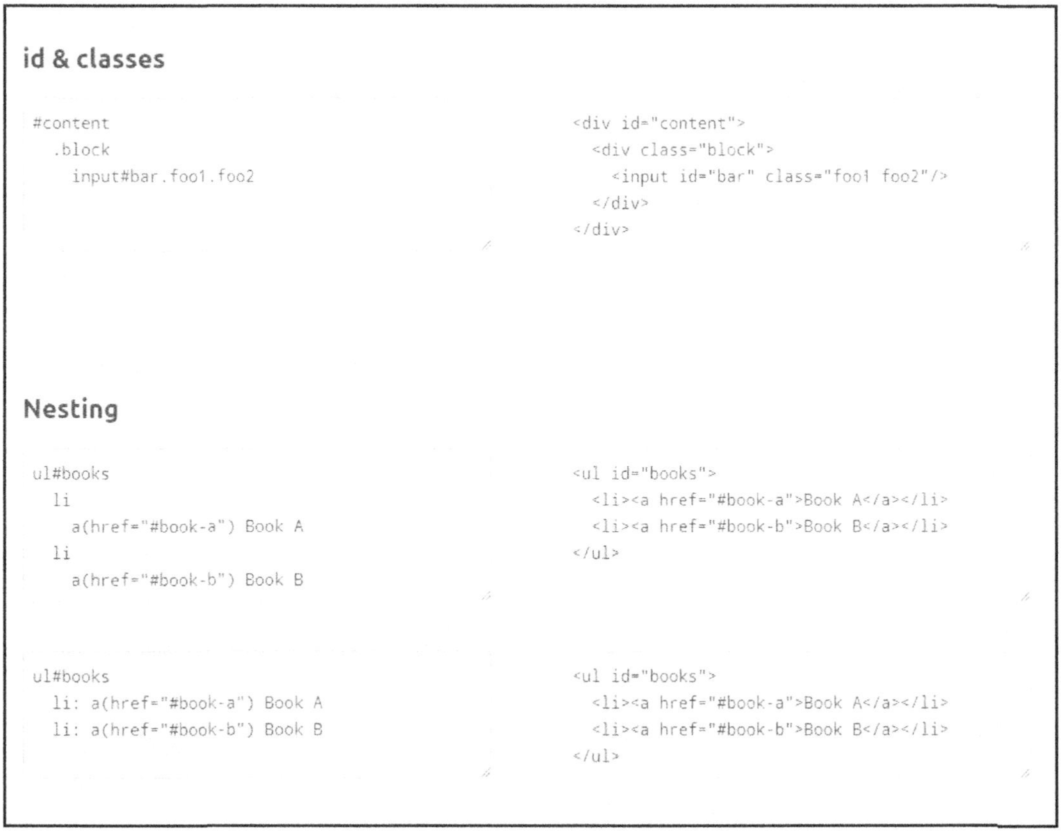

Nesting

In Nesting, we have a `ul` here with an `li` and inside that we have an `a` tag. So this is how you would, you would create a link, the text and then you put the attributes inside of parenthesis. Alright, and you can see that that gives us just a standard link:

Nesting

```
ul#books
  li
    a(href="#book-a") Book A
  li
    a(href="#book-b") Book B
```

```
<ul id="books">
  <li><a href="#book-a">Book A</a></li>
  <li><a href="#book-b">Book B</a></li>
</ul>
```

```
ul#books
  li: a(href="#book-a") Book A
  li: a(href="#book-b") Book B
```

```
<ul id="books">
  <li><a href="#book-a">Book A</a></li>
  <li><a href="#book-b">Book B</a></li>
</ul>
```

Text

When you use text you want the text to be on the same level as its tag, because if you don't, for instance let me just give you an example, if we type Hello World and we indent as shown in the following screenshot and maybe we're thinking we want this to be inside the `h3`, but if we save it and we go back and reload it's only seeing `World` and the reason for that if we do a *Ctrl* + *U* it's actually putting `Hello` inside of its own tag, alright because this this is being looked at as a tag alright, so that needs to be on the same line:

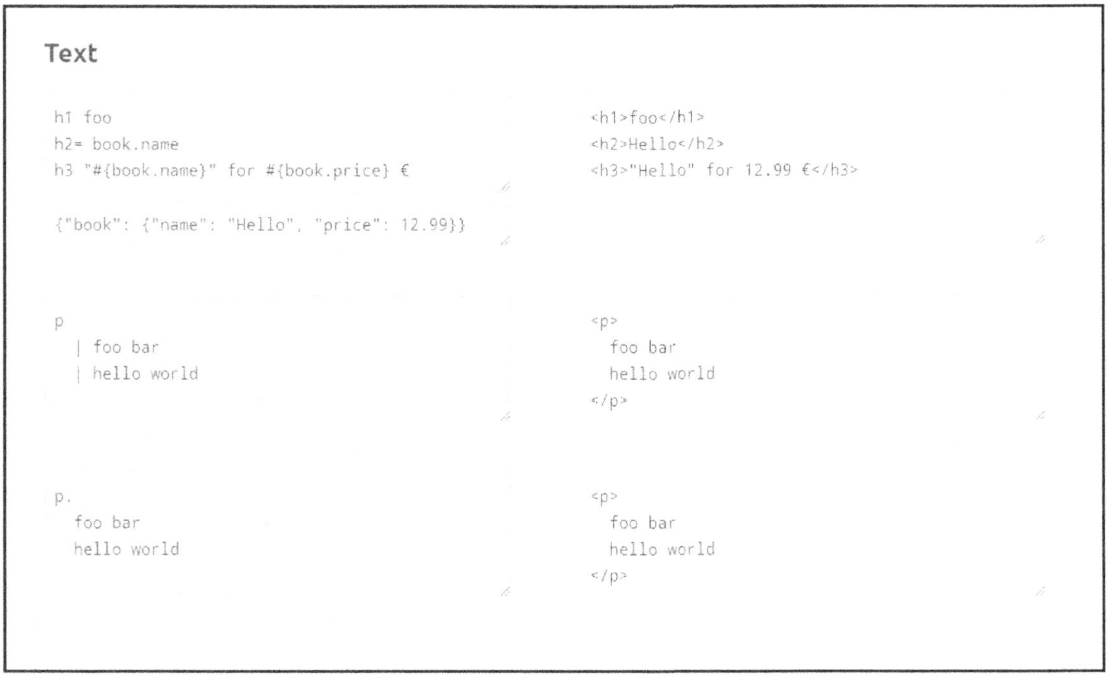

Alright, so hopefully that makes sense. Now let's talk about layouts.

> Jade is now renamed to Pug. So throughout the book, you will see Jade being named as Pug, although the principles remain the same for both. For more information, visit `https://pugjs.org/api/getting-started.html` and `https://github.com/pugjs/pug`.

Adding Layouts

We have an `index` file, which will probably have an `about` file as well. We don't want to have a menu in both views and then in every other view we create. So what we can do is we can surround our views in a layout, and then in that layout we can provide the code that we want to be on every page.

So in the `views` folder we'll create a new document and call this `layout.pug`. Let's open that up, grab the code right from the **Basics** window, and paste that into the `layout.pug` file:

```
doctype html
html
head
  title my jade template
body
  h1 Hello World
```

Let's save that!

> As mentioned before in the *Back to basics* section, the indents need to be either spaces or tabs. If these aren't formatted correctly you will get errors. I'm going to use spaces.

Now in the `index` file, we need to specify that we want to use that layout. So what we'll do is at the top, we'll use `extends layout` and then use `block content`. We'll then use `h3 Hello World` and this has to be inside `block content`, so we'll put a space (indent). We'll save that and see what happens:

```
extends layout

block content
  h3 Hello World
```

This is what you should now see when you run your browser:

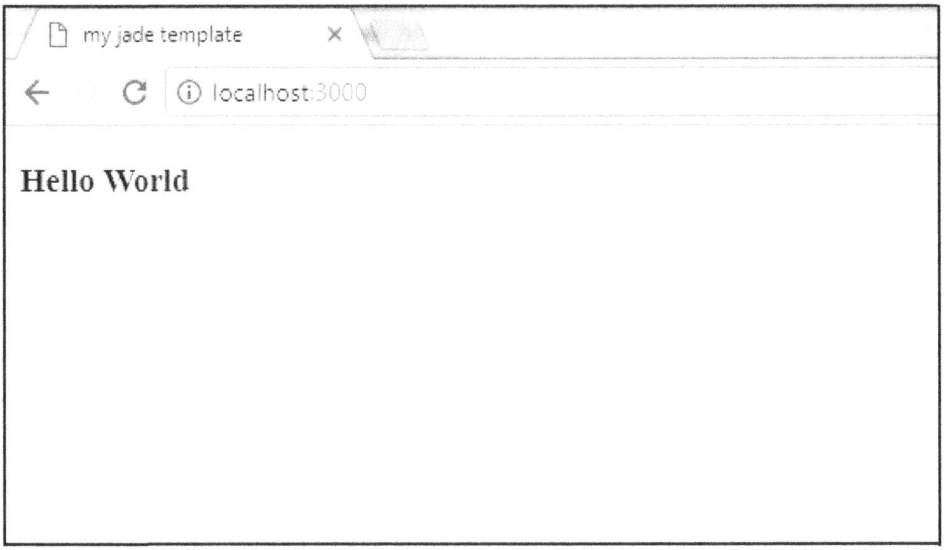

So now you can see we're getting the **Hello World**, which is in our `index`, but if you look at the tab it says `my jade template`, that's what's in the layout title. If we look at the source code you can see we now have our `doctype`, we have our `html`, `head`, and `body` tags. So we have this layout that we can wrap around any view we want as long as we just include these two things here.

Using Bootstrap - Jumbotron

Now I would like to use Bootstrap for our layout, so I'll go to `getbootstrap.com` and go to **Examples** and then **Jumbotron**:

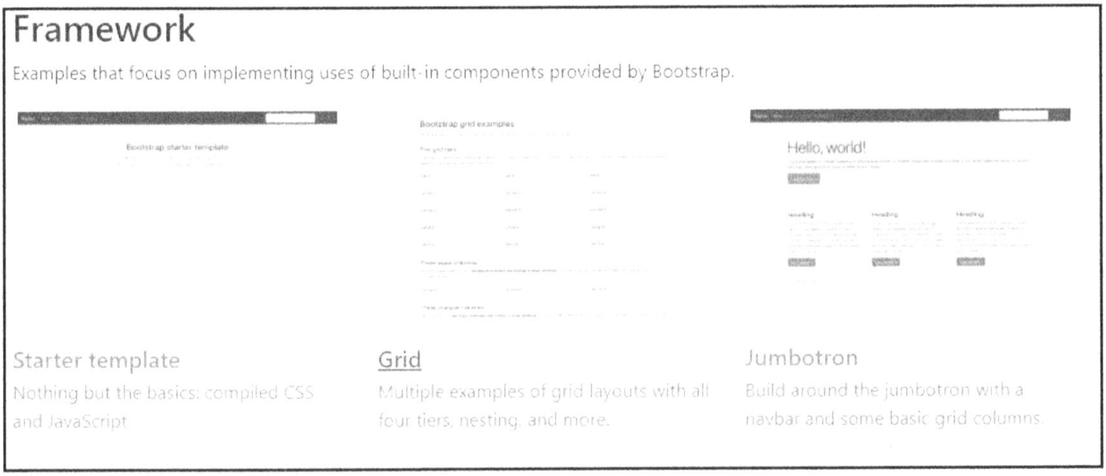

Creating the Home page view

1. Let's do a *Ctrl + U* inside the **Jumbotron** page. Let's grab all the code, and then let's open up another new file just to paste this in for now so we can edit it. There will be a lot of unnecessary code lines. We will have to get ride of them. Also, for convenience, we'll use a Jade converter that will give us the Pug code back once we paste the HTML in.
2. Now, I'm going to do is just get rid of a bunch of the `meta` and `link` tags that we don't need. We don't even need the `lang` attribute. Now for the stylesheet, let's look at our folder. The style sheets are going to go in a folder called `public`, alright so we need to create that. Then inside public let's create a folder called `stylesheets`, and we'll grab Bootstrap.
3. We'll just bring the `bootstrap.css` over. Now before we get to this we need to specify in our `app.js` that we want the `public` folder to actually be the `public` folder, or the `static` folder. So we'll go to the middleware and we'll type in the line highlighted in bold in the following code snippet:

```
app.use(bodyParser.json());
app.use(bodyParser.urlencoded({extended: false}));
app.use(express.static(path.join(__dirname, 'public')));
```

4. We'll save that and let's go back to our HTML. So for this, I'll have just the `css/bootstrap.css`. Then we can get rid of the rest of this stuff in the `head` tag:

```
<!-- Bootstrap core CSS -->
<link href="/css/bootstrap.css" rel="stylesheet">
```

5. Then for the `navbar`, let's change the project name and let's say this is a computer repair shop, so we'll just type in `PC Repairs`:

```
<a class="navbar-brand" href="#">PC Repairs</a>
```

6. Then we don't have any links. So let's use `div id="navbar"` I'm going to grab the `div` tag and just replace it in the HTML tag:

```
<nav class="navbar navbar-expand-md navbar-dark bg-dark fixed-top">
  <a class="navbar-brand" href="#">Navbar</a>
  <button class="navbar-toggler" type="button" data-toggle="collapse" data-target="#navbarsExampleDefault" aria-controls="navbarsExampleDefault" aria-expanded="false" aria-label="Toggle navigation">
    <span class="navbar-toggler-icon"></span>
  </button>

  <div class="collapse navbar-collapse" id="navbarsExampleDefault">
    <ul class="navbar-nav mr-auto">
      <li class="nav-item active">
        <a class="nav-link" href="#">Home <span class="sr-only">(current)</span></a>
      </li>
      <li class="nav-item">
        <a class="nav-link" href="#">Link</a>
      </li>
      <li class="nav-item">
        <a class="nav-link disabled" href="#">Disabled</a>
      </li>
      <li class="nav-item dropdown">
        <a class="nav-link dropdown-toggle" href="http://example.com" id="dropdown01" data-toggle="dropdown" aria-haspopup="true" aria-expanded="false">Dropdown</a>
        <div class="dropdown-menu" aria-labelledby="dropdown01">
          <a class="dropdown-item" href="#">Action</a>
          <a class="dropdown-item" href="#">Another action</a>
          <a class="dropdown-item" href="#">Something else here</a>
        </div>
      </li>
    </ul>
    <form class="form-inline my-2 my-lg-0">
      <input class="form-control mr-sm-2" type="text" placeholder="Search" aria-label="Search">
      <button class="btn btn-outline-success my-2 my-sm-0" type="submit">Search</button>
    </form>
  </div>
</nav>
```

7. We have `Home`. After `/`, I'll get rid of `class active` and for the `About` page we type in `About`, resulting in `/About`; similarly for `Contact`, it will be `/Contact`:

```
<div class="collapse navbar-collapse" id="navbarsExampleDefault">
  <ul class="navbar-nav mr-auto">
    <li class="nav-item active">
      <a class="nav-link" href="/">Home<span class="sr-
only">(current)</span></a>
    </li>
    <li class="nav-item">
      <a class="nav-link" href="/about">About</a>
    </li>
    <li class="nav-item">
      <a class="nav-link disabled" href="/contact">Contact</a>
```

```
      </li>
    </ul>
  </div>
```

8. We can now get rid of the `Jumbotron` comment and I'll get rid of all the JavaScript stuff present at the end of the file as well. So now we have a very simple template. So I'll just grab all of the code from this file and navigate to `html2jade.org`:

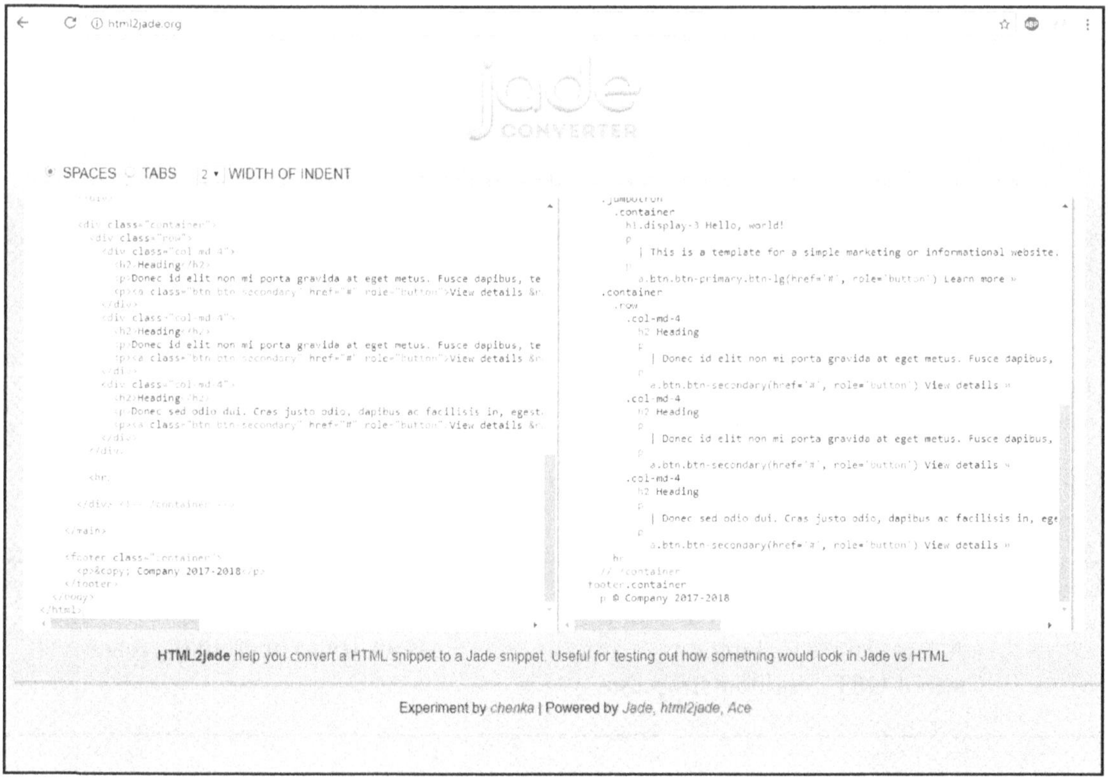

9. We'll paste this over and it's going to give us the Pug code. So we'll copy that and then let's go to our `layout.pug` file. We'll just replace this, save, and check out our app:

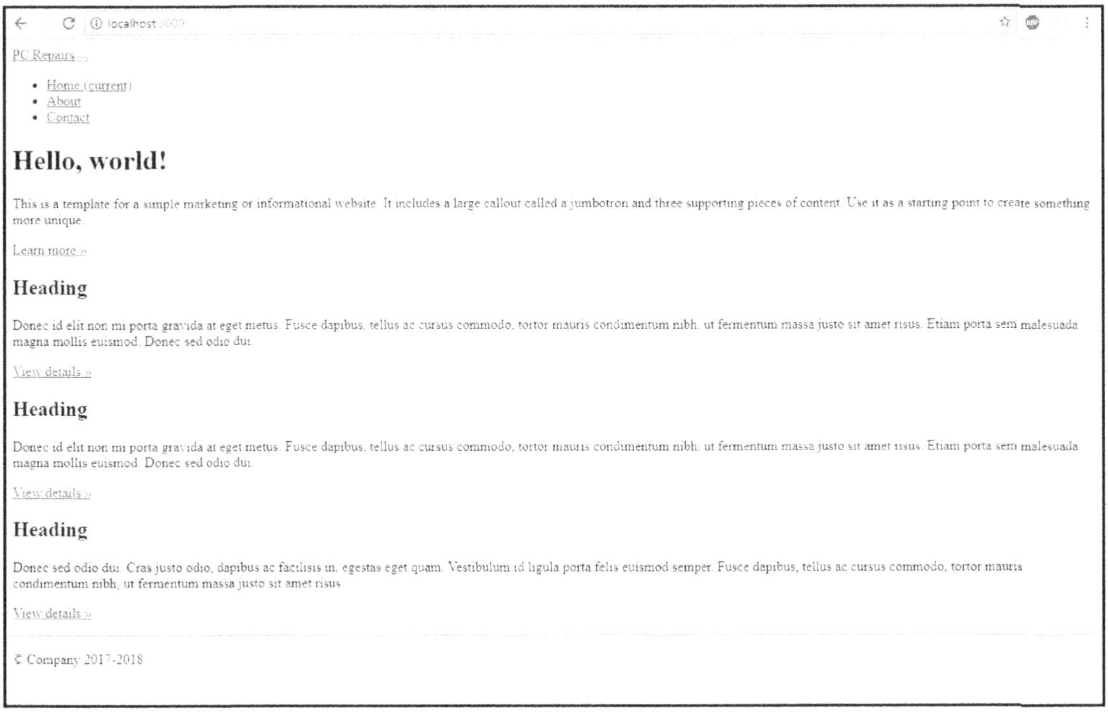

So what's going on here is that it's not seeing the CSS file if we do *Ctrl* + *U*, and you can see it's looking `css/bootstrap.css`. If we try to open that, we get **Cannot GET /css/bootstrap.css**:

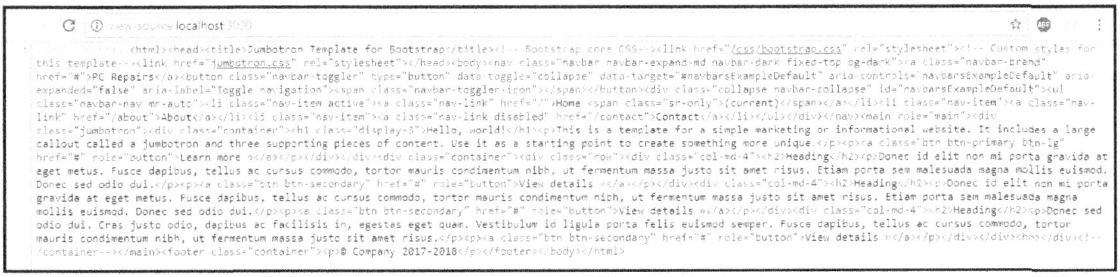

This is wrong and I know why, because we didn't restart the server. so let's do that:

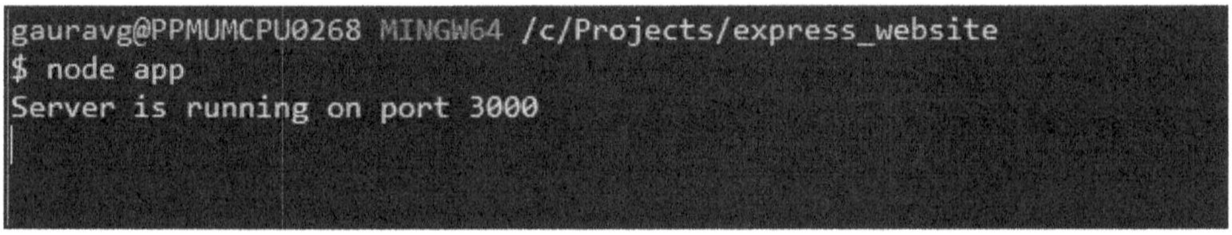

10. So we now have a template. Right now, everything that you see is inside `layout.pub` and that's not what we want; we want Jumbotron and the **Heading** area below:

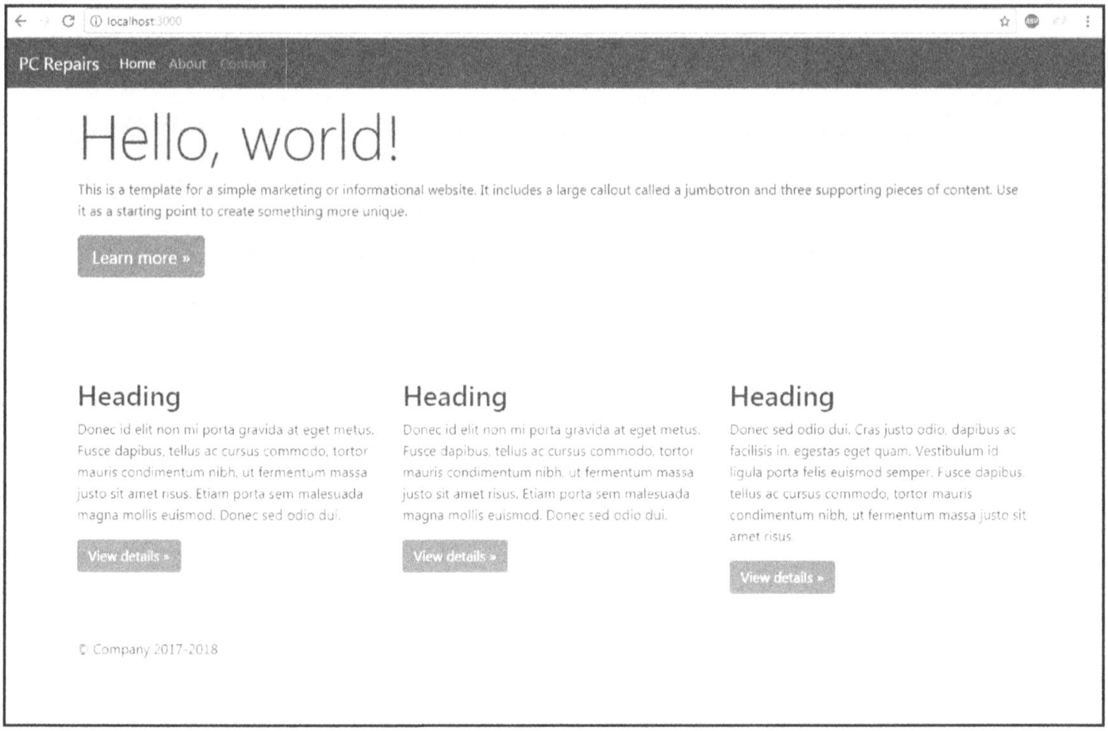

11. We want that to be in the `index` page. So let's go back to `layout.pug` and we'll grab from the `.jumbotron` tag down to right above `hr` as shown in the following screenshot:

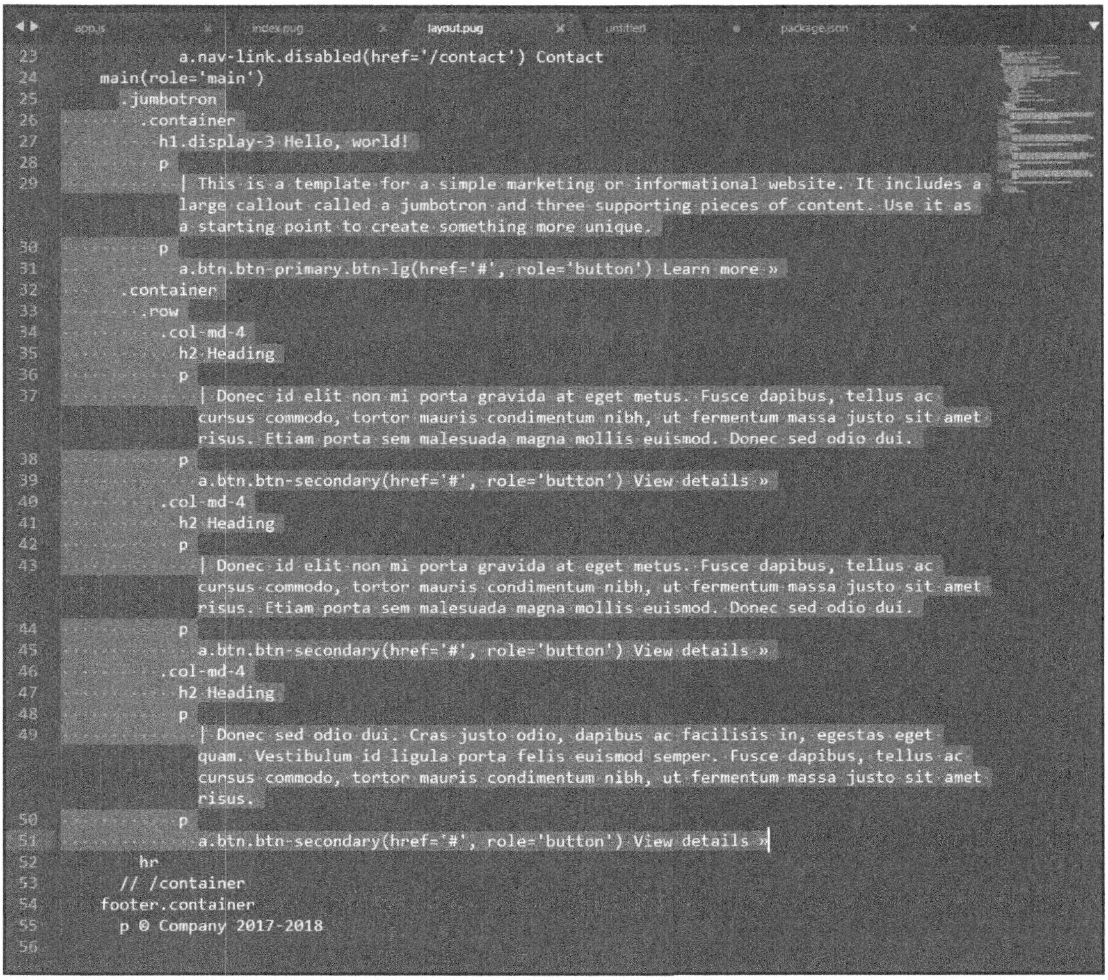

12. We'll cut that, and then right above the `hr` tag, we will type in `block content`. Save it, go to `index.pug`, and let's try to reload that.
13. You'll see we're getting **Hello World**. We want to replace that with the Pug code that we just cut. Paste it in and save it. Oops, it looks like we have something wrong! I think the `block content` needs to be over one:

```
block content
hr
footer.container
 p(class='text-center') © Company 2017-2018
// /container
```

Remember using spaces for indents not tabs. I will have this `block content` to be on the same level as the `nav`. Then I'll bring the `hr` and the `footer` along the `block content` level. So now we have our `footer`.

I actually want to give that paragraph in the footer a class, so we'll type in `(class='text-center')`. We'll now have the footer center-aligned on the page.

Now what we want to do is we want this `About` page to work. Let's go back to `app.js` and I'll copy some lines of code and modify it to `about` and render `about`:

```
app.get('/about', function(req, res){
  res.render('about');
});
```

Passing variable to view

Now if we want to pass variables through we can do that. For instance, we'll add another parameter, open some curly braces, and let's say `title`; we'll set `title` to `Welcome`. Now if we go to `index`, let's go up to the `h1` and we'll replace the `Hello, world` with `#{title}` We're going to have to restart the server though because we changed that. So go back and now we get **Welcome:**

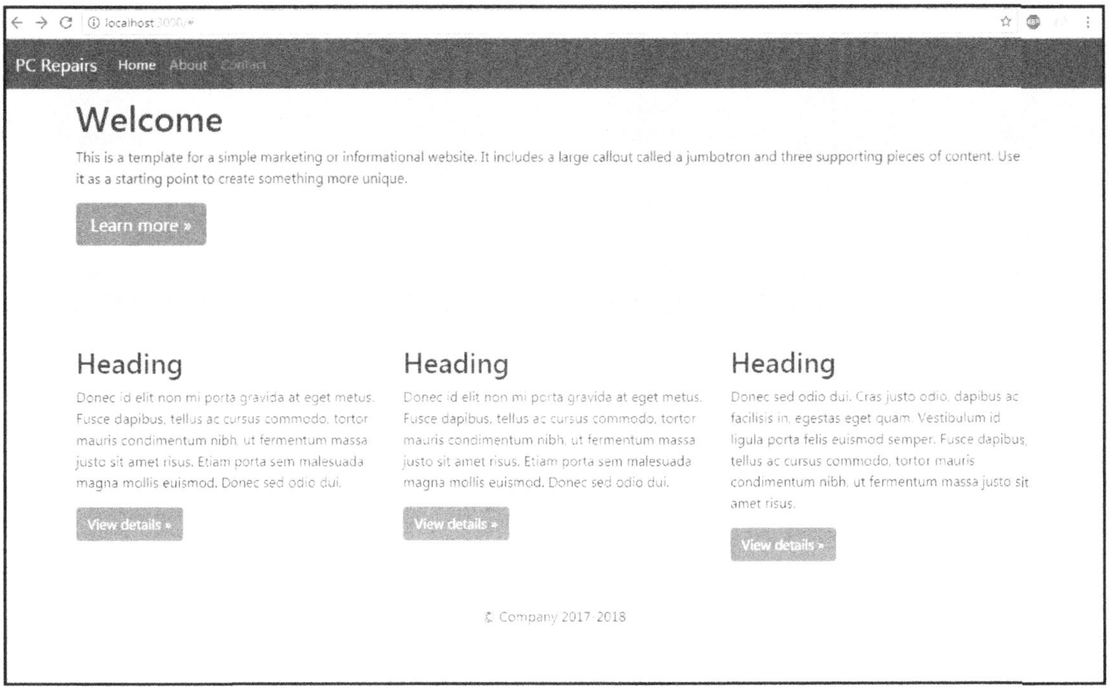

So that's how we can pass stuff to our view. As we have it that's just a string with `Welcome` but this could in fact be something that we pull back from a database; it could be an array of stuff we pulled from a database, and we can pass the results to the view very easily.

Creating an About page view

Now we need to create an about view, so let's go to `views` and we'll create a new file here called `about.pug`. We'll open that up and all I need from here really is this:

```
extends layout.pug

block content
  h1 About Us
```

Then we'll just put `h1` and we'll say `About Us`. We'll save that. We then go to `layout.pug` and get rid of the `navbar-fixed-top` class. There we go, so we get **About Us**:

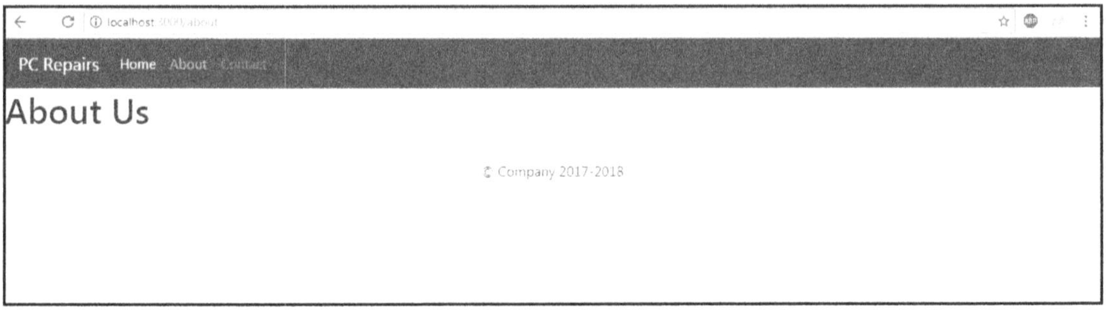

We probably want to put a container around that. So down before `block content`, we'll enter `.container`. We want the block inside it, so I'm just going to indent that like so:

```
.container
 block content
hr
footer.container
 p(class='text-center') © Company 2017-2018
// /container
```

Now we want a paragraph in the `About us` page.

Now with paragraphs, it's a little different. To avoid any kind of error, we can use the pipe (`|`) character so we can go like that:

```
extends layout.pug

block content
  h1 About Us
  p
    | This is the about page.
```

We'll save, and now we get the about page:

Alright, so we have our Home page and our About page. We'll work on the Contact page in the next section because we'll implement Nodemailer, which is a module that will allow us to have a contact form.

The Nodemailer contact form

We need to create our Contact form now!

1. If I click on Contact now, we get an error because we didn't create that route or that view. Let's go to app.js, copy the app.get code, and edit it by typing in /contact and render the contact view:

```
app.get('/contact', function(req, res){
  res.render('contact');
});
```

2. Let's save that and then inside the views folder, we'll create a new file and save it as contact.pug.

3. Inside this file, we paste the following code. Copy the highlighted code lines as you would want the name and email of the customer visiting the contact form. First, we implement the name section:

```
extends layout.pug

block content
 .container
 form(method='post', action='contact/send')
 h1 Contact
 .form-group
 label Name
 input.form-control(type='text')
```

You want these to be on the same level, and this one is going to be `Email` and we're going to give this one a type of `email`. The code should now look like so:

```
extends layout.pug

block content
 .container
 form(method='post', action='contact/send')
 h1 Contact
 .form-group
 label Name
 input.form-control(type='text')
 .form-group
 label Name
 input.form-control(type='email')
```

4. We also need a name for these, so inside after `type` we want to say `name='name'` and we'll also give it a `placeholder`. Same thing after `type` we want to have name and that's going to be `email`, and then we'll have `placeholder`. Now we have one more down here, this one is going to be `Message`, and we'll not have an input but a text area. So let's change `textarea` and have `message`. Let's also use `placeholder`, say `Enter Message`, and that should be good. So now we need a `button`, make sure you have the correct indentation so `btn.btn-default` and that's going to have a `type` of `submit`. Then we'll just have the text `Submit`. The code should now look like the following:

```
extends layout.pug

block content
 .container
 form(method='post', action='contact/send')
```

```
h1 Contact
.form-group
label Name
input.form-control(type='text', name='name',
  placeholder='Enter Name')
.form-group
label Email
input.form-control(type='email', name='email',
  placeholder='Enter Email')
.form-group
label Message
textarea.form-control(name='message',
  placeholder='Enter Message')
button.btn.btn-default(type='submit')
Submit
```

5. Let's go ahead and save that.
6. Restart the server.
7. There's our `Contact` form:

You'll see that the text and button are not showing up, let's troubleshoot:

```
textarea.form-control(name='message', placeholder='Enter Message')
 button.btn.btn-default(type='submit') Submit
```

We don't want Submit (highlighted in the preceding code snippet) to be on a separate line, which is why it's actually creating a `submit` tag. So we use the preceding code, refresh the page, and there we go:

More about the basic website

We have our form, so let's now go back to `app.js`, go to the bottom and copy `app.get`, and then this is going to be `post`. We will use `app.post('/contact/send')` and `console.log('Test')`:

```
app.post('/contact/send', function(req, res){
  console.log('Test');
});
```

We'll then just restart the server real quick. We'll be logging it, so let's reload the page and **Submit**, and you can see we get `Test`:

OK, so we know that the form is submitting. We already included `nodemailer` right here so we have access to that. Let's get rid of `console.log('Test')` and create a variable called `transporter`. Set that to `nodemailer.createTransport`. Inside this, we'll have some options: `service` and `auth`. Inside this object, we're going to have the `user` and `pass`:

```
app.post('/contact/send', function(req, res){
  var transporter = nodemailer.createTransport({
    service: 'gmail',
      auth: {
        user: 'garyngreig@gmail.com',
        pass: ''
      }
  });
});
```

Now we want to go right here and we're going to set up our mail options. This should still be within the post but outside of the `transporter` variable. Alright, so we'll say `var mailOptions` and this is going to be an object. So we'll use `from` and you can put the same one you entered above, and you can use the name and then the `email` address format, so put the name and then we'll go just like that.

Then we need to specify where we want the `email` to go. I'll use another email address of mine. We now want to specify a `subject`, OK we'll say `Website Submission`. Next thing is going to be the plain text version. We'll just say `You have a submission with the following details....` Let's just say `Name` and then we need to concatenate the submitted name. We can get that with `req.body.name`. We'll then type in `Email`, and then use `req.body.email` and `Message` that will say `req.body.message` with a comma.

So that's the `text` attribute. Next line is going to be the `html` attribute. For this, we'll use paragraphs and we can make this look a little better since we're using HTML so we're going to create an unordered list. Let's do the ending tag and then in here we want `li`, and we need to concatenate in the name. We'll do another `li` and put the text `Name`. We'll do the same thing in `Email`, and then we have the `Message`, just like that:

```
var mailOptions = {
  from: 'Gary Greig <garyngreig@gmail.com>',
  to: 'gauravg@packtpub.com',
  subject: 'Website Submission',
  text: 'You have a submission with the following details... Name:
'+req.body.name+'Email: '+req.body.email+'Message: '+req.body.message,
  html: '<p>You have a submission with the following details...</p><ul>
```

```
<li>'+req.body.name+'</li><li>Email: '+req.body.email+'</li><li>Message:
'+req.body.message+'</li></ul>'
};
```

That should do it for the `mailOptions`. Now what we want to do is go down and we'll use `transporter.sendMail` and then we want to pass in the `mailOptions` and then we need a function and that function will take a couple of parameters:

```
transporter.sendMail(mailOptions, function()){}
```

It's going to take `error` and `info`. Then we're going to test for an error. I'll use `if(error)` and then use `console.log(error)`. We'll then redirect we can do that with `res.redirect` and we want to go to the `Home` page, which will be a `/`. We also want an `else` on this, so let's just `console.log` and use `console.log('Message Sent')`. Let's then concatenate `info.response`. Then finally we want to redirect to the `Home` page so we'll copy `res.redirect`:

```
transporter.sendMail(mailOptions, function(error, info){
  if(error){
    console.log(error);
    res.redirect('/');
  } else {
    console.log('Message Sent: '+info.response);
    res.redirect('/');
  }
});
```

So now I need to enter my password so I'll do that and I hope you will do the same! So I have my password set up. Now with Gmail in order for you to use their email service in the way we're using it, you need to actually go to this `URL`:

Now what we're going to do is **Access for less secure apps**, I'm going to **Turn on**:

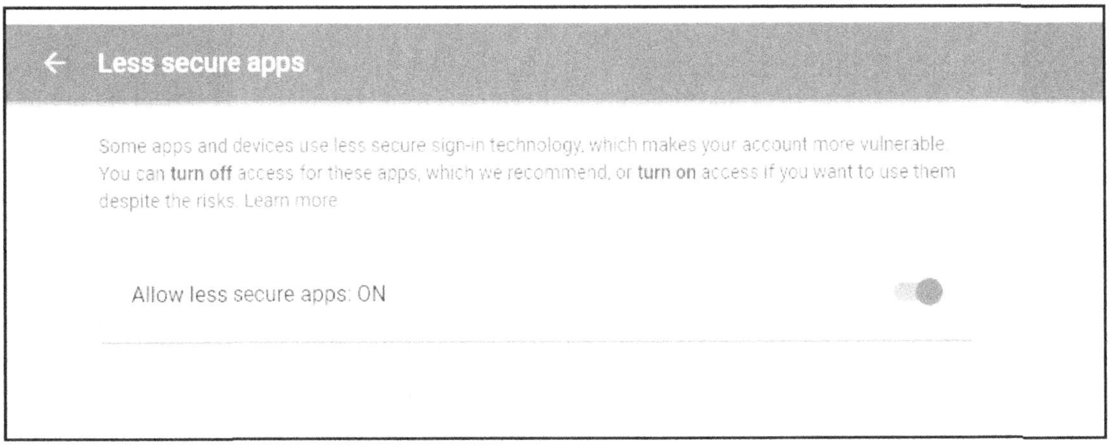

Gmail isn't the only service you can use with Nodemailer you can basically use any SMTP server.

Let's go back to our application and I'm going to just restart the server.

We'll go to the `Contact` page and let's go ahead and just enter `John Doe` as **Name**, `Test message field` as **Message**:

Alright, so let's submit and we get redirected and you can see `Message Sent`:

So now what I'm going to do is just open my Gmail and remember it's coming from my email ID since that's what we're logged in as, so it says **me**, and there's our submission. We have the **Name**, the **Email**, and the **Message**. So that's pretty much it as far as the functionality goes.

If you want to kind of add some content to this you could do that. For instance, let's go to our `app.js` file and we could say a `Computer Not Working`. And for instance in the `index.pug` page the three `h2` boxes down we could say like `Virus Removal`, `Hardware Issues`, and `Software Issues` instead of the headings. Restart the server and here we see it:

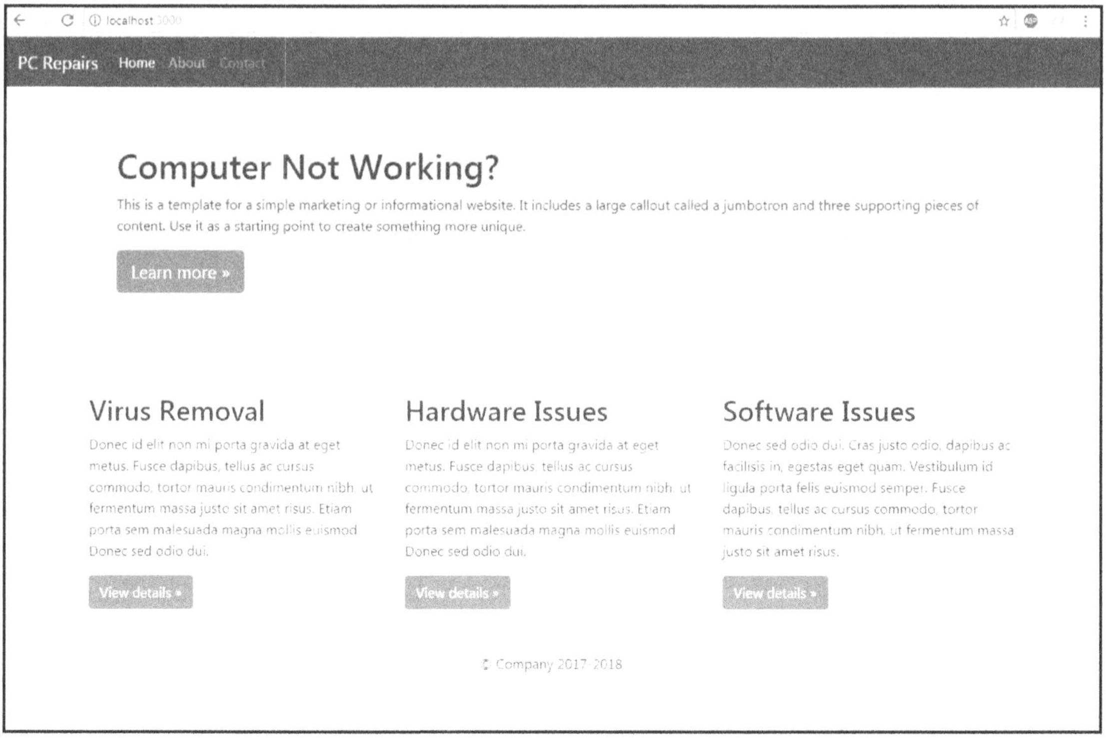

Of course you can continue to add pages, maybe you want a `Services` page. All you would have to do is just copy one of these and have our services route and then render a file called `services.pug` in the views.

Summary

With the concepts that we learned in this project, we have now created a basic Express website using Express and Node.js. It's easy, so feel free to do what you want, experiment with it, but that's going to be it for this project.

3
The User Login System

In this project we'll build a user authentication system using Node.js, Express, and Passport. Passport is a very flexible authentication system for Node.js and if you look at the documentation, there's a lot of good stuff, a lot of good knowledge, and it shows you how to do anything from logging in using a local database like we'll be doing, up to logging in with Facebook, Twitter, or Google. It's very flexible.

Let me just give you a quick idea. First we'll register for an account, say email will be `harry@gmail.com`, username will be `harry`, and you can also upload an avatar. Register and it'll say we're registered, and we can log in. Let's log in, and it'll redirect us to the Members Area. We'll not do anything further than this because it's just the authentication system. You also see we have a **Logout** button; if I click on that it logs us out. That's what we'll be doing, pretty simple but flexible in terms of using it with with another application.

In addition to learning Passport, in this chapter, we will also learn:

- Getting started with MongoDB – part A
- Getting started with MongoDB – part B
- App and middleware setup
- Views and layout
- Register form and validation
- Models and user registration
- Password hashing with bcrypt
- Passport login authentication

Getting started with MongoDB – part A

In this project we'll be creating an authentication system where users can go and they can register, log in, and we can implement some kind of access control. It's going to be kind of a big project compared to the the first two.

There are a few different modules and technologies. We'll be using MongoDB, which is a NoSQL database; it's quite different from a relational database. If you've never used NoSQL specifically, MongoDB is a document NoSQL database. So it holds what's called documents, and all documents really are are JSON objects, that's how they're formatted. They're really easy to use, are scalable, and these databases were created to just hold just tons and tons of data!

Installing MongoDB

We're on Windows, so we'll install MongoDB.

1. If we go to `mongodb.org/downloads` you'll see a page like this:

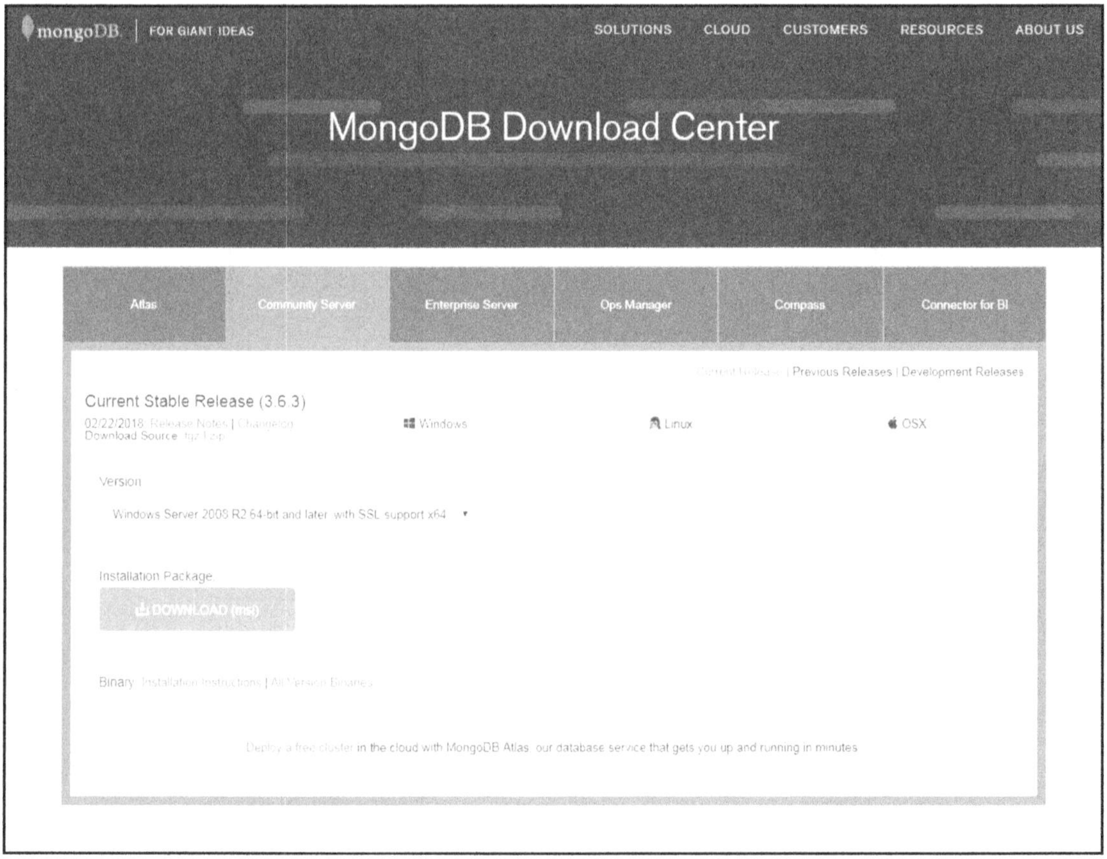

I'm on a Windows 64-bit machine so I'll download the file.

2. We'll save that file. It's about 93 megabytes so it might take a minute. The main module that we'll be using for user registrations and all that is called **Passport**, which is a really well-known module for authentication with Node.js. We'll also be using something called `bcrypt`, which will allow us to encrypt our passwords. Because you don't want to save plaintext passwords in your database by any means, you don't want to do that ever. So it's important to have something to encrypt the passwords.

3. I'll open the downloaded setup, accept the agreement, and click on **Next**:

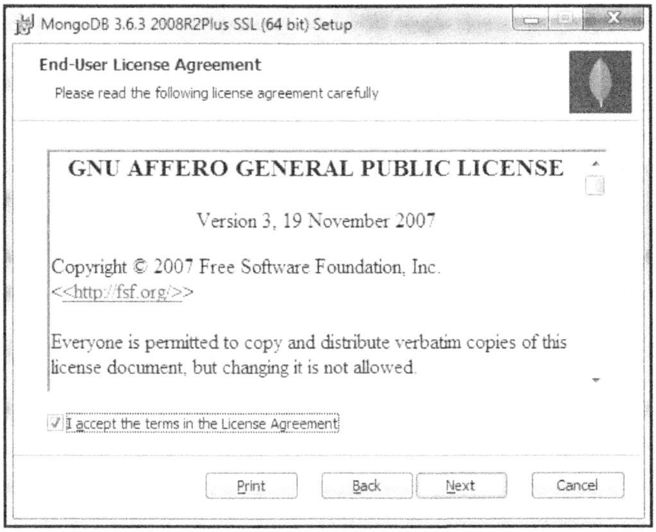

4. By default, it's probably going to install it in the `Program Files` folder, but I don't want to do that. I want it in my `C:` drive, so I'll change the installation location. Now, click on **Browse**, and I'll go to `C:` and create a new folder named `mongodb`:

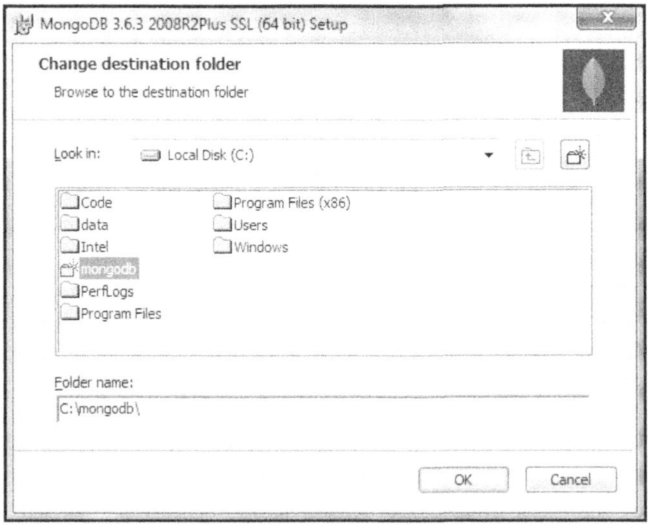

5. So we want to install it right there. We'll click on **OK**, then **Next**, and then **Install**. So once it's finished installing, there are a few things we have to do before we can actually use it, so let's go into the `C:` drive and then `mongodb`.
6. It basically just gave us this `bin` folder, that's where all the programs are including `mongo.exe` and `Mongod.exe`, which is the daemon. What we want to do is create a couple of folders inside the `mongodb` folder, we want one called `data` and inside this folder, we want another folder called `db`. Alongside `data` and `bin`, we want a `log` folder.
7. Now what we want to do is open a Windows command prompt and we want to open it as administrator. Actually if you go to search, we want the `cmd` program we want to run as administrator.
8. Now what we'll do is navigate to that `mongodb` folder:

```
cd mongodb
```

We can see we have the `bin`, `data`, and `log` folders. Now we want to go into the `bin` folder so `cd bin`, and what we want to do is we want to enter `mongod` and add a bunch of different flags. This is because we need to tell it where the `data` folder is and where the `log` file is going to be.

9. So, the first flag will be `--directoryperdb` and then we'll type in `--dbpath`. That's going to be in our `C:\mongodb\data\db`. The next thing will be the `--logpath` flag and this is going to be in our `C:\mongodb\log`, and then the name of it will be `mongodb.log`. Then we will specify `--logappend` and the reason we're doing that is because we don't want the log files to get overwritten, we want to just append them to the end. We then need to add two more things: `--rest`, which will allow us to use the REST interface and `--install`, which will let us run it as a service:

```
mongod --directoryperdb --dbpath C:\mongodb\data\db --logpath
C:\mongodb\log\mongodb.log --logappend --rest --install
```

10. Let's run the command. Now we want to try to run the service, so we'll enter `net start MongoDB`:

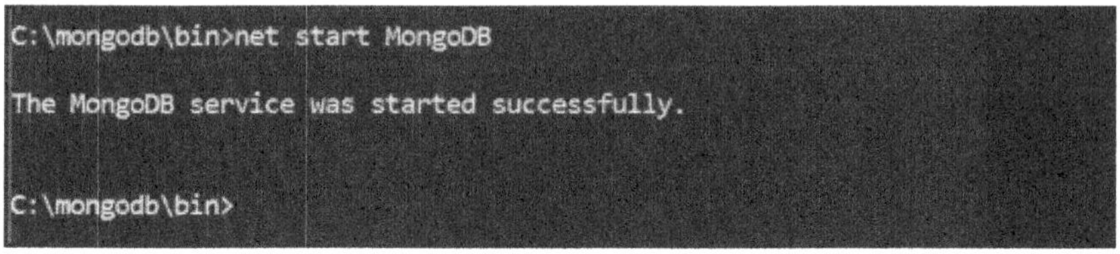

It says **The MongoDB service was started successfully**.

Now there's also a shell program that comes with Mongo. As long as we're in the `bin` folder, we should be able to run it with the `mongo` command. This opens up a nice shell interface:

```
C:\mongodb\bin>mongo
MongoDB shell version: 3.2.3
connecting to: test
Welcome to the MongoDB shell.
For interactive help, type "help".
For more comprehensive documentation, see
        http://docs.mongodb.org/
Questions? Try the support group
        http://groups.google.com/group/mongodb-user
Server has startup warnings:
2016-03-08T10:20:37.161-0500 I CONTROL  [main] ** WARNING: --rest is spec
ified without --httpinterface,
2016-03-08T10:20:37.162-0500 I CONTROL  [main] **          enabling http
interface
>
```

We can use this shell interface and we can do things like create databases, create documents, update, delete, and pretty much anything we want. We can also manage our collections. If you've never used MongoDB or a NoSQL database collections can be, I guess they could be compared to tables in a relational database. So for instance if we have a database for our blog we might have a post collection, we might have a categories collection and so on, and users. Now we're not going to go in depth with the syntax in this section but I will show you a few things.

So if we just say `db` that's going to tell us what database we're currently in. So by default, we're in the `test` database:

```
interface
> db
test
>
```

If we want to create a new one and go into it we can use `use`. So let's just say `use customers`:

```
> use customers
switched to db customers
```

You can see that it created the database customers and switched us to it. So if we say `db`, it'll show us that we're in `customers`. We can also use `show dbs` and that will show us all the available databases:

```
> show dbs
local  0.000GB
>
```

Now the reason you don't see `customers` or `test` is because there's nothing in it. If there's nothing in it, it's not going to show it. So what we want to do is create a collection. We'll say `db.createCollection` and we'll put the collection name in collection; let's call it `customers`:

```
db.createCollection('customer');
```

And it gives us this {"**ok**" : **1**} result. Now if we say `show dbs`, you can see we have a `customers` database:

```
> show dbs
customers  0.000GB
local      0.000GB
>
```

We named the database and the collection `customers`, which we probably shouldn't have done but it's fine. We can also use a command called `show collections` and you can see we have one collection called `customers`:

```
> show collections
customers
>
```

So in the next part of this section, we'll actually create the database for our project and also show you how to add data and also how to fetch it.

Getting started with MongoDB – part B

In the last section we went ahead and installed MongoDB, I showed you how to log into the shell and create a database, as well as create a collection. Now what we'll do is create the database for our application, for our `nodeauth` application. We'll insert some data and I'll also show you how to fetch that data from the shell.

Data fetching from the shell

So let's create a new database:

1. To do that we can simply use `use` and then name it. I'm going to call this `nodeauth`:

   ```
   use nodeauth
   ```

2. You can see we switch to `nodeauth` and we want to create a collection called users. Let's say `db.createCollection` and I'll call this `users`:

   ```
   db.createCollection('users');
   ```

   We'll run that and now if we say `show collections` we have `users`.

3. Now to insert a user, we can simply use `db.users.insert` and then insert a document, which is basically just a JSON object. So we need our curly braces and the first thing we'll give it is a `name`, I'll use my name.
4. The next thing we want is `email`. Next is `username`. For username, I'll put `brad` and we also want a password. Now when we build our application we'll enter the password. The password will be encrypted, but for now I'll put a plaintext password as `1234`:

   ```
   db.users.insert({name: 'Brad Traversy', email:
   'techguyinfo@gmail.com', username: 'brad', password: '1234'});
   ```

5. So that looks good; let's run that:

```
> db.users.insert({name: 'Brad Traversy', email:'techguyinfo@gmail.com',u
sername: 'brad', password:'1234'});
WriteResult({ "nInserted" : 1 })
>
```

You can see we get `"nInserted" : 1`. Now if we want to see the records in our database, we can say `db.users.find` and that gives us our user:

```
> db.users.find()
{ "_id" : ObjectId("56def05ec752750afa4ec8c4"), "name" : "Brad Traversy",
 "email" : "techguyinfo@gmail.com", "username" : "brad", "password" : "12
34" }
>
```

6. So let's add one more. I'll change some stuff. For `username`, we'll say `john` and change `email` and `name`:

```
db.users.insert({name: 'John Doe', email: 'jdoe@gmail.com', username:
'john', password: '1234'});
```

7. Let's run that. Now if we use `db.users.find`, it gives us both users:

```
> db.users.find()
{ "_id" : ObjectId("56def05ec752750afa4ec8c4"), "name" : "Brad Traversy",
 "email" : "techguyinfo@gmail.com", "username" : "brad", "password" : "12
34" }
{ "_id" : ObjectId("56def08ec752750afa4ec8c5"), "name" : "John Doe", "ema
il" : "jdoe@gmail.com", "username" : "john", "password" : "1234" }
>
```

There's also a helper function we can add on to this called `.pretty` and that gives us a nicely formatted list:

```
db.users.find().pretty()
```

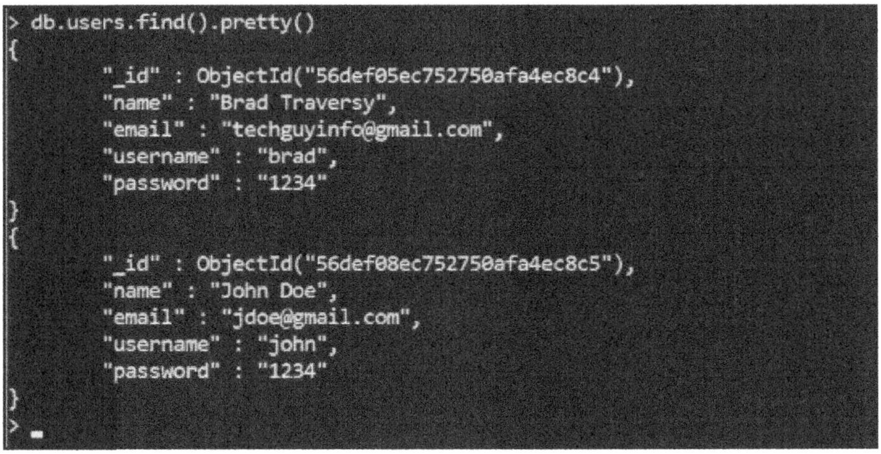

Now you'll notice that we have this `_id` and we didn't create that. MongoDB creates `ObjectId` for us automatically, which is really nice because it is unique. So we can use it in our application as a primary key.

Create, read, update, and delete using MongoDB

The next thing I'll show you is how we can do an update. So to do that, we'll say `db.users.update` and then we'll pass in the first parameter, which will go inside the curly braces, and let's use `username`. Our `username` equals `john`. We'll put the next parameter in curly braces and we'll say `$set` and then that will have its own set of curly braces. We will change that to, let's say `email`. So we'll say email and let's change it to `jdoe@yahoo.com`. Press *Enter*. Now if we go and we say `find`, you will see that `John Doe` has a Yahoo email:

```
db.users.update({username: 'john'},{$set:{email:'jdoe@yahoo.com'}});
```

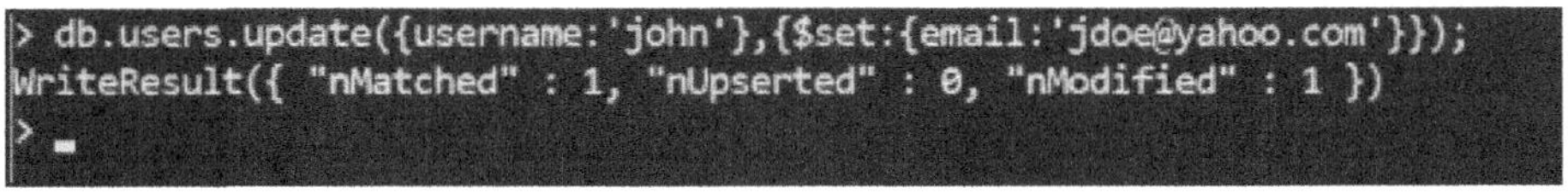

And using that set you want to use that `$set` because if you don't then it's just going to change the email. but it'll get rid of everything else, and you don't want that usually. So that's how we can update. Now let's go ahead and let's add one more.

I'm going to change `username` to `mike` and I'm going to keep that as it is because what I'm going to do is show you how to remove a record:

```
db.users.insert({name: 'John Doe', email:'jdoe@gmail.com', username:
'mike', password:'1234'});
```

If we use `find`, you can see the name is still is `John Doe` but the user name is `mike`:

```
> db.users.find().pretty()
{
        "_id" : ObjectId("56def05ec752750afa4ec8c4"),
        "name" : "Brad Traversy",
        "email" : "techguyinfo@gmail.com",
        "username" : "brad",
        "password" : "1234"
}
{
        "_id" : ObjectId("56def08ec752750afa4ec8c5"),
        "name" : "John Doe",
        "email" : "jdoe@yahoo.com",
        "username" : "john",
        "password" : "1234"
}
{
        "_id" : ObjectId("56def15dc752750afa4ec8c6"),
        "name" : "John Doe",
        "email" : "jdoe@gmail.com",
        "username" : "mike",
        "password" : "1234"
}
>
```

So what we want to do is delete `mike`. To do that, we'll say `db.users.remove` and then we'll pass where `username` is equal to `mike`:

```
db.users.remove({username:'mike'});
```

If we use `find` again, you can now see that `mike` is gone:

So that's how we can do create, read, update, and delete using MongoDB. We're going to keep this database as is because we'll be using it in our project.

App and middleware setup

In this section, we'll create our application. We'll be using Express and we'll use something called the Express generator, which will allow us to just type in a command and have it generate a bunch of files and folders for us that we can use in our app.

Let's create a folder, you can create it wherever you want, and mine's going to be in my `Projects` folder. We'll call it `nodeauth`. Now inside the folder, I'll open my command line in that folder using Git Bash. So you want to make sure you have Express installed globally so you can access it from anywhere and also the Express generator. So we'll run the following command:

```
npm install -g express
```

Then we also want to run the following command:

```
install -g express-generator
```

Now while we're in the `nodeauth` folder, let's just use `express`. It will create a bunch of stuff for us. It gave us a `bin` folder, `public`, `routes`, `views`, `app.js`, and our `package.json`. What we'll do is open up the `package.json` file and I'll add this project to my editor. Inside `package.json` you can see that it's actually added a bunch of dependencies for us, `body-parser`, `cookie-parser`, `debug`, `express` of course, `pub` which is the template engine, `morgan` and `serve-favicon`:

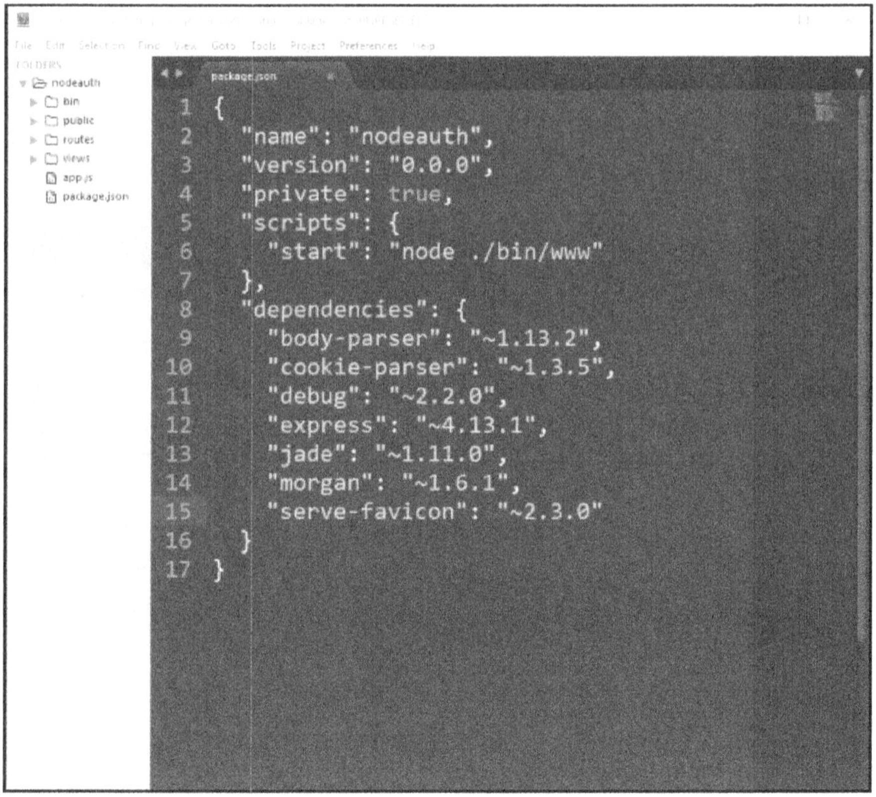

There are actually quite a few dependencies that we need to add. The first one will be `mongodb`, and I'll be using the latest version of all of these. We also want something called `mongoose` which is an ORM. It will give us a way to easily interact with our database through our application. There are a few different ones, `mongoose` is one of the most popular, and it's really easy to use. We also need something called `connect-flash` and that has to do with the ability to add messages. So for instance, when we log in we want something to say you're now logged in. Then we need something else to go with that, which is called `express-messages`.

Next one we need is the `express-validator` so we can have form validation. Now we'll be using something called Passport, that will be for our login and our registration, so we want Passport. Then we want something called `passport-local` and Passport actually comes with a few different modules. For instance, there's a Facebook one, there's Twitter, etc. You can actually log in using those, but the last Passport one we'll want is `passport-http`. Then we also want something called `multer`, and that's a module that will allow us to upload images if we want:

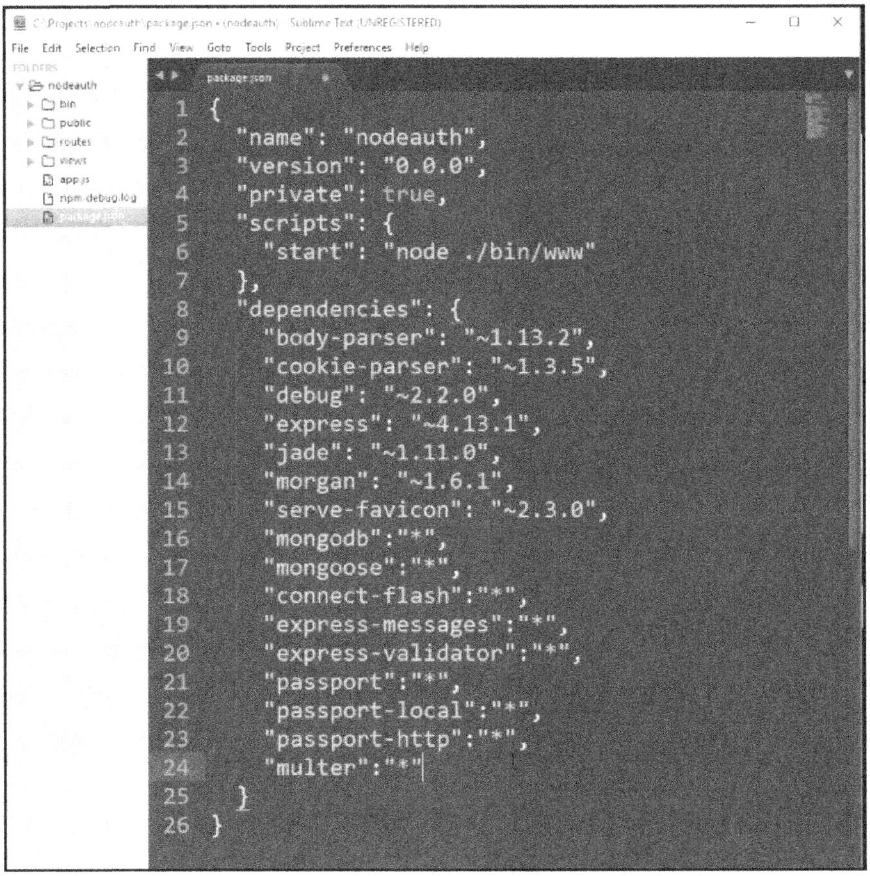

So let's save this and then we're going to go back into the command line and we'll use `npm install`. It might take a minute or two because there are quite a few dependencies for it to install. Now we have the `node_modules` folder with a whole bunch of different things in it. We'll not need to go through that, as very rarely will you need to edit `node_modules`.

Now what we'll do is close the `package.json` file and open up `app.js`. Let's go under the `bodyParser` require and you can see that all of the modules that the generator included are installed, it required them automatically. Let's insert one thing that we forgot, `express-session`, we didn't have that. We could just add it inside `package.json` and do an `npm install`. But I also just want to show you that we can say `npm install` and then whatever the module is, it will be `express-session`:

```
npm install express-session
```

Now as it is installed, it won't add the module to the `package.json` file. If we want it to add, we need to add `--save`. Now you can see `express-session` inside `package.json`. Let's go back to our app file and include it, actually this is going to be `var session = require('express-session')`.

After that let's include `passport`. Then with `passport` we have to create what's called a strategy, and I'd like to put it right under the `passport` inclusion. So we'll say `var LocalStrategy = require` and this is where we want to require `passport-local`, but we also want to add `.Strategy` at the end. After that, let's do `multer`. We also want our `connect-flash`, then we want `mongodb` and then `mongoose`. Now under `mongoose`, we want to create a `db` variable and I'll set that equal to `mongoose.connection`. Moving along you can see that we have two variables `routes` and `users`, and we're setting those to the `index` file inside of the `routes` folder, and then the `users` file inside the `routes` folder:

```
var session = require('express-session');
var passport = require('passport');
var LocalStrategy = require('passport-local').Strategy;
var multer = require('multer');
var flash = require('connect-flash');
var mongo = require('mongodb');
var mongoose = require('mongoose');
var db = mongoose.connection;

var routes = require('./routes/index');
var users = require('./routes/users');
```

Now in the last project, we put our `routes` directly in the `app.js` file. We had `app.get`, then the route, and then a function with whatever we want to happen when we hit that route. In this case, we have them in their own separate files, so you can see in our `index.js` file, we have `router.get` and you know we have the rest of the route. Now when doing this, we need to have the `module.exports = router` line. That's what's going to allow us to access it from a different file; in this case, the `routes` variable. If we don't have the file, it's not going to work.

Now in the users.js file, you'll see we also have router.get. However, since this is in the users file the way we have it set up, what this means is really if we go to /user or users. Now if we put, let's say, /edit, then it's really going to be going to /users/edit. So let me just save it. Inside app.js file, we'll instantiate the app variable with Express. We tell the system we want to use Pug, and then there is just middleware stuff, nothing we really have to pay attention to right now.

This line here, app.use(express.static(path.join(__dirname, 'public')));, is saying that we want public to be the static folder, and then in app.set('/users', users) since we have our routes in separate files, we have to make sure we use app.use. That way, you know the route and then the name of the variable that holds the file. That's what we don't really need to care about. Now there is a bit of middleware we have to add; for instance, to use multer for file uploads, let's say Handle File uploads, what we need to do is use app.use(multer) and then that's going to be a function. In there, we just want to pass in a destination. So we want to say dest and let's say ./uploads:

```
// Handle File uploads
app.use(multer({dest:'./uploads'}));
```

Middleware for sessions

So now we want to do the middleware for sessions. In app.use and we use sessions and then inside, let's use secrets. This could be anything, but I'll type in secret. We also want one called saveUninitialized. That's going to be true, and then we want resave and that's also going to be true:

```
// Handle Sessions
app.use(sessions({
  secret: 'secret',
  saveUninitialized: true,
  resave: true
}));
```

Down below, after the session, let's do our Passport middleware. Passport again is the authentication system, so let's say app.use and we use passport.initialize, which is a function, and then we use passport.session:

```
// Passport
app.use(passport.initialize());
app.use(passport.session());
```

The next thing is `Validator`. In here, we use `expressValidator`, which we should have up and ready. And here's our usage, **Middleware Options**, this is what we want:

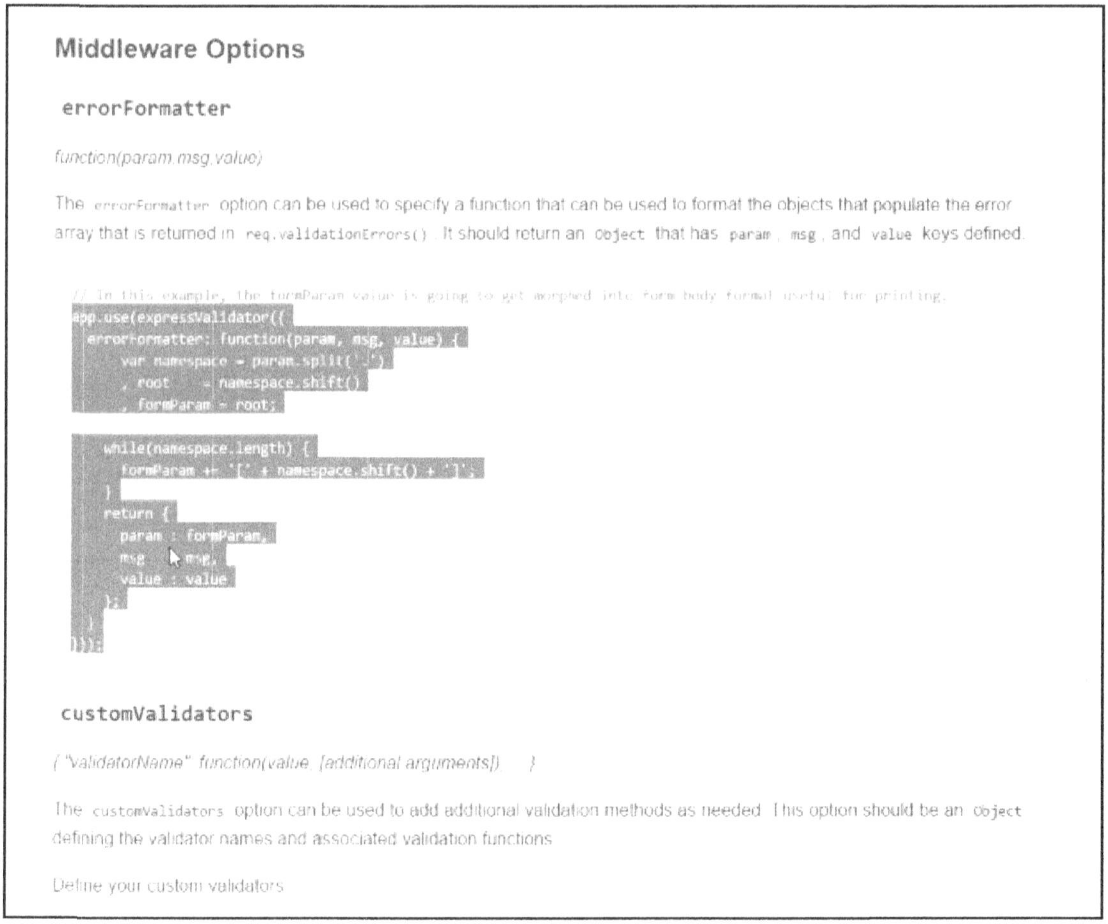

Middleware Options

errorFormatter

function(param,msg,value)

The `errorFormatter` option can be used to specify a function that can be used to format the objects that populate the error array that is returned in `req.validationErrors()`. It should return an `Object` that has `param`, `msg`, and `value` keys defined.

```
// In this example, the formParam value is going to get morphed into form body format useful for printing.
app.use(expressValidator({
  errorFormatter: function(param, msg, value) {
      var namespace = param.split('.')
      , root    = namespace.shift()
      , formParam = root;

    while(namespace.length) {
      formParam += '[' + namespace.shift() + ']';
    }
    return {
      param : formParam,
      msg   : msg,
      value : value
    };
  }
}));
```

customValidators

{ "validatorName": function(value, [additional arguments]), ... }

The `customValidators` option can be used to add additional validation methods as needed. This option should be an `Object` defining the validator names and associated validation functions.

Define your custom validators:

I'll grab the whole code, copy it, and paste it into `app.js`.

Middleware for messages

Now we also need our middleware for the messages, so let's say `connect-flash`. Actually, I want to look at the Express messages. Let's grab the code from here:

Express 3+

Install connect-flash and add them as middleware:

```
app.use(require('connect-flash')());
app.use(function (req, res, next) {
  res.locals.messages = require('express-messages')(req, res);
  next();
});
```

Adding Messages

On the server:

```
req.flash("info", "Email queued");
req.flash("info", "Email sent");
req.flash("error", "Email delivery failed");
```

For further information see connect-flash.

I'll put that right inside of `app.js`. It's quite a bit of middleware that needs to be configured just because we'll be so many different modules. So let's try to save and run the server. We'll say `npm start`. Let's see, we have an error here, **app.use requires middleware**. So we include `multer`. Let's say `var upload = multer` and then we can put in our destination. Let's put the validator right under `passport`. It looks like it's running. Let's go to `localhost3000` and we get **Express**:

We open the **Console** and it looks like we have no errors. Good! So we have our middleware set up. In the next section, we're going to get into our views and layouts.

Views and layouts

We'll now get into the views and layouts part of our application. I want to use Bootstrap, so I get `bootstrap.com`. I'll download it and open that up, and let's also open up the application folder:

All this stuff will go in the `public` folder. We will put `bootstrap.css` in the `stylesheets` folder, in the `javascripts` folder is where we'll put `bootstrap.js`. Let's go back to our `views` folder and you can see we have `layout` file, if we open that up. Basically, the generator gave us these templates and it just has `html`, `head`, `body` tags, and things like that:

```
doctype html
html
  head
    title= title
    link(rel='stylesheet', href='/stylesheets/style.css')
  body
    block content
```

It includes the `style.css` sheet in the `public` folder. Now for the layouts, in your project files, you'll have a file called `_layout.pub` and that's going to include just a very basic boilerplate for a Bootstrap page. This is basically just the `navbar` and the content area. We have our `doctype html`, the head area. We'll Bootstrap along with `style.css`. In our `body`, we have a `navbar`, we have the unordered list right here with the list items, then we have a `container` div and inside that `container` we have our `content`, and then at the bottom we'll include `jquery` and our `bootstrap.js`:

```
.container
block content
script(src='https://ajax.googleapis.com/ajax/libs/jquery/1.11.1/jquery.min.
js')
script(src='javascripts/bootstrap.js')
```

Let's save that and check it out. Actually that doesn't look right, as the navbar should go all the way across. I think, the problem is in the `style.css` file. So let's go ahead and open that up, that's in `public/stylesheets`. We see that we have a `padding: 50px` for the `body`. We don't want that, so let's just get rid of all that. And there we go:

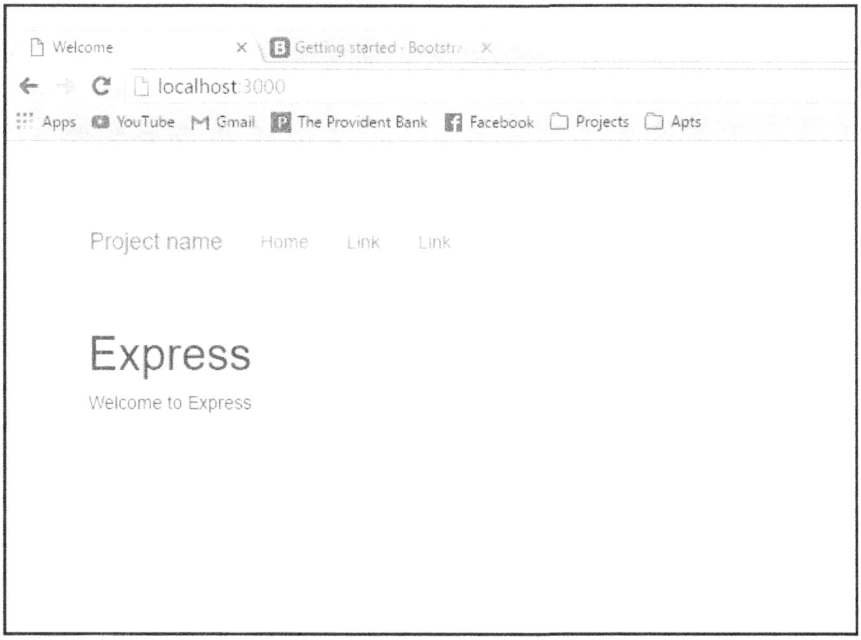

We have our navbar. Let's go ahead and change the project name to `NodeAuth`, and for the link present, we'll say `Register`. That will go to `/users/register`. The other one will be `Login`, so that one's going to go to `users/login`:

```
a.navbar-brand(href='#') NodeAuth
.navbar-collapse.collapse
  ul.nav.navbar-nav
    li
      a(href='/') Home
    li
      a(href='/users/register') Register
    li
      a(href='/users/login') Login
```

Let's also add a `Logout`. I want to put `Logout` on the right-hand side. So let's go on the same level as `ul`, and we'll say `ul.nav.navbar-nav` and with `navbar-right`:

```
ul.nav.navbar-nav.navbar-right
```

We'll put a space and paste the `Login` code, change this to `Logout`, and there we go:

```
li
  a(href='/users/login') Logout
```

Now **Logout** isn't going to be showing when we're not logged in. Similarly, we won't see **Register** and **Login** when we are logged in, but we'll have to do that later:

Let's go to some of the other views.

Index

The index is going to be the members page or the dashboard, the page that you'll go to after you log in. When we're done our final product, you won't be able to actually visit the members' page unless you're logged in; if you do, you'll get redirected to the `Login` page. But for now, let's take the index and for the `h1`, let's say `Members Area`, and the paragraph will say `Welcome to the members area`:

```
extends layout

block content
  h1 Members Area
  p Welcome to the members area
```

We can actually change the home link. I'll change that to `Members`:

```
li
  a(href='/') Members
li
```

The next thing I will do is take care of the register route, because if we click it now, we get a **Not Found** error message:

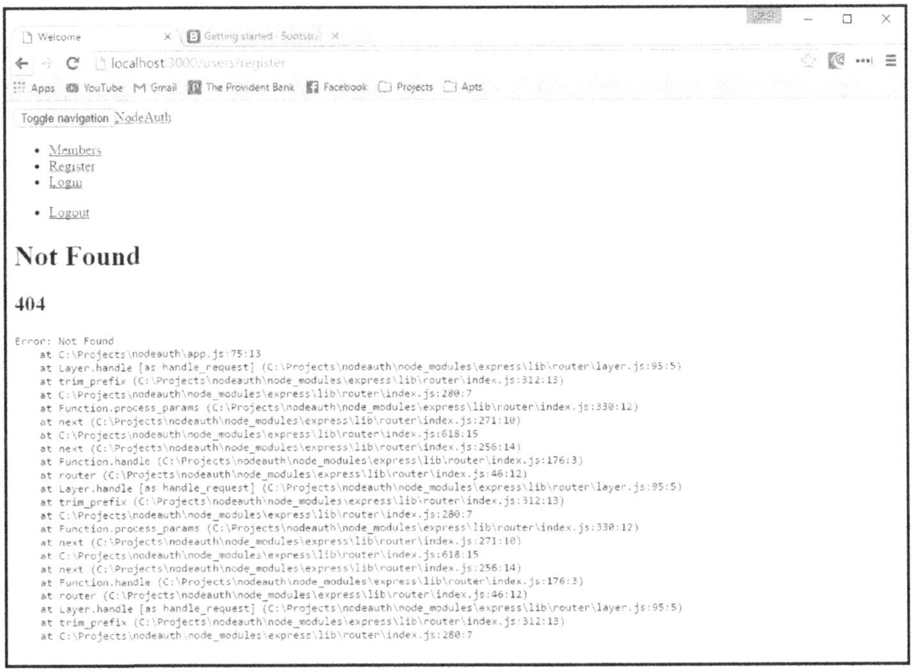

We'll now go to `users.js` inside our routes and let's copy this:

```
router.get('/', function(req, res, next) {
  res.send('respond with a resources');
});
```

This will be `/register`. Now remember since we're in the `users` route, this will be `/user/register`. What we want to do here is say `res.render` and we want to render `register`:

```
router.get('/register', function(req, res, next) {
  res.render('register');
});
```

So we'll save this. Now we need to create a register. Let's go to `views`, create a new file, and save it as `register.pub`. So in `register.pug` we'll use `extends layout` and then we add `block content`. Let's put in an `h2`, give it a class of `page-header`, and we'll say `Register` and put a paragraph as shown in the following code snippet:

```
extends layout

block content
  h2.page-header Register
  p Please register using the form below
```

Let's actually just make sure that this will load if we go to our `users/register`. Let's restart the server:

We're getting it but for some reason the CSS isn't showing:

If we look at the source code, we have `stylesheets/bootstrap` and that's not found. I think we just need to add a `/` in front of that. Let's go to our `layout.pug` file and put a `/` before both our `stylesheets`:

```
link(href='/stylesheets/bootstrap.css', rel='stylesheet')
link(href='/stylesheets/style.css', rel='stylesheet')
```

There we go. So there's our register page:

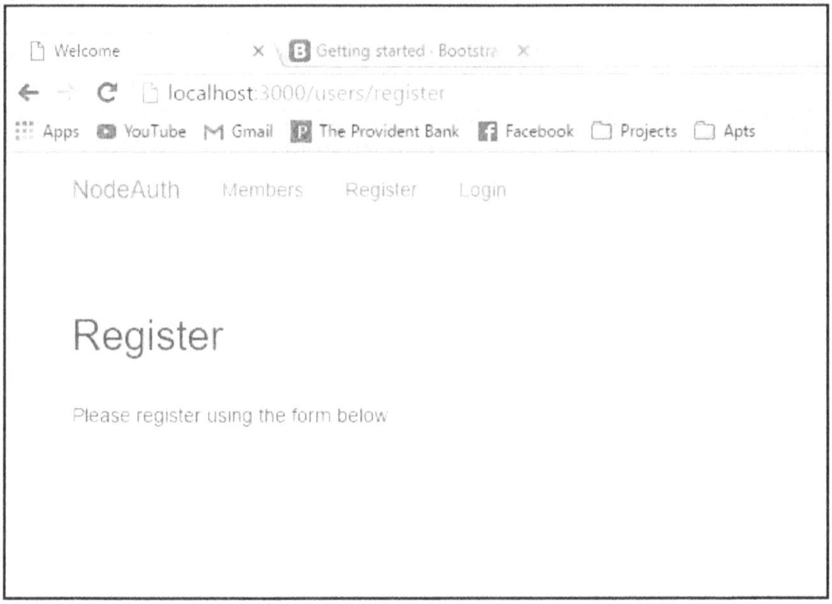

Creating a form

We'll now create a form, so let's go back to `register.pub`. We'll put in a form, give it a `method` of `post`, and let's give it an action, `/users/register`. Now we'll have a file upload, a profile image, and we need to make our form multipart. We'll give to give it an `enctype` and that's going to be `multipart/form-data`. That has nothing to do with Node, that's just HTML. If you want to upload a file, you need to add that attribute. Now we'll add a class called `form-group`, and I'll space that and let's give this a label of `Name`. Then we want an `input.form-control`. We'll give it a name of `name`:

```
extends layout

block content
  h2.page-header Register
  p Please register using the form below
  form(method='post', action='/users/register', enctype='multipart/form-
data')
    .form-group
    label Name
    input.form-control(name='name', type='text', placeholder='Enter Name')
```

Let's give it a `type` of `text`. Then we'll give it a `placeholder`. We'll copy the `.form-group` code, because we'll need a couple more of those.

After `name` will be `email`, so this will be `name='email'` and the `type` will also be `email`. The next thing will be the `username`, that's going to be `text`, and then we need a `password`. Don't forget to change the labels as you type the code! We'll want the confirm password field, so I'm going to copy this and we'll call this `password2`:

```
.form-group
label Email
input.form-control(name='email', type='email', placeholder='Enter
Username')
.form-group
label Username
input.form-control(name='username', type='text', placeholder='Enter Email')
.form-group
label Password
input.form-control(name='password', type='password', placeholder='Enter
Password')
.form-group
label Password
input.form-control(name='password2', type='password', placeholder='Confirm
Password')
```

Finally, we want our profile image. So for this label, we'll say `Profile Image`. Then we'll have our form control; the name will be `profileimage`, `type` would be `file`, and we don't want a `placeholder`. Alright, so those are the fields, now we'll also need a button so let's go right in the code, and this will be `input type` we'll say `submit` and we need to put this in parentheses. I also want to give it a class, so we'll say `.btn` and `.btn-primary`. That'll make the button blue. Then we need the type `submit`. Let's also give it a name of `submit` and we also need a `value`, we'll say `Register`:

```
  .form-group
  label Profile Image
  input.form-control(name='profileimage', type='file')
input.btn.btn-primary(type='submit', name='submit', value='Register')
```

Alright, let's take a look at it. So there's our form:

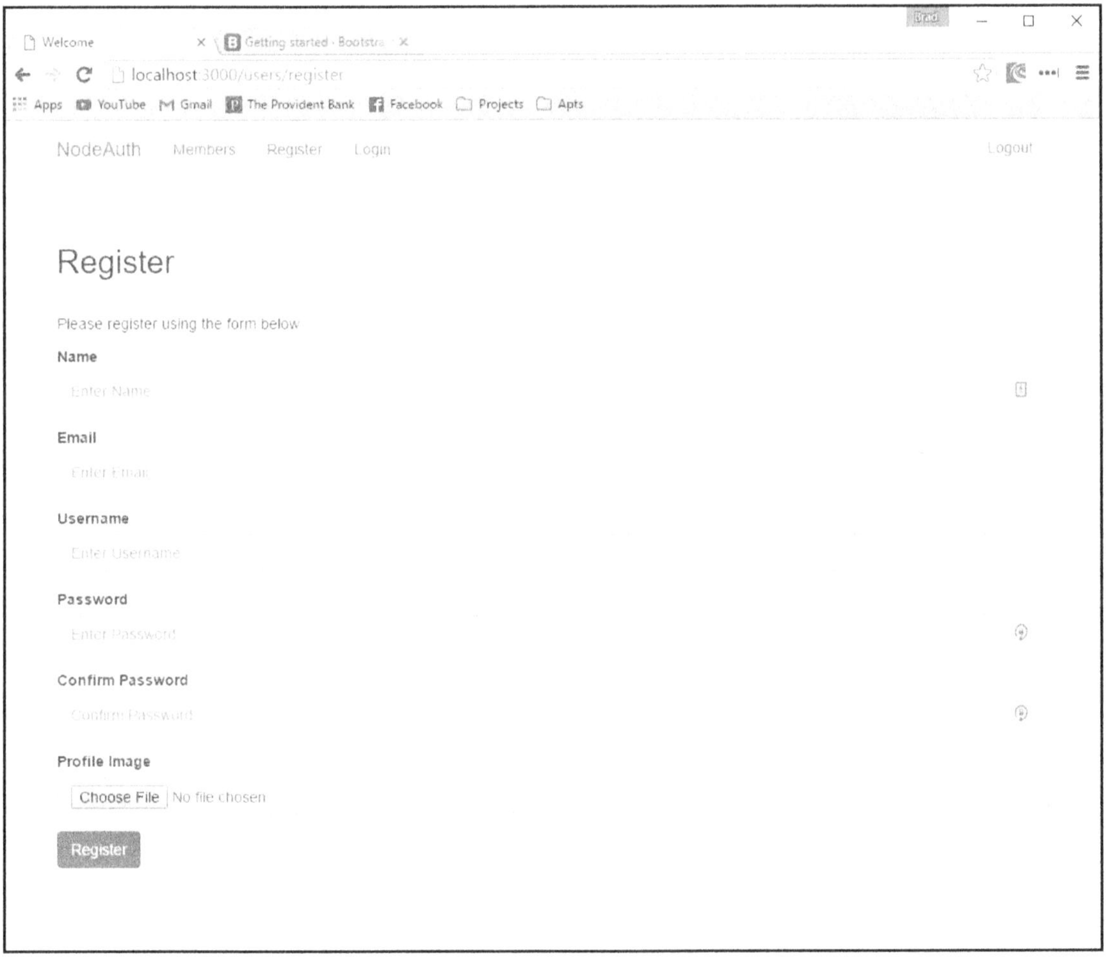

We're not going to handle the submission yet. What I want to do is get the login view done.

Creating the login view

I'll copy the form code because it's going to be very similar to the registration form:

```
extends layout

block content
  h2.page-header Login
  p Please login below
  form(method='post', action='/users/login')
  label Username
  input.form-control(name='username', type='text', placeholder='Enter
Email')
  .form-group
  label Password
  input.form-control(name='password', type='password', placeholder='Enter
Password')
input.btn.btn-primary(type='submit', name='submit', value='Login')
```

But we'll create a new view and let's save this as `login.pub`. We'll paste the preceding code completely and we'll change a couple of things: we'll use `Login` and say `Please login below`. It will go to `user/login` and we don't need the `enctype` attribute. All we want is the `Username` and `Password`, so we'll get rid of the rest and we'll change `Register` to `Login`. Alright, so let's save that and then we need to go back to our `users.route` file and restart the server:

```
/*GET users listing. */
router.get('/', function(req, res, next) {
  res.send('respond with a resource');
});

router.get('/register', function(req, res, next) {
  res.render('register');
});

router.get('/login', function(req, res, next) {
  res.render('login');
});

module.exports = router;
```

We'll go to **Login** and there's our `Login` page. Alright, so we have our views:

One last thing I would like to do is have these highlighted with the active class. So what we can do is let's go to index and see how we're passing a `title: 'Express'`. Let's change this to `title: 'Members'`. Then also in the `users` route we'll add a `title`. So the first one will be `Register` and the next one will be `Login`:

```
/*GET users listing. */
router.get('/', function(req, res, next) {
  res.send('respond with a resource');
});

router.get('/register', function(req, res, next) {
  res.render('register',{title: 'Register'});
});

router.get('/login', function(req, res, next) {
  res.render('login',{title: 'Login'});
});

module.exports = router;
```

Now if we go to our layout file where our links are, we can test for those. So in the `li` tag, let's add parentheses and say `class=`. Let's then add another set of parentheses and say `title` is equal to `Members`, then the class will be `active`. If not, we can do that with a colon; this is just a shorthand `if` statement . If not, then the class will be nothing. Alright, so we want to just grab the `li` tag and paste that again:

```
ul.nav.navbar-nav
  li(class=(title == 'Members' ? 'active' : ''))
    a(href='/') Members
  li(class=(title == 'Register' ? 'active' : ''))
    a(href='/users/register') Register
  li(class=(title == 'Login' ? 'active' : ''))
    a(href='/users/login') Login
```

For one of them we'll change to `Register`, and for the other one we'll change to `Login`. Restart the server and you can see **Members** is highlighted. If I click on **Register**, that gets highlighted, and the same thing with **Login**:

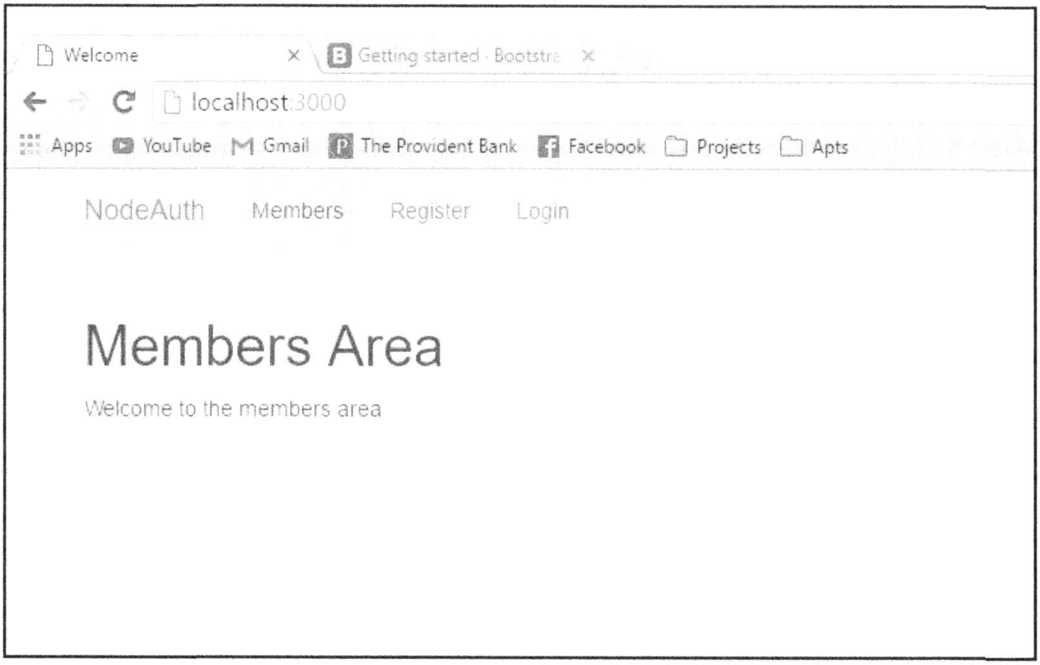

So our views and layouts are all set up. In the next section, we're going to take a look at registration and we'll create that functionality.

The register form and validation

Now that we have our views and layouts all set, we want to be able to register a user. So we have our form and if we open up `routes/users`, you can see we have a couple of requests but we have all get requests. We need a post request to `user/register`. So I'll copy the `route.get` method and I'll change `get` to `post`, and let's get rid of `res.render`:

```
router.get('/register', function(req, res, next) {
  res.render('register',{title: 'Register'});
});

router.get('/login', function(req, res, next) {
  res.render('login',{title: 'Login'});
});

router.post('/register', function(req, res, next){

});
```

Now it's really important to understand that when we submit a form and we can grab the data using `req.body.email`. We usually do that using `body-parser`, which we have installed and set up, but `body-parser` cannot handle file uploads and we have the profile image upload, that's where `multer` comes in. If we look at our `app.js` file, you can see we have this, and we'll set our upload directory. So what we actually need to do is copy the `multer` code from `app.js`, and we'll paste that up here in `users.js`:

```
var express = require('express');
var router = express.Router();
var multer = require('multer');
var upload = multer({dest: './uploads'});
```

There's a little extra step, we need to add an extra parameter as shown below. What we need to do is say `upload.single()` and put the name `profileimage`. Alright, so that's what we want to use. So now we should be able to get values for the fields. To test things out, let's say `console.log` and let's say `req.body.name`:

```
router.post('/register', upload.single('profileimage'), function(req, res,
next){
  console.log(req.body.name);
});
```

We'll save that. Make sure you restart, reload, and inside the **Name** we'll just say `Test`. Let's submit and you can see we get `test`. Now what I want to do when we submit is I want to put all those values into their own variable.

For instance, let's say `var name`, I'll set that to `req.body.name`. We'll do that to all of them, so I'll copy this line. The first one here will be `email`, the next one will be `username`, then `password`, and then `password2`. Now `password2` isn't being submitted into the database; we'll use it for validation, which we'll get to in a second:

```
router.post('/register', upload.single('profileimage'), function(req, res,
next){
  var name = req.body.name;
  var email = req.body.email;
  var username = req.body.username;
  var password = req.body.password;
  var password2 = req.body.password2;
});
```

This takes care of the text fields now, and now we have our image field to take care of. So I will do kind of a little test and say `console.log` and it should be under a `req.file`. If it was an array, instead of using single like we are using here we would use `req.files`. Alright, but let's just try that out:

```
  console.log(req.file);
});
```

We need to restart the server and I got a sample image just some balloons, so I'll try to upload that. Let's reload the page and **Choose File**, and I'll grab that image and **Register**. You can see what `req.file` gave us; it gave us a bunch of information, the field, the filename, or the fieldname, the original image name, the encoding, mimetype, destination, filename, path, and size. You can do all kinds of validations here if you want a certain size or certain, certain mimetypes, and things like that.

The first thing we want to do is test to see if the file has actually been uploaded or not. So let's try this using `if` and `else`:

```
if(req.file) {
  console.log('Uploading file...');
} else {
  console.log('No File Uploaded...');
}
```

Let's try this out. If we upload it, we get `Uploading File....` Now if we go back and we don't choose to upload, we get `No File Uploaded....` Alright so that's what we want!

Now if we go to our `nodeauth` folder you can see we have an `uploads` folder and if we look in, we actually have some files present in there. So these are image files and they'll display in the browser if we point them. But I'll delete those because they're pretty much all the same thing. We know that that's working, and now we grab that filename. So if there is a file uploaded, we'll create a variable called `profileimage = req/file.filename`. Now if there isn't one uploaded, then we create the same variable, `profileimage`, and set it to `noimage.jpg` because if there isn't one, then we'll just have a standard image that we can load to show instead of the image that's not there. So that should take care of all the file uploading stuff:

```
if(req.file) {
  console.log('Uploading file...');
  var profileimage = req.file.filename;
} else {
  console.log('No File Uploaded...');
  var profileimage = 'noimage.jpg';
}
```

Now what we want to do is we want to add some form validation. Remember we're using the Express validator, so let's just put that stuff:

```
    // Form Validator
    req.checkBody('name', 'Name field is required').notEmpty();

    // Check Errors
    var errors = req.validationErrors();

    if(errors){
      console.log('Errors');
    } else {
      console.log('No Errors');
    }
});
```

To do this, we'll say `request.checkBody`, and then in here we want the field name; in this case, `name`. Then we need a description, we'll say `Name field is required`. Next, we need a property, let's say `.notEmpty`. It's actually a function. Now before I go and add the rest of them, I just want to finish this so we can actually test it first. So the next thing we need to create a variable called `errors` and set it to `req.validationErrors`. Then we'll check for errors. So if `(errors)` then let's `console.log('Errors')`, else `('No Errors')`. Alright, let's try this out.

We'll go to the `Register` page and let's just click on it. We can see it says `Errors`. If I put a name in there and submit, we get `No Errors`. Alright, so we know that's working.

Let's add the rest of our fields here:

```
// Form Validator
req.checkBody('name', 'Name field is required').notEmpty();
req.checkBody('email', 'Email field is required').notEmpty();
req.checkBody('email', 'Email is valid').notEmail();
req.checkBody('username', 'Username field is required').notEmpty();
req.checkBody('password', 'Passwordfield is required').notEmpty();
req.checkBody('password2', 'Passwords do not
match').equals(req.body.password);
```

I'm going to copy `req.checkbody`. So we want the email to also be required. Let's put in `email`, `notEmpty()` let's just change this, we also want it to be a valid email and we have to just change this from `notEmpty()` to `isEmail`. Next one is going to be `username`, that's going to be required, next one is `password`, it's also going to be `required`, then we want `password` to match the confirm password. So this one is going to go on to `password2` and the message would be `Passwords do not match`. Instead of this `notEmpty()` we're going to change that to `equals()`, and then as a parameter we have to put in the field that we want it to equal which will be `req.body.password`.

Alright so what do we want to happen when there is or isn't any errors? Well we're going to want to render if there are errors, then we're going to want to rerender the page, so we know that so let's say `res.render`:

```
var errors = req.validationErrors();

if(errors){
  res.render('register', {
    errors: errors
  });
} else {
  console.log('No Errors');
}
```

We'll render the register and pass along errors. So let's save that and now let's restart. So we're at the `Register` page and it's just re-rendering this for us, but what we want is we want it to not only re-render, but also see what's the problem and what we need to do.

So we need to go to our `register.pub` file. Let's go right under the `p` tag and create a `ul`, we'll say `ul.errors`. Then I'll say `if errors`. Then we'll do a loop through the errors, so `each error, i in errors`. Then we want to spit out a list item, it's going to have a class of `alert` and `alert-danger`. Then we just want to spit out the error so we can say `error.msg`:

```
p Please register using the form below
ul.errors
  if errors
    each error, i in errors
      li.alert.alert-danger #{error.msg}
```

Alright, so we'll save that, and there we go, it's giving us all of our errors. Actually you know what let's not use a list item, let's get rid of `ul` and then here we will just have a `div`. All this needs to be indented. Alright, so **Register**, there we go. So if I put a name in, **Name Field is required** doesn't show up anymore. Let's just see if we can do a successful submission. So we know that the validation is working.

Models and user registration

In the last section we created our `Register` form, where we have some form validation and we could upload an image. Now we still can't add a user to the database because we haven't added our schema yet. So when you're working with Mongoose, which is an ORM module for MongoDB, you need to create what's called a schema and also a model; the schema is going to be inside a model.

Let's go to the root of our application and create a new folder called `models`. Inside this folder, we'll have a file called `user.js` with the following content:

```
var mongoose = require('mongoose');

mongoose.connect('mongodb://localhost/nodeauth');

var db = mongoose.connection;

// User Schema
var UserSchema = mongoose.Schema({
  username: {
    type: String,
    index: true
  },
  password: {
    type: String
```

```
    },
    email: {
      type: String
    },
    name: {
      type: String
    },
    profileimage: {
      type: String
    }
  });
```

We'll bring in Mongoose and then connect using `mongoose.connect`. We put the URL of our database, so this will be `mongodb://localhost`, followed by what you called it (I called mine `nodeauth`) and then we need a variable that's going to hold the connection, so `mongoose.connection`. We'll now define our user schema. So we'll create a variable called `User Schema` and set that to `mongoose.Schema`. Here, we'll open up some curly braces and have a username. This is going to be a string, so we will say `type: String` and set `index: true`. The next thing will be a `password`, where `type` will be `String`. Next up will be `email` with `name` and `type` will be `String`. And lastly, `profileimage`. So they're all strings. That's the schema:

```
var User = module.exports = mongoose.model('User', UserSchema);

module.exports.createUser = function(newUser, callback){
  newUser.save(callback);
}
```

Now we want to create a variable down below called `User` and set that equal to `module.exports` We want to be able to use this outside of this file, so we'll export `mongoose.model` and pass in the model name which is `User`, and also the `UserSchema variable`. We'll create a function that will be available from outside called `createUser` and type in `module.export.createUser`. We'll set that to a function, which will take in `newUser` as well as the `callback`. Then we'll put `newUser.save` and pass in that `callback`. That's it!

Let's save that, go to our `route/users`, and we'll go right above the first `router.get` function. We'll bring in that model. We'll go the `User = require` and put `../models/user`. So we now have access to that `User` object:

```
var User = require('../models/user');
```

Now we can go down where we have our registration and get rid of `console.log`. We'll now create a variable called `newUser`, set it to `new User()`, and pass in some stuff:

```
if(errors){
  res.render('register', {
    errors: errors
  });
} else {
  var newUser = new User({
    name: name;
    email: email,
    username: username,
    password: password,
    profileimage: profileimage
  });

  User.createUser(newUser, function(err, user){
    if(err) throw err;
    console.log(user);
  });
}
```

Remember, we have all this stuff and variables. So we have a name `variable`, `email` `username`, `password`, and `profileimage`. Then right below we'll put `User.createUser`. Remember, we put that in our model as well, so we'll put `User.createUser`, then pass in our `newUser` that we just created, and have our `callback`. This `newUser` and our `callback` matches what we have in `user.js` and then we'll call save. So in here all we want to do is check for an error. We'll say `if(err)` and throw the error. This takes the error parameter and the user. Then, let's just put `console.log(user)`.

That will go ahead and create the new user. Then we want to redirect to a location. So I'll put `res.location` and set that to just the `Home` page. We also want to put `res.redirect` to redirect to the `Home` page. Let's save it and see what happens:

```
res.location('/');
res.redirect('/');
```

Let's restart the server and go to `Register`. Let's say the name's `Mike Smith`, we'll put the username as `mike`, enter the password (password is not going to be encrypted yet), and for the image we'll grab that balloons image. So let's see what happens; we got redirected. Now if we want to check this out and actually see if Mike was entered, we have to go to our command line and go to our Mongo shell.

Open up just the standard Windows command line. So let's go to `\mongodb\bin mongo`. Now let's say `show dbs`. We have our `nodeauth`, so we'll say `use nodeauth` and then `db.users.find().pretty`. There he is, **Mike Smith**:

```
> db.users.find().pretty()
{
        "_id" : ObjectId("56def05ec752750afa4ec8c4"),
        "name" : "Brad Traversy",
        "email" : "techguyinfo@gmail.com",
        "username" : "brad",
        "password" : "1234"
}
{
        "_id" : ObjectId("56def08ec752750afa4ec8c5"),
        "name" : "John Doe",
        "email" : "jdoe@yahoo.com",
        "username" : "john",
        "password" : "1234"
}
{
        "_id" : ObjectId("56df2c0646776d742cb91919"),
        "name" : "Mike Smith",
        "email" : "msmith@yahoo.com",
        "username" : "mike",
        "password" : "1234",
        "profileimage" : "b8b8128c5c235eba5707339d31ff869d",
        "__v" : 0
}
> _
```

We now know that we can add users, we can register, and that's exactly what we want. Now one thing that I want to mention is that when we registered, we got redirected to the `Home` page, but we didn't have any kind of message. So we want to be able to use messages.

Let's go back to `user.js`. I want to go right before we did our redirect and put `req.flash` (remember we installed that `connect-flash` module, that's what we're using here). We want a success message and then we want the actual message. We'll say `You are now registered and can login`:

```
req.flash('success', 'You are now registered and can login');
```

We'll save that. It's not going to do it yet, as we need to actually add something to our layout. So in our layout, we'll go right above our `block content` and put in `!=` and then `messages()`:

```
.container
!=messages()
block content
```

Let's save that and restart. We'll go to `Register` and put the name, `Tom Williams`. You can then enter **Email**, **Username** as `tom`, **Password**, put the **Profile Image**, and click on **Register**:

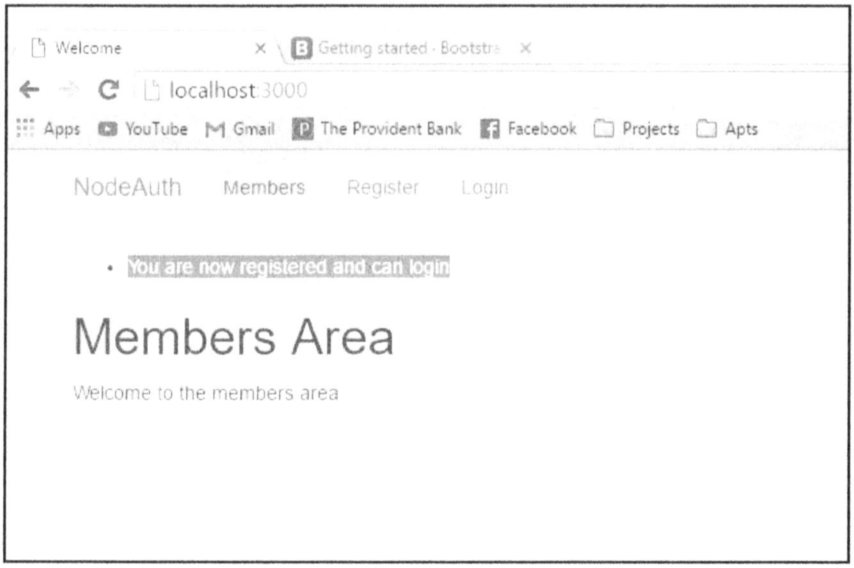

You can see we have a message, **You are now registered and can login**. Now we can change the look of this a little bit. If we go to our little element highlighter, we'll see that we have a `<ul class = "success">` and then an `li`. We'll go into our CSS; let's go to `public`, `stylesheets`, `style.css`, and we'll put `ul.success li` and paste some stuff in here as shown in the following code snippet—some padding and margin, border, and then also some color:

```
ul.success li{
  padding: 15px;
  margin-bottom: 20px;
  border: 1px solid transparent;
  border-radius: 4px;
  color: #3c763d;
```

```
    background-color: #dff0d8;
    border-color: #d6e9c6;
    list-style: none;
  }
```

Now for the error, we'll say `ul.error` and change the color, and we'll leave that stuff:

```
  ul.error li{
    padding: 15px;
    margin-bottom: 20px;
    border: 1px solid transparent;
    border-radius: 4px;
    color: #a94442;
    background-color: #f2dede;
    border-color: #ebccd1;
    list-style: none;
  }
```

This will make it red. Let's save that. Now if we go and try again, there we go! We get a nice looking alert:

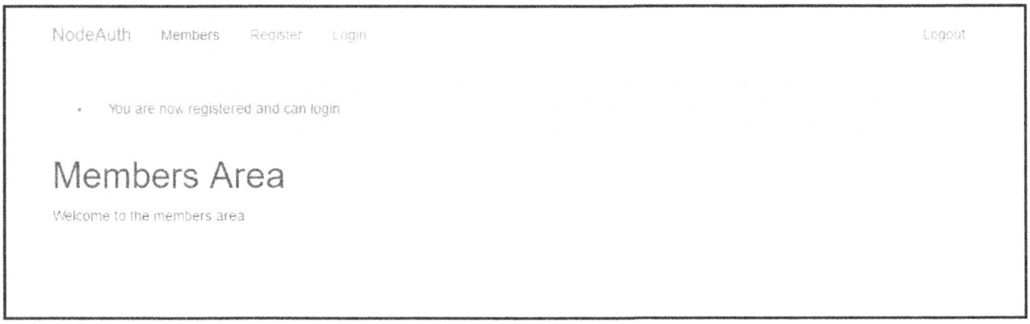

So we now can interact with our database and can add data. In the next section, we're going to get into logging in and authentication and also password encryption.

Password hashing with bcrypt

In this section, we're going to learn to encrypt passwords because right now we're storing passwords as plain text and that is a horrible idea. So there are a few different things that we can use to do it. We're going to use bcrypt, more specifically we're going to use `bcrypt.js`. You could use bcrypt but there's a ton of dependencies you need to have; for instance, Visual Studio, OpenSSL, and a bunch of other stuff:

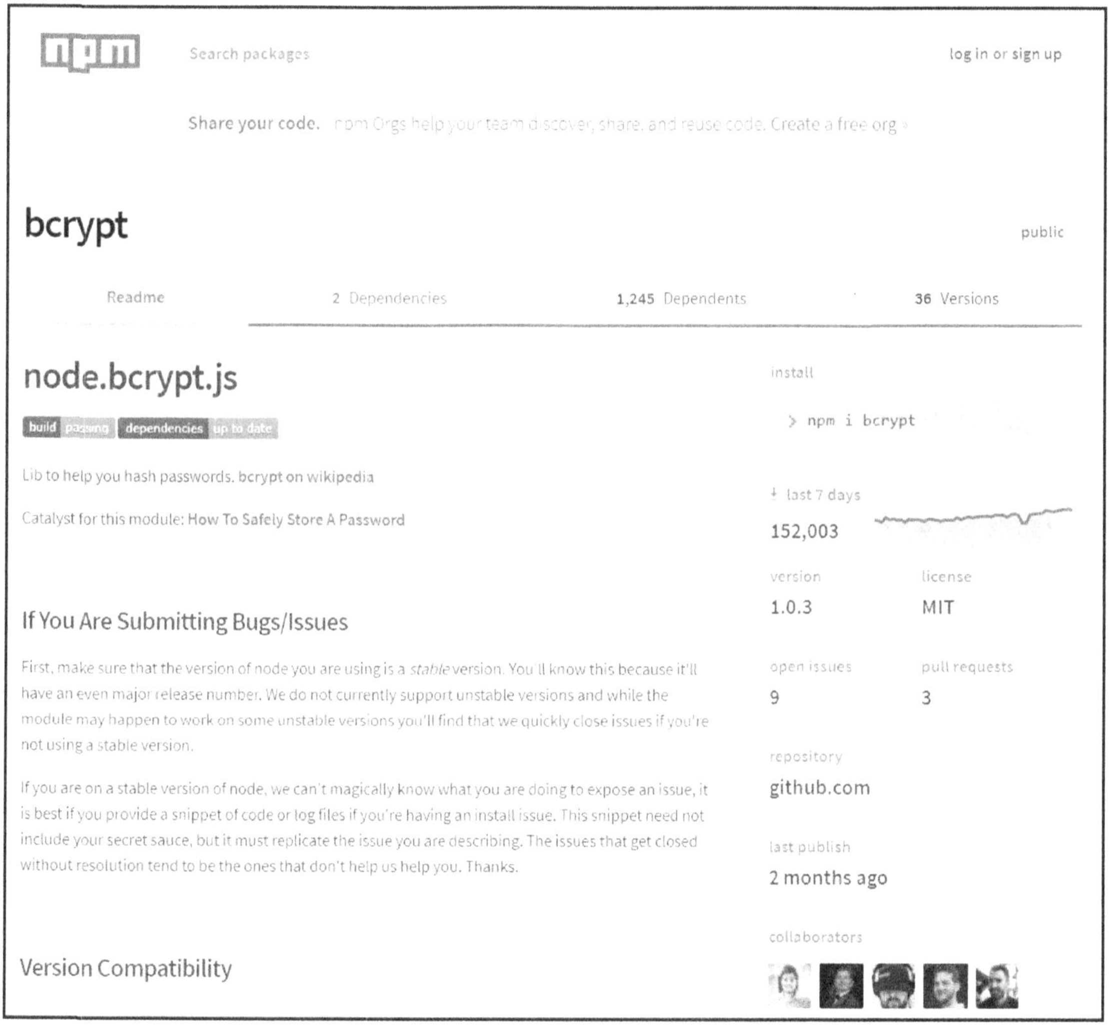

So this you can see is bcrypt in plain JavaScript with zero dependencies. It gives you some of the code examples down as well. We'll go ahead and install it.

Installing bcrypt

I'll stop the app from running and we'll run `npm install bcryptjs` and save that in our `package.json` file. So just to check, if we go to `node_modules`, you can see we have `bcryptjs` right there:

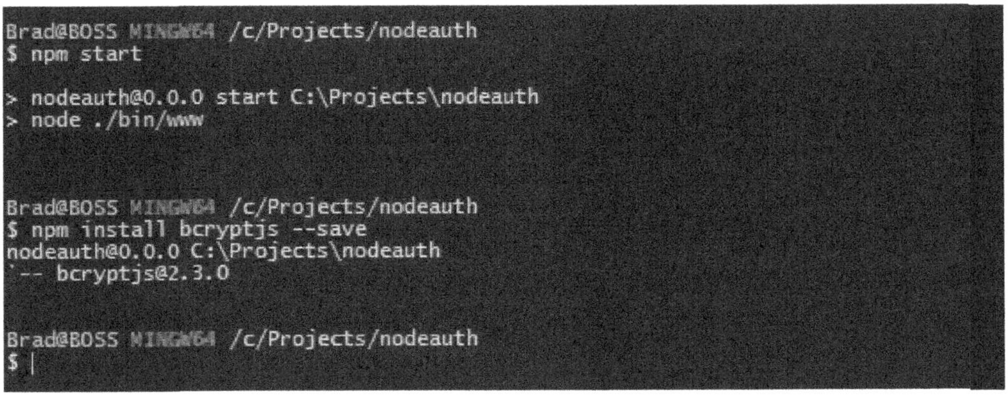

So let's open up `app.js`. We'll enter the `bcrypt` variable and we'll require `bcryptjs` just like that:

```
var bcrypt = require('bcryptjs');
```

Make sure that's saved and then we'll go to our `users` route, and I'll copy what we just did and put that in the model as well that's in `models/users.js`. Now down in `createUser` is where we'll implement this. If we look at the documentation, as far as usage is concerned you can do this synchronously or asynchronously. In case of synchronous it's going to do line by line, one at a time, which is going to be a little slower than asynchronous; so we'll use asynchronous, which means we have to use it through callbacks:

Usage

async (recommended)

```
var bcrypt = require('bcrypt');
const saltRounds = 10;
const myPlaintextPassword = 's0/\/\P4$$w0rD';
const someOtherPlaintextPassword = 'not_bacon';
```

To hash a password:

Technique 1 (generate a salt and hash on separate function calls):

```
bcrypt.genSalt(saltRounds, function(err, salt) {
    bcrypt.hash(myPlaintextPassword, salt, function(err, hash) {
        // Store hash in your password DB.
    });
});
```

Technique 2 (auto-gen a salt and hash):

```
bcrypt.hash(myPlaintextPassword, saltRounds, function(err, hash) {
  // Store hash in your password DB.
});
```

Note that both techniques achieve the same end-result.

Now let's copy the preceding code from the documentation. We'll go right into our `createUser` function and paste that in. Now instead of the `hash` function, we'll replace it with `newUser.password` because that's what we want to `hash`, and `newUser` will come from the following code:

```
var User = module.exports = mongoose.model('User', UserSchema);
module.exports.createUser = function(newUser, callback){
  bcrypt.genSalt(10, function(err, salt){
    bcrypt.hash(newUser.password, salt, function(err, hash){
      newUser.password = hash;
      newUser.save(callback);
    });
  });
}
```

Next, we'll take this, cut it, and put that right in `user.js`, and the hash is actually going to be passed in right here. So we put `newUser.password` is going to equal `hash`. It will get saved. So it's just hashing the password before it gets saved. Let's see if this works. Make sure you save it. Let's go to our Git Bash console and run `npm start`.

We'll open our application and go to `Register`. This will say `Paul Smith`, **Email**, **Username**. We'll say `paul`, password as `12346`. Choose the profile image file; actually he doesn't need a profile image, so let's register. That went good, and you can see in here password is this:

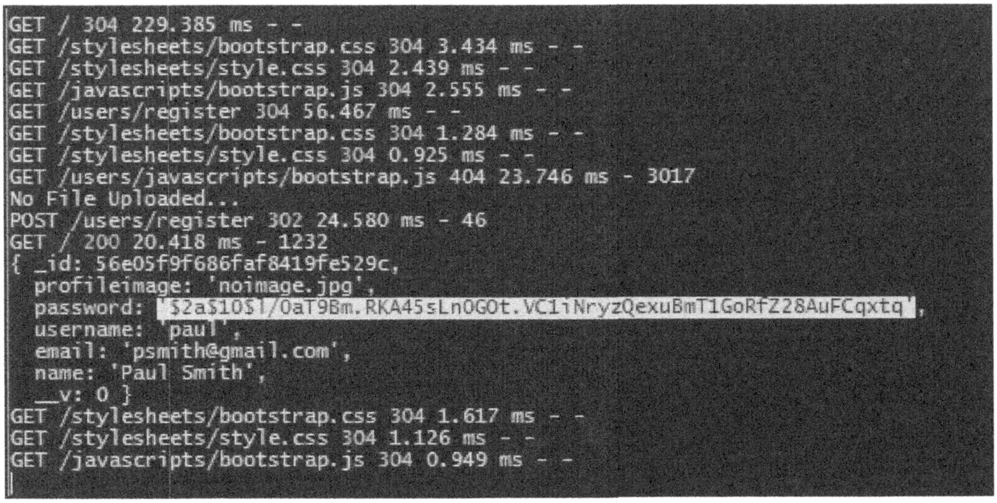

Now have a safe and secure hashed password.

Passport login authentication

In the last section, we went ahead and hashed our passwords using bcrypt. We'll now get into our login functionality. We'll use Passport with it, which is an authentication module for Node.js. What's great about Passport is that it's highly customizable; it just gives you a simple layer that sits on top of your application and you can kind of do what you want with it. You can use the `LocalStrategy`, which is what we'll be doing. This means we'll have a username, password, and a local database. But you can also use things like Facebook login, Twitter login, and a bunch of other types of logins:

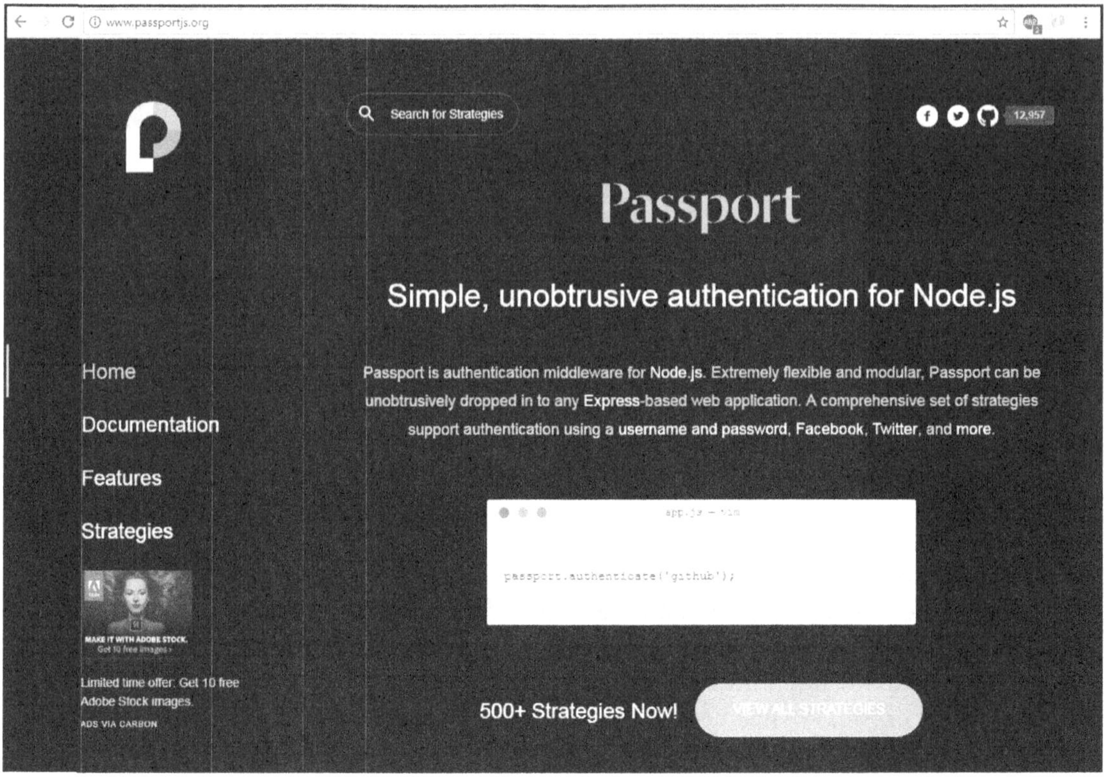

Let's go to the **Documentation** page and then go to **Authenticate**. This is going to show us that we need a post route to our login and we also need to include this `passport.authenticate`:

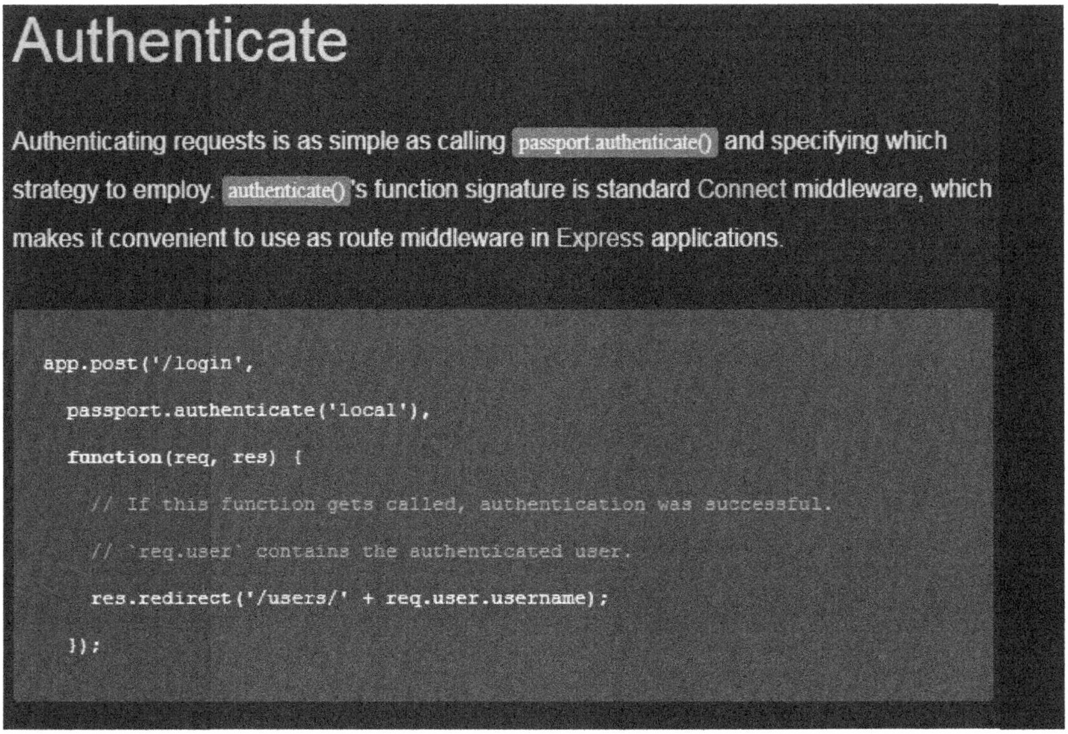

I'll copy the preceding code and go into `routes/users.js`. We'll go down to login. Paste that in right below it and instead of app, we'll use our router, `router.post('/login', authenticate`. We're using a `LocalStrategy`, then we have our function. I will add an extra parameter in the `authenticate` function. This is going to be an object and we'll add in `failureRedirect`. We just need to specify where we want the app to go if it's a failure, and we'll want it to go just to our login. We'll say `/users/login`. We also want a message if it's a failed login, so let's say `failureFlash`. That will just say `Invalid username or password`. Now inside there, we'll say `req.flash` and this is going to be a success message. Let's say `You are now logged in`. Then we want to redirect to the `Home` page. That's our route, now what we need to do is since we're using local in the code, we need to create a `LocalStrategy`, so I'll put that right below it. What we need to do is include passport first, and I can grab that from `app.js`:

```
var LocalStrategy = require('passport-local').Strategy;
```

We'll want passport but we'll also want `LocalStrategy`. Now in `users.js`, I'll put `passport.use` and then inside open a `new LocalStrategy` and have a function. This function is going to have a `username`, `password`, and `done`, which is a callback. Then inside, we'll call a `model` method that we haven't created yet but we will, which be called `getUserByUsername`. Then, we'll pass in username and then a callback function. This will take in an error and user, and we'll check to see if there's an error. If there is, we'll throw the error and then check to see if there's a user or not. If there's no user, then we'll get return done, and pass in a couple of parameters, `null` and `false`. Then we need an object with a `message`. For the message, we'll put `Unknown User`:

```
passport.use(new LocalStrategy(function(username, password, done){
  User.getUserByUsername(username, function(err, user){
    if(err) throw err;
    if(!user){
      return done(null, false, {message: 'Unknown User'});
    }
  });
}));
```

That will check for the username. After that, we'll call another function that we'll create called `comparePassword`. In here, we'll pass in password and the actual password, which will be `user.password`, and then our callback. This will take in error and also `isMatch`, to see if the password matched any. So in here, we'll check for the error. If there is an error, then let's use `return done` and pass in the error. Now we get a check for `isMatch`. So if `if(isMatch)`, we'll use `return done(null, user)`. This is also going to have an `else`; that is, if there isn't a match, then too we'll use `return done`, but we'll pass in `null`, `false`, and then a message:

```
User.comparePassword(password, user.password, function(err, isMatch){
  if(err) return done(err);
  if(isMatch){
    return done(null, user);
  } else {
    return done(null, false, {message: 'Invalid Password'});
  }
});
```

This is very simple. We're getting a user by the username that's passed in. If there is no user found, then we'll use `return done` along with faults. Here, we're comparing the user's password. If it does match, then we'll use `return done` and pass along the user; if it's not a match, we'll use `return done` and pass along `false`. Let's save that.

Now there are two other methods or functions we need to include, `serializeUser` and `deserializeUser`, and I think we should have an example. What we want is this:

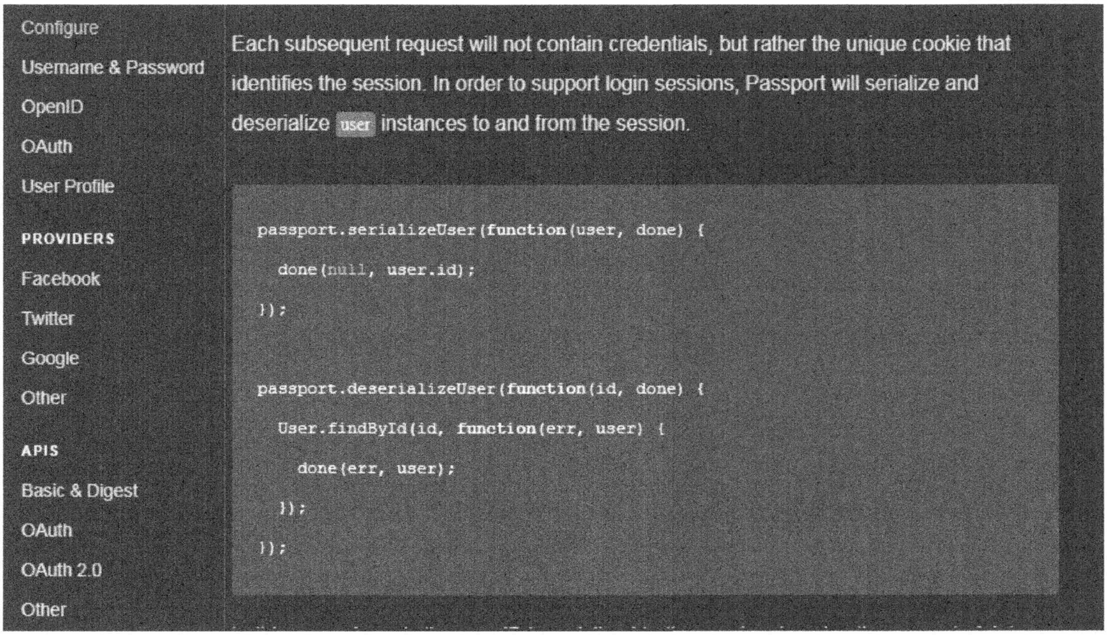

We copy that and then put it right above the strategy. We'll use our `getUserById`, which we'll create, instead of `findById`. That's what I mean by flexible; we can just use whatever ORM and functions we want. So that looks good. Let's save that:

```
passport.serializeUser(function(user, done) {
  done(null, user.id);
});
passport.deserializeUser(function(id, done) {
  User.findById(id, function(err, user) {
    done(err, user);
  });
});
```

Now let's take a look at the login view. Open up `login.pub` and you can see that this is going to `users/login`. We now need to create some functions here. We need to `getUserById` and `comparePassword`. We'll put that inside the model. So let's go down to the bottom and let's put `getUserById`; since we're using these outside the file, we'll use `module.exports` and it will be `getUserById`. This will take in an `id` and `callback`, and then we'll put `user.findById` and pass in `id` and `callback`:

```
module.exports.getUserById = function(id, callback){
  User.findById(id, callback);
}
```

Notice that in the documentation they used `findById` right from the route, but we want to have all of our user functions inside our models, so we're doing it all through here.

The next one will be `getUserByUsername`. That will obviously take in a `username` and `callback`. We'll set a variable called `query` and let's set that to an object `username: username`. Then we will call `user.findOne`, which will get one record and we pass in our `query` and `callback`. Then we create our `comparePassword` and that should be the last one. This will take in a `candidatePassword`, `hash`, and `callback`:

```
module.exports.getUserByUsername = function(username, callback){
  var query = {username: username};
  user.findOne(query, callback);
}
```

Now inside this function, we need to use our `bcrypt` method. So let's open up the documentation for bcryptjs and we need to use compare. Let's grab the following code from the documentation:

```
// Load hash from your password DB.
bcrypt.compare(myPlaintextPassword, hash, function(err, res) {
    // res == true
});
bcrypt.compare(someOtherPlaintextPassword, hash, function(err, res) {
    // res == false
});
```

We'll paste that into `users.js`. Now we want to include `candidatePassword` so we'll replace it and have `hash`. Let's say it will have `isMatch`, and then we want our `callback`, and that will take in `null` and `isMatch`:

```
module.exports.comparePassword = function(candidatePassword, hash,
callback){
  bcrypt.compare(candidatePassword, hash, function(err, isMatch){
    callback(null, isMatch);
  });
}
```

Make sure we save that and our `users` route make sure that's saved. Let's restart the server. We know that Paul has an encrypted password, so let's use him. Rather, let's do a test with something that's not a username, something like **Invalid username or password**. So if we say Paul with the wrong password, it will display this error. If we say Paul with the correct password, we'll now be logged in. Awesome! It's working now!

Now we need a way to actually tell if we're logged in, we also need a way to log out, and we need to implement some kind of access control for the members' area. We will do that next.

Logout and access control

I should be currently logged in, so we'll create a route for our logout. Let's go to `routes` and then `users.js`. We'll go down to the bottom and say `router.get`, and the route is going to be `/logout`, which will be `users/users/logout/`. We'll pass in `req` and `res` and then all we need to do to logout is a `req.logout`. Then we'll create a message, we'll say `req.flash`, and that's going to be a success message and the text for that will just say `You are now logged out`. We want to simply redirect, so we need `res.redirect`. Now we'll redirect back to the `Login` page because the index page or the `Members` page we're not going to be able to access that. We'll put some restrictions on that, so this will go to `/users/login`:

```
router.get('/logout', function(req, res){
  req.logout();
  req.flash('success', 'You are now logged out');
  res.redirect('/users/login');
});
```

Let's save that and let's restart. Now the link you see goes to user's `Logout`. So if I click on that it brings us to the `Login` page and tells us we're logged out. Now if I click on **Members**, we'll still able to see the page and we don't want that.

Let's go to our `index` routes which we haven't even touched this file at all really. It's just a route to the index, so we go in between the route and the function and have another parameter, `ensureAuthenticated`. We have to also create a function, so let's go down and say function `ensureAuthenticated` and I'm going to pass `req`, `res`, and `next` into that. I'll say `if (req.isAuthenticated())`, so if `isAuthenticated` then we'll do `return next`. If not, we'll say `res.redirect` and we'll get redirected back to the `Login`, `/users/login`. Alright, let's save that:

```
router.get('/', ensureAuthenticated, function(req, res, next){
  res.render('index', {title: 'Members'});
});

function ensureAuthenticated(req, res, next){
  if(req.isAuthenticated()){
    return next();
  }
  res.redirect('/users/login');
}
module.exports = router;
```

We'll save it. Let's restart the server! If we go back now we can't get to the `Members` page, so let's login and now we can. So the next thing I want to do is I don't want to show **Register** and **Login**. Similarly, if we're logged out, I don't want to see **Logout**. So let's go to our `layout.pub` file, we need a global variable that is going to let us know if we're logged in or not. We'll put it in here but first we'll create it in `app.js`.

We'll create a global variable, `res.locals.example`. In this case, `example` will be `messages`. Let's say `app.get` so we'll make a get request to any page and you can do that with an asterisk. So any page this is going to run, it will take in `req`, `res`, and `next`. We will then say `res.locals.user`, and that's going to be equal to `req.user` or `null`. And then we just say `next`. Let's save that:

```
  res.locals.messages = require('express-messages')(req, res);
  next();
});
app.get('*', function(req, res, next){
  res.locals.user = req.user || null;
  next();
});
```

We'll then go into our `layout.pub` file again and go where we have our links. Let's say `if !user` and then we just want to space these out as shown in the following code snippet. So if not user, then it's going to show **Register** and **Login**. Down at `Logout`, we want to say `if user` and we'll just space that out. So let's save that and restart:

```
ul.nav.navbar-nav
  li(class=(title == 'Members' ? 'active' : ''))
    a(href='/') Members
  if !user
    li(class=(title == 'Register' ? 'active' : ''))
      a(href='/users/register') Register
   li(class=(title == 'Login' ? 'active' : ''))
      a(href='/users/login') Login
ul.nav.navbar-nav.navbar-right
  if user
    li
      a(href='/users/logout') Logout
```

So now we have **Register** and **Login**, and **Members**. We could leave **Members** or you could get rid of it. Actually, we'll just get rid of it so up at `members`, we'll say `if user`. So now if we log in, you cannot see register and login pages, which is what we want.

We now have a full user login system, login and registration, logout, and there we go. Alright, so I know that this project had a lot of sections to it, it's good stuff. It's stuff that you can keep reusing.

Summary

In this chapter, we started with understanding Passport along with the basics of MongoDB in two parts. With the knowledge of MongoDB, we went ahead to explore the app and the middleware setup. Once thorough with the middleware setup, we learned the views and layouts. After that, we moved on to understand forms and it's validation. We then went on to explore our validations with user registration and models. To replace plaintext passwords, we executed password hashing with `bcrypt`. Finally, we experimented the Passport Login authentication.

In the next project, we're going to create our models using Mongoose so that we can get ready to actually add a user to our database.

4 The Node Blog System

In this project, we will be building a simple blog system using Node.js and Express. We will use a few other things that we haven't used before. We will use something called Monk, which is similar to Mongoose; it's an ORM that is used to interact with our MongoDB database. We will use form validation with the Express validator. We will be able to upload images using a module called multer; also, we will use a module called moment, which allows us to format dates and times.

Let's first look at a simple example. We have two posts with a featured image. When we click on the post link, it takes us to the single view and gives us a comment form where we can add comments:

To test this, let's say `Hey, great post` and click on **Add Comment**; you can see that now that comment has been added. We don't have the login functionality because it would just make the section exhaustive; however, you can use the `nodeauth` program that we built in the previous chapter, and implement it. We have a way to `Add Post`; we only have to say `Another post`, and you can choose **Category**, and we also implemented a WYSIWYG editor called CK Editor:

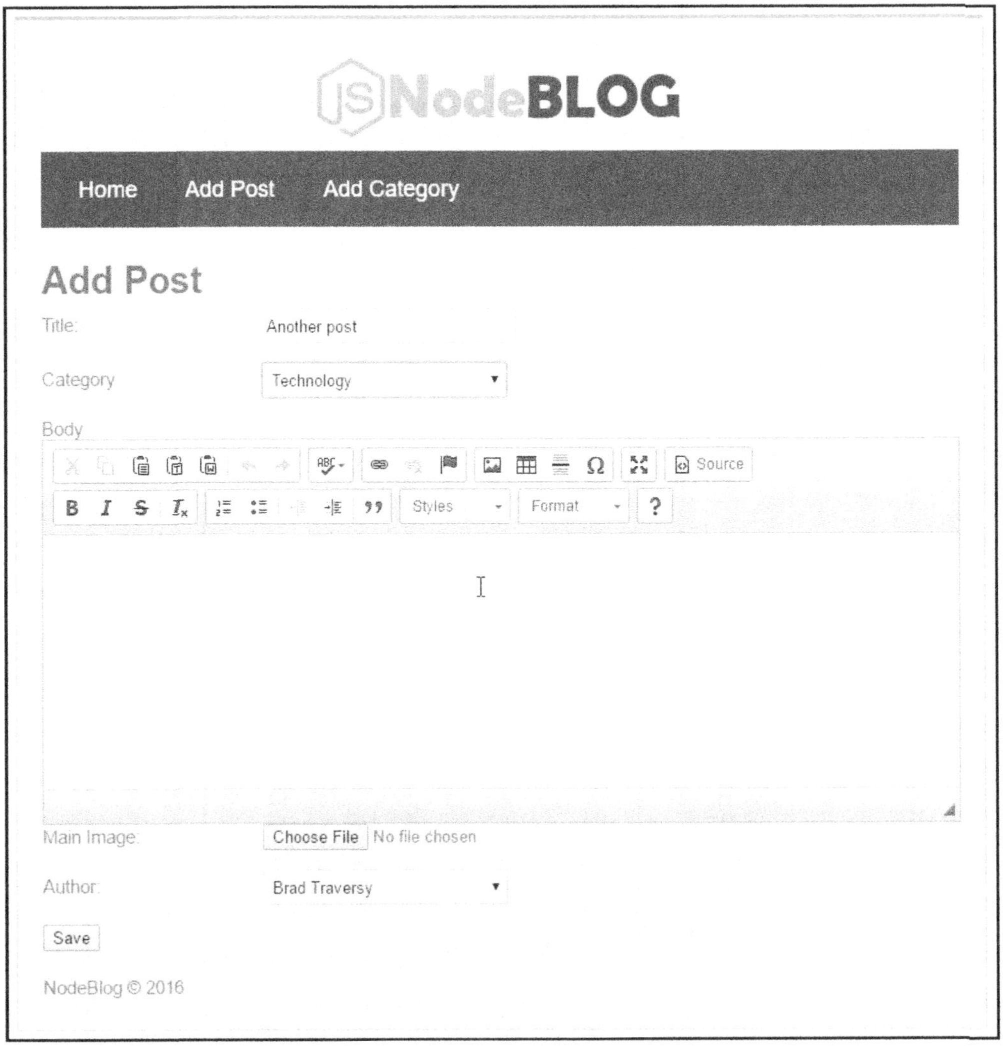

We can use this, say `This is a post`, and we have the ability to add an image and author. So, if we save this now, you can see that we have our post:

We can also add categories; so let's say `Test Category`. Now when we add a new post and go to **Categories**, you can see that we have the post available. So this is what we'll build—pretty simple! Let's get into it and get started.

In this chapter, we will also learn:

- App and module setup
- A custom layout template
- Homepage posts display
- Adding posts
- Text editor and adding categories

- Truncating text and categories view
- Single post and comments

App and module setup

In this project, we will build a blog system using Node and Express. In this blog system, we'll have posts and categories, but we will not have a login system because that would make the project a little too big. We already did a project dedicated to an entire user login and registration system, so it wouldn't be difficult to implement that project with this project.

The first thing we will do here is to open up a command line in the `projects` folder. I'm using **Git Bash**; we will also use the Express generator. If you don't have Express and the generator installed globally, you must enter `npm install -g express`, and to run that, use `generator`:

```
$ npm install -g express-generator
```

Since I have it already installed, we will say `express nodeblog`:

```
$ express nodeblog
```

This will create a bunch of files and folders; let's go into `nodeblog`:

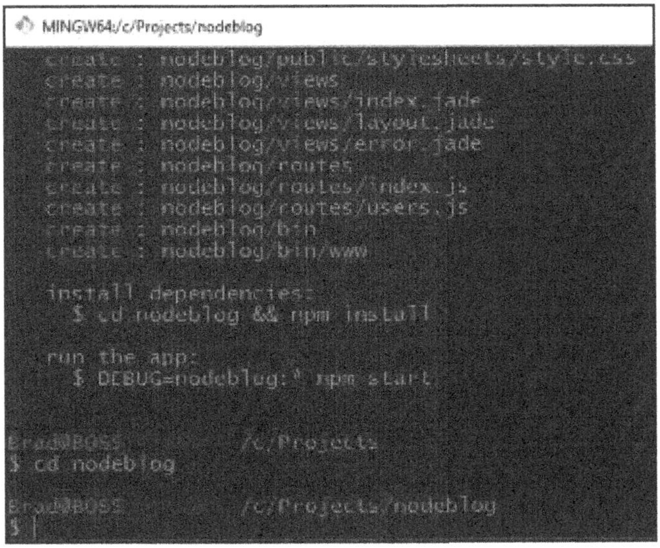

I'll also open it up in Sublime Text. Let's open up `package.json`; there are a bunch of `dependencies` that we will have to add here. The first one we will add is `monk`, which is very similar to Mongoose which we used in the previous project.

It's an ORM that allows us to interact with MongoDB pretty easily. We can use Mongoose, but I just wanted to give you something else to try and you can decide which one you like better. When we say `monk`, there's an issue with this if we just use the asterisk. Since the version is `1.0.1`, we will use the little tilde sign (~) here and then say `1.0.1`:

```
{
   "name": "nodeblog",
   "version": "0.0.0",
   "private": true,
   "scripts": {
     "start": "node ./bin/www"
   },
   "dependencies": {
     "body-parser": "~1.13.2",
     "cookie-parser": "~1.4.3",
     "debug": "~2.6.9",
     "express": "^4.16.3",
     "jade": "^1.11.0",
     "morgan": "~1.9.0",
     "serve-favicon":"~2.3.0",
     "monk": "~1.0.1",
   }
 }
```

The next thing that we will want is `connect-flash`; actually, I'll just paste these in, and they are pretty much the same things that we used in the previous project. So we have `connect-flash` and `express-messages`, and these work together to give us flash messages:

```
{
   "name": "nodeblog",
   "version": "0.0.0",
   "private": true,
   "scripts": {
     "start": "node ./bin/www"
   },
   "dependencies": {
     "body-parser": "~1.13.2",
     "cookie-parser": "~1.4.3",
     "debug": "~2.6.9",
     "express": "^4.16.3",
     "jade": "^1.11.0",
```

```
    "morgan": "~1.9.0",
    "serve-favicon":"~2.3.0",
    "monk": "~1.0.1",
    "connect-flash": "*",
    "express-validator": "*",
    "express-session": "*",
    "express-messages": "*",
    "multer": "*",
    "moment": "*",
  }
```

We have the `validator`, `session`, and `multer` which allows us to upload files, and `moment`, which is a JavaScript library for date and time and for formatting dates. So, that should be good; let's save it and run `npm install` to get all the dependencies set up:

```
$ npm install
```

Now let's try and run the `package.json` file; we'll enter `npm start`:

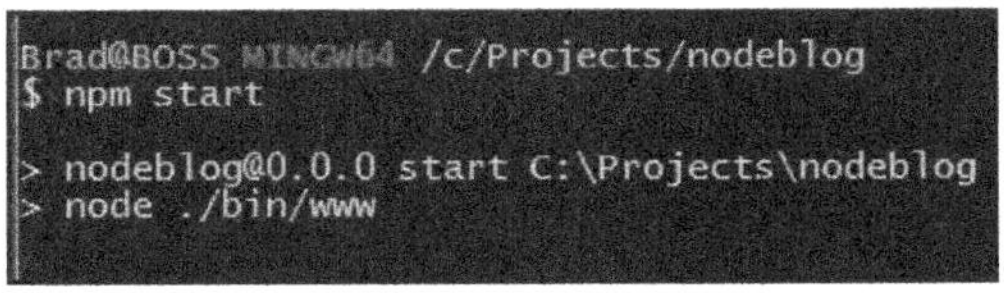

Let's go to `http://localhost3000`:

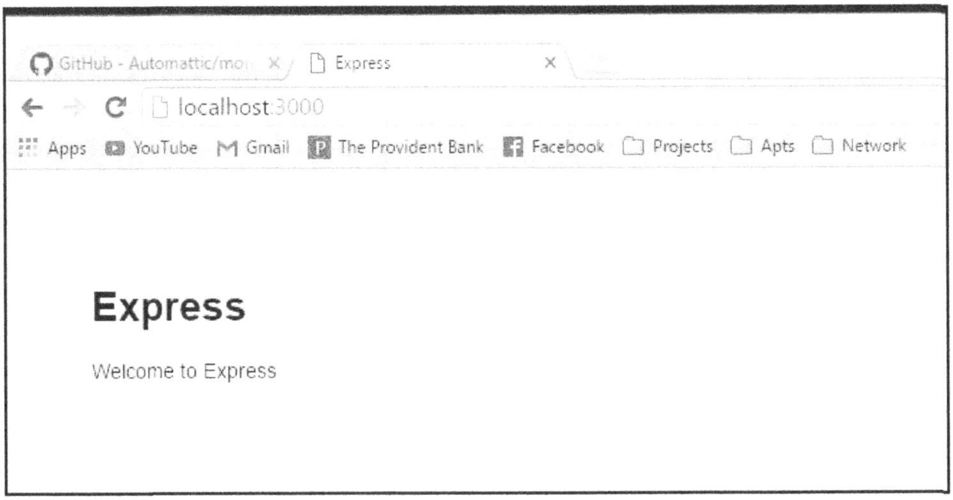

Next, let's open app.js; I have some stuff which I'll will paste in. We want to include session management using express-session. We also will need multer and moment:

```
var express = require('express');
var path = require('path');
var favicon = require('serve-favicon');
var logger = require('morgan');
var cookieParser = require('cookie-parser');
var bodyParser = require('body-parser');
var session = require('express-session');
var multer = require('multer');
var moment = require('moment');
```

Furthermore, we need express-validator to validate form fields. Now when we include monk, we actually create a variable called db, and we will set this equal to require('monk'). We also want to include our database name, so right next to ('monk') in parentheses we will enter localhost/ and call it nodeblog. Also, we shouldn't have to actually manually create the blog, the application should do this for us:

```
var express = require('express');
var path = require('path');
var favicon = require('serve-favicon');
var logger = require('morgan');
var cookieParser = require('cookie-parser');
var bodyParser = require('body-parser');
var session = require('express-session');
var multer = require('multer');
var moment = require('moment');
var expressValidator = require('express-validator');

var db = require('monk')('localhost/nodeblog');
```

Now, for the database variable, we also need to make it accessible to our router, so we will go down here and paste the below code in; it's just a middleware app.use function and we're only setting req.db = db:

```
app.use(function(req, res, next) {
    next(createError(404));
});
```

We also have some middleware to set up for this stuff; we need `Connect-Flash`, so I'll put that down here:

```
app.use(flash());
app.use(function (req, res, next) {
  res.locals.messages = require('express-messages')(req, res);
  next();
});
```

I'll also put `Express Validator` here:

```
app.use(expressValidator({
  errorFormatter: function(param, msg, value) {
      var namespace = param.split('.')
      , root = namespace.shift()
      , formParam = root;
    while(namespace.length) {
      formParam += '[' + namespace.shift() + ']';
    }
    return {
      param : formParam,
      msg : msg,
      value : value
    };
  }
}));
```

This is exactly the same thing as in the previous project; that's why I'm pasting this stuff in. The `session` object also needs some middleware, so provide a secret `saveUninitialized:true` and `resave: true`:

```
app.use(session({
  secret: 'secret',
  saveUninitialized: true,
  resave: true
}));
```

Now `multer` has a little bit of middleware, which we need to set up. I don't have it on me though, so we got to search for it:

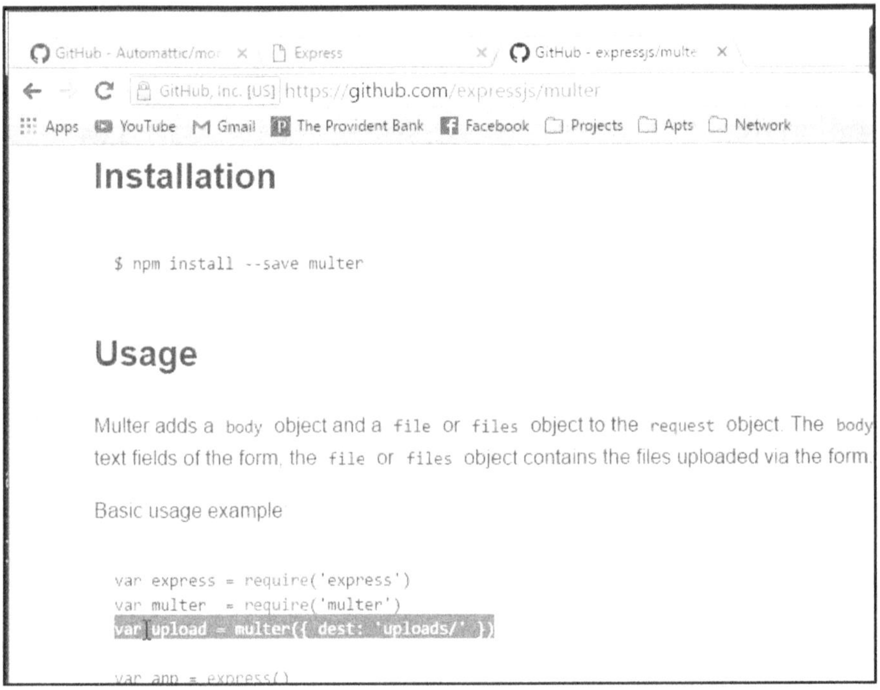

We need to create a variable called `upload` and then provide the destination, as shown here:

```
var express = require('express');
var path = require('path');
var favicon = require('serve-favicon');
var logger = require('morgan');
var cookieParser = require('cookie-parser');
var bodyParser = require('body-parser');
var session = require('express-session');
var multer = require('multer');
var upload = multer({ dest: 'uploads/' })
var moment = require('moment');
var expressValidator = require('express-validator');
```

Let's save this, and we'll try to run it again. Make sure that we don't get any errors. We do not find the `mongodb` module because we did not include MongoDB. Therefore, in the `package.json` file, we will specify that we want `mongodb`, and we'll just use the asterisk (`*`). Let's go back and enter `npm install`:

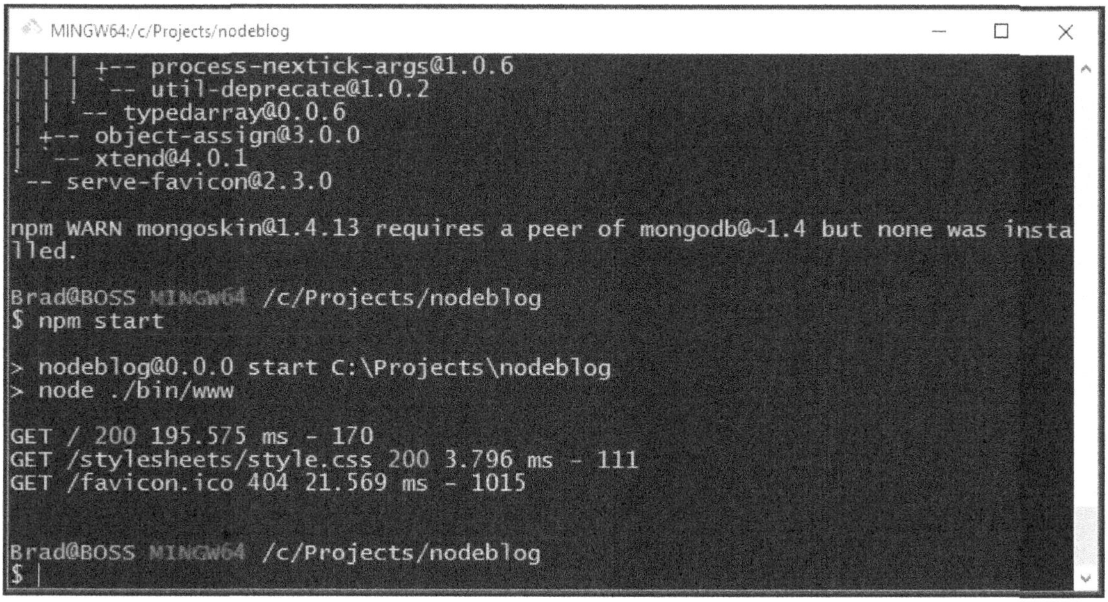

Next, we'll get this `mongoskin`, which requires a peer of `mongodb@~1.4`. So I've had this before, and I think the solution is here somewhere:

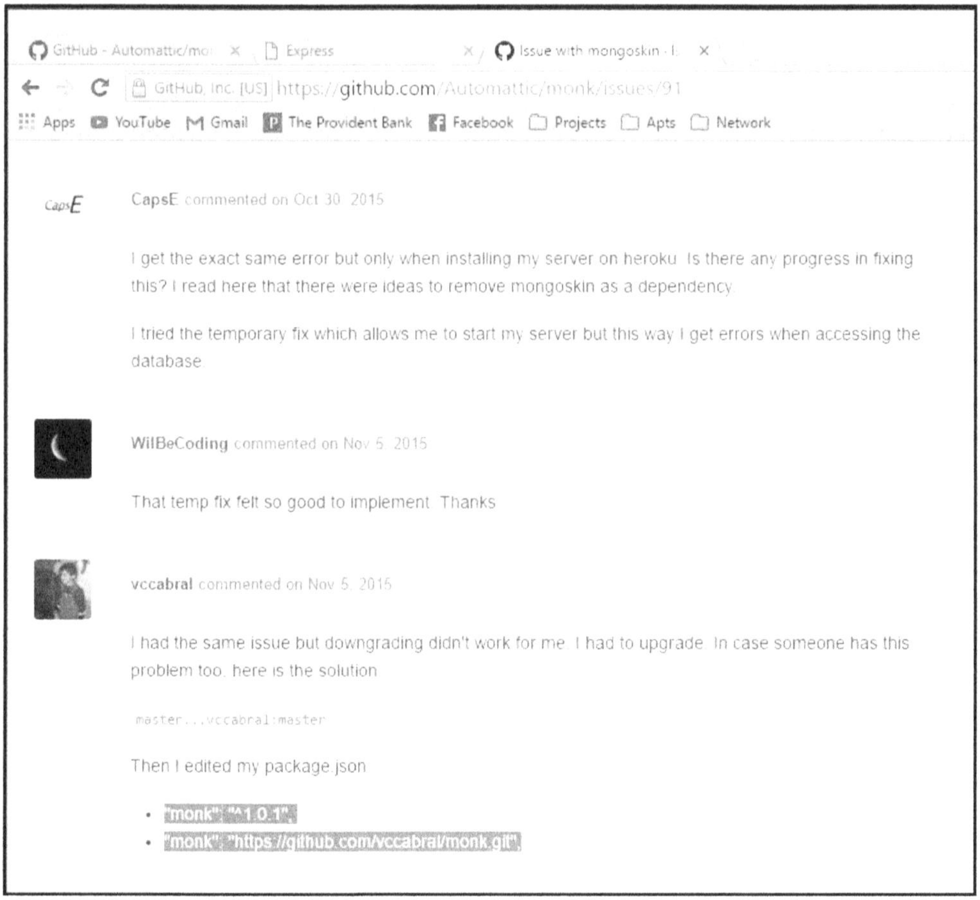

We will add the above code to `package.json` so that we can override this right here:

```
},
"dependencies": {
  "body-parser": "~1.13.2",
  "cookie-parser": "~1.3.5",
  "debug": "~2.2.0",
  "express": "~4.13.1",
  "jade": "~1.11.0",
  "morgan": "~1.6.1",
  "serve-favicon": "~2.3.0",
  "mongodb":"*",
  "monk": "^1.0.1",
  "monk": "https://github.com/vccabral/monk.git",
```

Next, we'll install npm:

```
$ npm install
```

This requires a peer of `mongodb@~2.0`, but none was installed. Let's include it in `app.js`; I will go right above `monk`, the `db` and save `var mongo mongodb`:

```
var mongo = require();
var db = require('monk')('localhost/nodeblog');
```

Another thing that we need to do right here is that we have to change `app.use(flash)`. We need the below code, which is in `express-messages`:

Now let's try to run `npm start`:

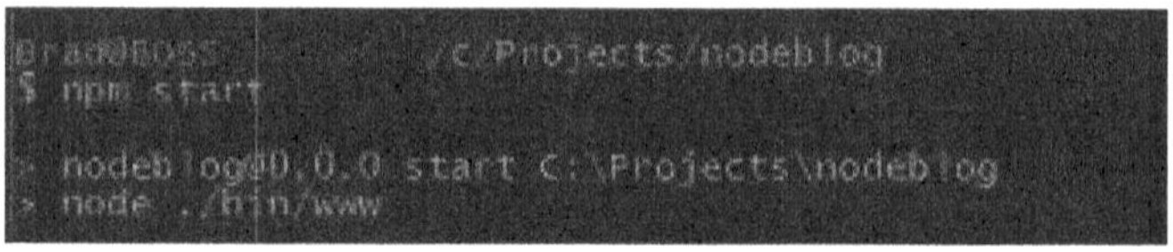

So the middleware is now fully set up.

A custom layout template

We will now create a custom template for our application. The first thing that we will do is to go into the `views` folder and open `layout.jade`; there are a few things that we need to do here. We will set up just a very basic structure, so we will go right under the `body` tag here and add a space and create a class called `container`:

```
doctype html
html
  head
    title= title
    link(rel='stylesheet', href='/stylesheets/style.css')
  body
   .container
    block content
```

In the `container` class, we will create an `img` tag using Jade, giving it a class of `logo` (I'll give it an `src` attribute); we'll set this to `/images/nodebloglogo.png`, and this will be in your files:

```
.container
img.logo(src='/images/nodebloglogo.png')
```

In this container, we will create a `nav` tag, and inside this, we'll have a `ul`; next, we'll have `li`, and then, we'll have the `a` link, let's give it an `href` attribute, which will go to `/`, and after this, we'll say `Home`:

```
.container
 img.logo(src='/images/nodebloglogo.png')
 nav
  ul
   li
    a(href='/') Home
   li
```

Next, let's place another `li` and give it another link. We will set this to `/post/add` and say `Add Post`:

```
    li
     a(href='/posts/add') Add Post
  block content
```

This one here will be to add a category, so it will go to `categories/add`:

```
   a(href='categories/add') Add Category
```

Within the `block content` statement, let's put `footer` that'll contain a paragraph, and we'll say `NodeBlog © 2016` and save it:

```
  block content
  footer
    p NodeBlog &copy; 2016
```

This doesn't look like much; we actually have to put the image in there, so let's open that next. To add images, go to `projects`, `nodeblog`, `public`, it will go into public images and I will paste that in, so there's our logo:

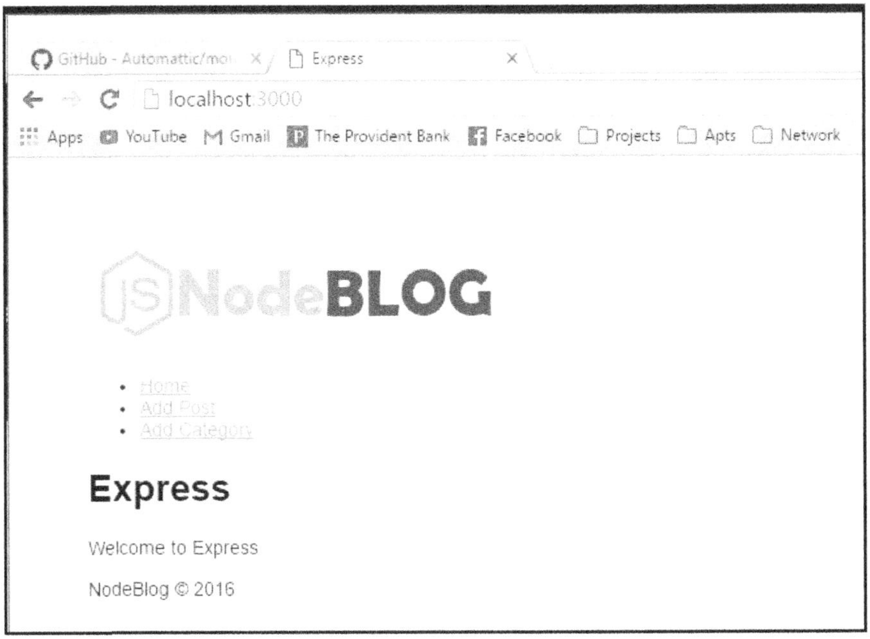

Now, in our public folder, we also have the style sheets, so we will open up `style.css`. Let's get rid of the `body` padding. Also, let's get rid of `Lucida Grande` because we don't need it, and then, let's change the font size to `15`. The body will also have a very light gray `background`, but the color of the text will be a darker gray. Now we will look at `logo`. Let's set `text-align` to `center` and `margin` to `auto`, and we'll add `display:block`:

```
body {
  font: 15px Helvetica, Arial, sans-serif;
  background: #f4f4f4;
  color:#666;
}
.logo{
    text-align: center;
    margin:auto;
    display:block;
}
a {
  color: #00B7FF;
}
```

Now for the `container`, we will give it `width` of `750px` and `border` of `1px` with solid and gray. We will give `margin` of `20px` on the top and bottom and `auto` on the left and right; we'll do `padding:20`, and we'll set `border-top` as `83cd39` and make this `3px` and `solid`:

```
.container{
    width:750px;
    border: 1px solid #ccc;
    margin: 20px auto;
    padding:20px;
    border-top: #83cd39 3px solid;
}
```

Next, let's create a class called `clr` for clearing the floats, so we'll say `clear: both`. For `ul`, we will set `padding` to `0` and `margin` to `0` by default:

```
.clr{
    clear: both;
}
ul{
    padding:0;
    margin:0;
}
```

We'll use `h1`, `h2`, and `h3` for headings and `p` for paragraphs; for these, let's set `padding:5px 0` and `margin-bottom` to `0`, and then, for paragraphs, we'll set all `margins` to `0`:

```
h1,h2,h3,p{
    padding:5px 0;
    margin-bottom:0;
}
p{
    margin:0;
}
a {
    color: #00B7FF;
}
```

For the `nav` object we will set `background` of `404137`, `overflow` to `auto`, `height` to `40px`, `padding` to `20px 0 0 10px`, and `font-size: 18px`:

```
nav{
    background:#404137;
    color:#fff;
    overflow:auto;
    height:40px;
    padding:20px 0 0 10px;
    font-size: 18px;
}
```

Now, we will do `nav li` and use `float:left`; we will also say `list-style:none`:

```
nav li{
    float:left;
    list-style:none;
}
```

Next, we'll do the `nav` links, giving them a `padding` of `10px`, `margin` of `0` and `10px`, and `color` will be `white`:

```
nav a{
    padding:10px;
    margin:0 10px;
    color:#fff;
}
```

Let's now do the current nav link; for this, we'll say `nav a.current`, also, for hover, let's use `nav a:hover`, giving it `background` of `83cd29` and `color` as black:

```
nav a.current, nav a:hover{
    background: #83cd29;
```

```
        color:#000;
    }
```

Let's save this and take a look:

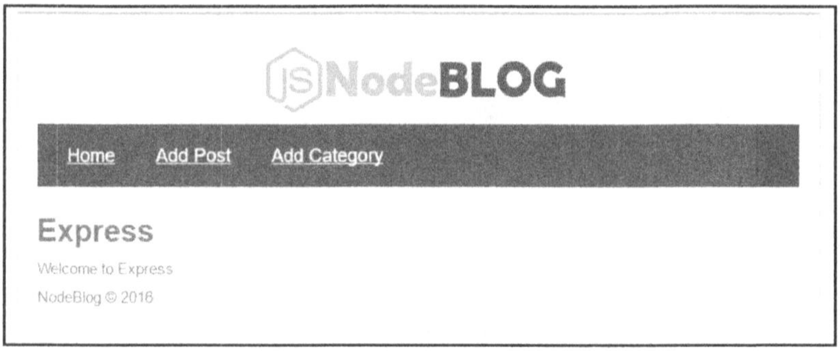

This is not the best looking template in the world but it'll do.

Let's take those underlines out. To do this, in our `nav a` tag, we'll say `text-decoration` and set it to `none`. So there's our template.

In the next section, we will add some posts and some categories through the Mongo shell. Then we'll create the functionality to get some posts displayed on the **Home** page.

Homepage posts display

In this section, I want to display posts on our Home page, but first we need to add some and we will use the Mongo shell to do this:

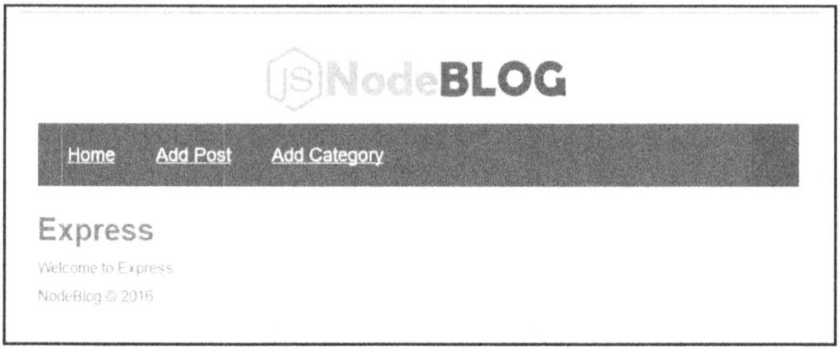

Let's go into a Windows Command Prompt here and go to our `mongodb` folder and then inside the `bin` folder:

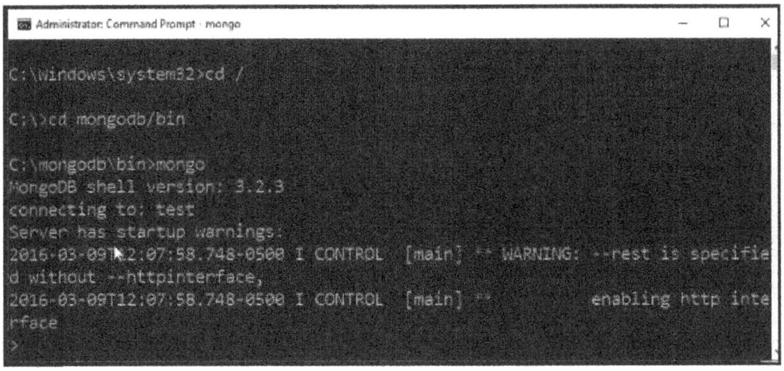

Now let's run `mongo`. We're now inside a shell, and we'll create a new database by saying `use nodeblog`; this will create the shell and it's will put us inside of it:

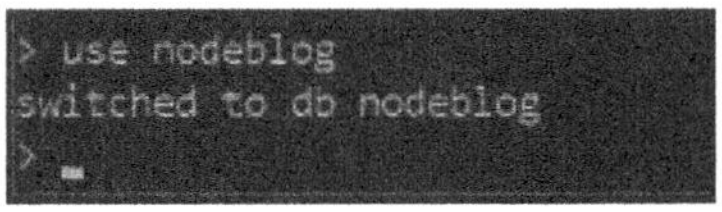

Next, we'll create two collections, one of which we'll call `db.createCollection` and the other, `categories`; we'll also create another one and call it `posts`:

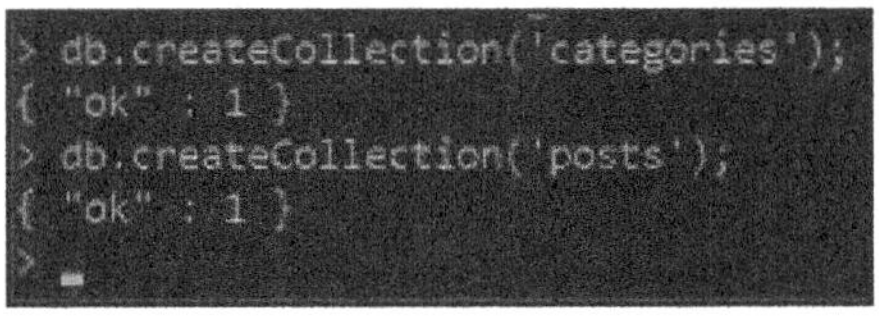

Now we have a comment functionality, but we'll not create a comments collection; I'll show you how we can actually embed comments inside our post collection.

We will first enter `db`. I'll just only few posts, so enter `db.posts.insert`; we will put a couple of things in here. We need to have `title`, and we'll just say `Blog Post One`. We will also have `category`, and for this, let's say `Technology` (I'll actually use double quotes for these). The next thing will be `author`:

Next, we'll need `body`, so I'll say `This is the body`. We also want `date`, and I want this to be an ISO date, so we will say `ISODate` and put parentheses after it:

```
> db.posts.insert({title:"Blog Post One",category:"Technology",author:"Brad T
raversy",body:"This is the body of the second post",date:ISODate()});
```

Let's go ahead and run this. We get `"nInserted" : 1`; let's create one more - `This is the body of the second post`. Let's change `author` to `John Doe` and `category` to `Science`, and then add `Blog Post Two`. Next, we'll enter `db.posts.find` and then `.pretty`:

```
Administrator: Command Prompt - mongo
rface
> use nodeblog
switched to db nodeblog
> db.createCollection('categories');
{ "ok" : 1 }
> db.createCollection('posts');
{ "ok" : 1 }
> db.posts.insert({title:"Blog Post One",category:"Technology",author:"Brad T
raversy",body:"This is the body",date:ISODate()});
WriteResult({ "nInserted" : 1 })
> db.posts.insert({title:"Blog Post Two",category:"Science",author:"John Doe"
,body:"This is the body of the second post",date:ISODate()});
WriteResult({ "nInserted" : 1 })
> db.posts.find().pretty()
```

Here are our two posts; you can see that there's an ObjectId that was automatically created:

```
Administrator: Command Prompt - mongo
{
        "_id" : ObjectId("56e092a5a3de45cf6802420f"),
        "title" : "Blog Post One",
        "category" : "Technology",
        "author" : "Brad Traversy",
        "body" : "This is the body",
        "date" : ISODate("2016-03-09T21:16:21.859Z")
}
{
        "_id" : ObjectId("56e092c7a3de45cf68024210"),
        "title" : "Blog Post Two",
        "category" : "Science",
        "author" : "John Doe",
        "body" : "This is the body of the second post",
```

Now we will go to routes and then `index.js`, and grab from `app.js`. We'll need these two code from `index.js` and let's paste those in `app.js`:

```
var mongo = require('mongodb');
var db = require('monk')('localhost/nodeblog');
```

For our `router.get`, we'll create a variable called `db`, and set it to `req.db`. Then we will create a variable called `posts` and set it to `db.get('posts')`. Next we'll say `posts.find` and inside it, we will first pass in just an empty set of curly braces; actually, I'll do this twice and then add our `function`:

```
var express = require('express');
var router = express.Router();
var mongo = require('mongodb');
var db = require('monk')('localhost/nodeblog');
/* GET home page. */
router.get('/', function(req, res, next) {
    var db = req.db;
    var posts = db.get('pots');
    posts.find({}, {}, function());
  res.render('index', { title: 'Express' });
});
module.exports = router;
```

This function will pass an `error` and also our `posts`. Then we'll take this render, cut it, and then, paste it right in as shown, along the `posts`:

```
extends layout
block content
  h1= title
  p Welcome to #{title}
```

We should have access to our `posts` inside our index view; so let's go into the `index.jade` file. First, we'll check for the post, so we'll say `if posts`, then we want to loop through them, so we will say `each post i in posts`:

```
extends layout

block content
  if posts
   each post, i in posts
```

Then we'll create a div with the `post` class. Inside this, we'll have an `h1`, which will have the `a` link, and we want this to go to `/posts/show/` and then whatever the ID. We can get this using this syntax, `post._id`.

On the next line, we will say `=post.title`. Let's save it and restart to see what this does:

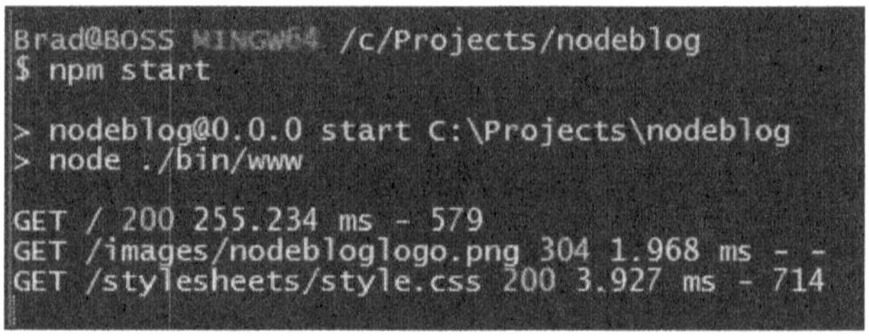

You can see that we're actually getting our post titles. Now, I don't like that color; so in our style sheet, so let's get rid of it:

Here, in `post a`, let's set `color` to dark gray and get rid of the underline.

```
.post a{
    color:#666;
    text-decoration: none;
}
```

So there's our new heading:

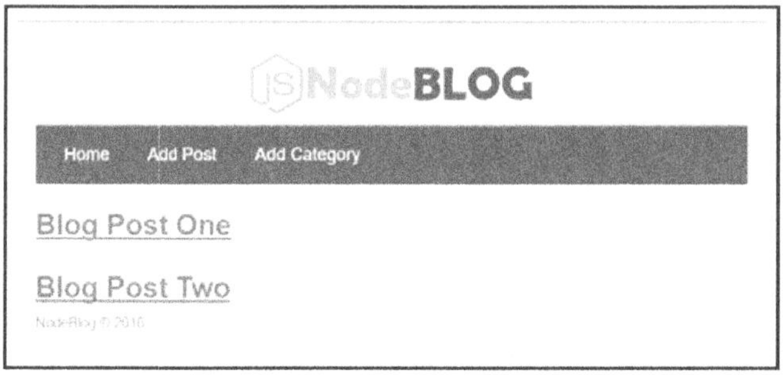

Back in `index`, we will have a paragraph that should be on the same level as `h1`; we will give this a class of `meta` and then say `Posted in` and `category`. Then we'll say `by`, followed by `author`, then, `on` and then the date:

```
extends layout

block content
  if posts
   each post, i in posts
    .post
    h1
     a(href='/posts/show/#{post._id}')
      =post.title
    p.meta Posted in #{post.category} by #{post.author}
```

We use `moment` because we want to format the `date`, so we'll say `moment` and inside it we say `post.date`; following this, we will say `.format` and put in a format—so month, day, and year. If you go to the `Moment.js` website, you'll see all the different formats that you can use. Since we want the body, we will say `=post.body` and then we need the link, let's give it a class of `more`. So you can see Jade is really easy after you get to know, if you get to use it a little bit:

```
extends layout
block content
  if posts
   each post, i in posts
    .post
     h1
      a(href='/posts/show/#{post._id}')
       =post.title
     p.meta Posted in #{post.category} by #{post.author} on #
     {moment(post.date).format("MM-DD-YYYY")}
     =post.body
     a.more(href='/')
```

So this will be `posts/show/`, and then, for the ID we say `post._id`. The text for this will just be `Read More`. So now we will save this, let's go and reload:

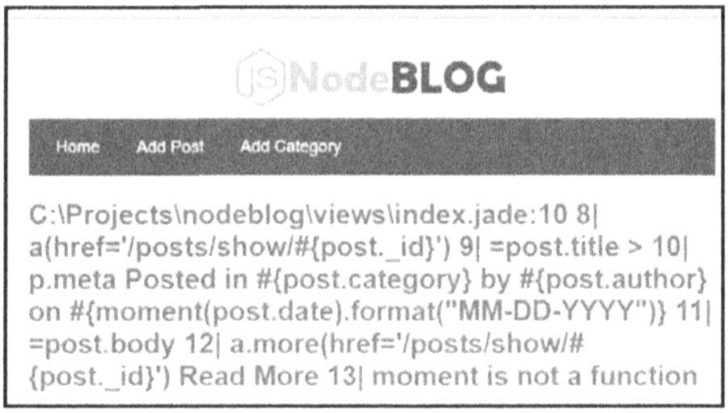

It looks like we're getting an error here, **moment is not a function**. So we'll need to make the function global and include `moment` globally.

Let's go to `app.js` and say `app.locals.moment` and then, set it to `require('moment')`:

```
app.locals.moment = require('moment');
```

Let's try the above code. We'll have to restart the server:

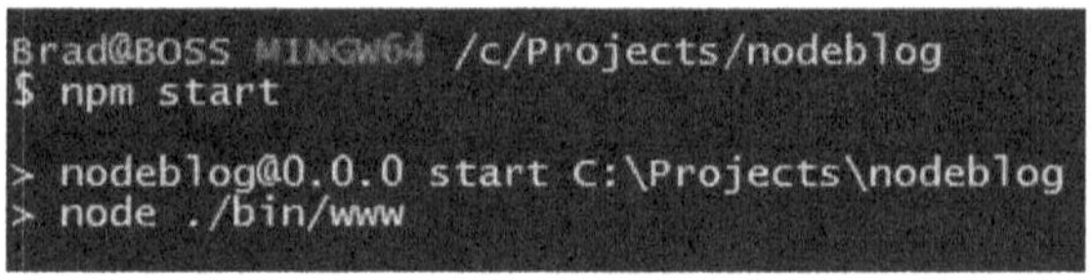

So we have our title, metadata, body, and **Read More**:

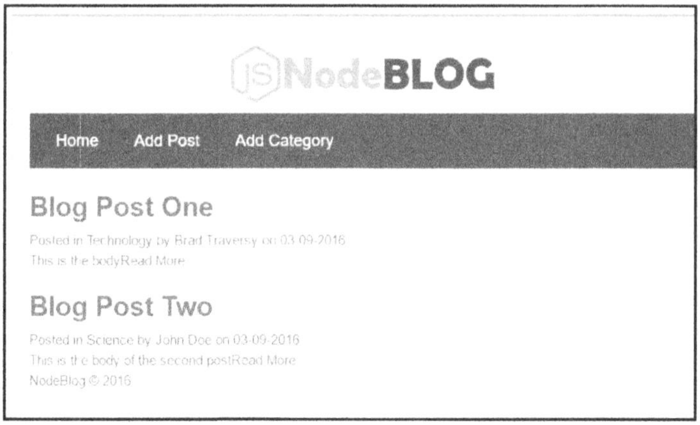

Now when we click on **Read More**, it will not work yet because we haven't created this show route.

I just want to throw some CSS in our style sheet down at the bottom and I paste the below code in.

```
.meta{
    padding:7px;
    border:1px solid #ccc;
    background:#ccc;
}
```

we have some styles for the meta class as well as the **Read More** link and the post itself. Let's save this and reload. The **Read More** link should actually be white so lets make the following changes in the code and save.

```
a.more{
    display:block;
    width:80px;
    background:#404137;
    color:#fff;
    padding:10px;
    margin-top:30px;
    text-decoration: none;
}
```

This may not be the best-looking blog in the world, but it'll do; the looks aren't really what's important, it's the functionality.

This may not be the best-looking blog in the world, but it'll do; the looks aren't really what's important, it's the functionality.

Adding posts

Our application can now read posts from our MongoDB database. Now we want to make the app in such a way that we can actually add posts through the application, because up to this point we've been adding them through the Mongo shell. To do this, we will need a post route, so let's open up Sublime. In our `routes` folder, we will create a new file and save it as `posts.js`. Also, we can actually just get rid of `users.js`; first I'll copy what's in it or cut it, paste it in `post.js`, and delete `users.js` file all together:

```
var express = require('express');
var router = express.Router();
/* GET users listing. */
router.get('/', function(req, res, next) {
  res.send('respond with a resource');
});

module.exports = router;
```

Next, we will use `GET Posts`. Actually, we don't want this yet because we're already doing it on the home. In the index view, we'll create the `add` route; so this will be `post/add`, and this is where we want the form to be. Now before we can do anything here, we need to go to `app.js` and require the `post` route, so I'll just change `users` to `posts`. Then, down, we also have to change to `posts` and add the `post` variable:

```
app.use('/', routes);
app.use('/posts', users);
```

Now back in our posts route, in our add route, we will render a form and the add template. So we'll say `res.render` and pass in `addpost` (that's what we'll call it); the second parameter will be an object, and let's just include `title`, which will just say `Add Post`:

```
var express = require('express');
var router = express.Router();
router.get('/add', function(req, res, next) {
  res.render('addpost',{
    'title': 'Add Post'
  });
});
module.exports = router;
```

We will now create a template, so let's go to the `views` folder and create a new file; we will save this as `addpost.jade`. Now we will paste this code in here because it's all the stuff that we've already done—it's just a form using Jade syntax. We have the `post` method, the `action` as `posts/add`, then we have a title. We also have a `category` select form; nothing is in it yet because the method will actually be fetched from the database. Also, we have a textarea, which is the body and a main image. We have an image file, the Author, which will be a select; this will just be a static select box, and then we have an input button. So let's go ahead and save this and restart the server:

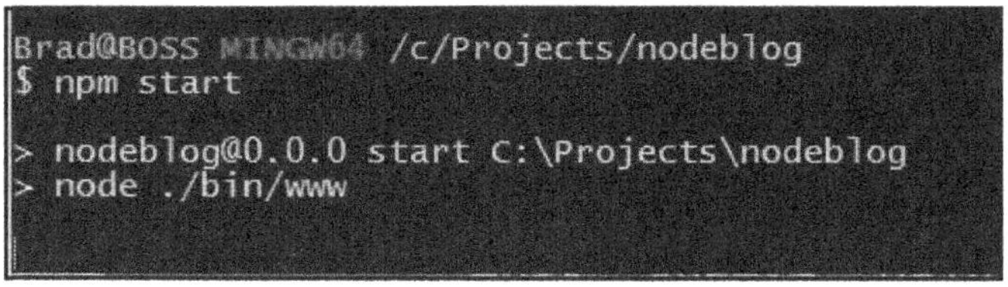

Now let's go to **Add Post**, and there's our form:

This doesn't look too good, so I'll paste in some CSS. To do this, we'll go to our style sheet, and at the bottom, we will paste the below code in. We have some margin on the bottom of the inputs.

The label will be a block, text fields will have some padding, height, and width, select will have a height, and textarea will have a heightened width:

```
input, select, textarea{
  margin-bottom:15px;
}
label{
  display:inline-block;
  width:180px;
}
input[type='text'], select, textarea{
  padding:3px;
  height:20px;
  width:200px;
  border:1px #ccc solid;
}
select{
  height:28px;
}
textarea{
  height:70px;
  width:400px;
}
```

Let's save this, reload, and now the form looks a lot better. When we submit this page, it will go to `posts/add`, but it's a post request; you have to create the route.

Now let's go back to our post route file and copy `router.get` method that what we have. We will change this `get` to `post`, and then, let's get rid of `res.render` method. Then, we want to get the form values, so we want the title. Also, if you look at the names, here we have name, title, category, body, main image, and author. So we have to create all these; we will set them to `req.body.title`. We'll just copy this.

Next we will have `category`, so we'll change the next one to `body`; the next one will be `author` and `date`. Now this here we'll actually use the `date` function, so I'll say `new Date`:

```
router.post('/add', function(req, res, next) {
  // Get Form Values
  var title = req.body.title;
  var category= req.body.category;
  var body = req.body.body;
  var author = req.body.author;
  var date = new Date();
});
```

To do a little test, let's use `console.log` and say `title`. We'll restart the server, reload our form here, and put in `Test` for the title and then save. We'll get undefined:

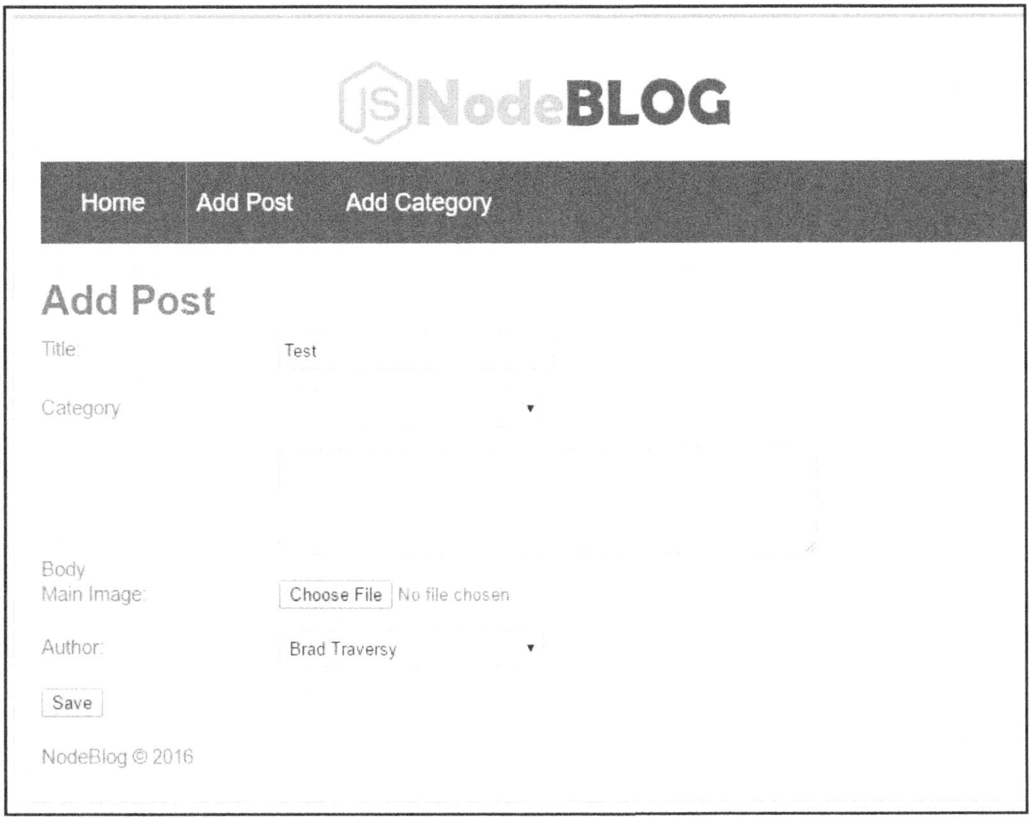

Now we'll use `multer`, so it has something to do with this. Let's go to the multer documentation. We should have the following code in our `app.js`, which we're pretty sure that we do, yeah we have it right:

```
var multer = require('multer');
```

Then, we will use a single file. We want to have this parameter in the middle of our route, so let's go back to our `router.post` and we want to paste this in the `app.js` file, except that we don't want it to be an avatar; it will be `mainimage`. So let's save this and restart. What have we got here `Upload is not defined`?

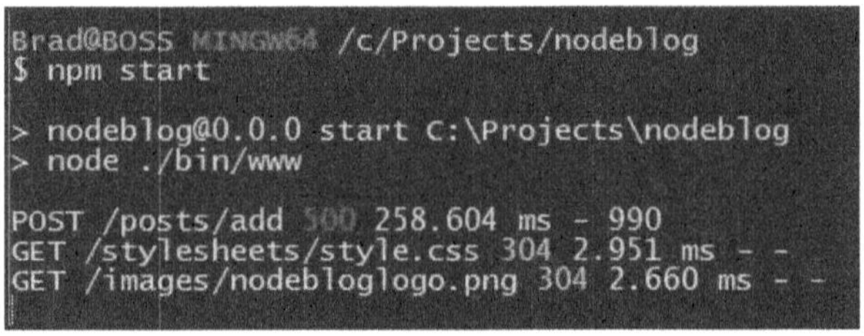

We need to include both of the following code lines in our posts file:

```
var multer = require('multer');
var upload = multer({ dest: 'uploads/' })
```

Let's save, and now you can see that we getting `Test` in the command prompt. Since this is working, let's get rid of `console.log`:

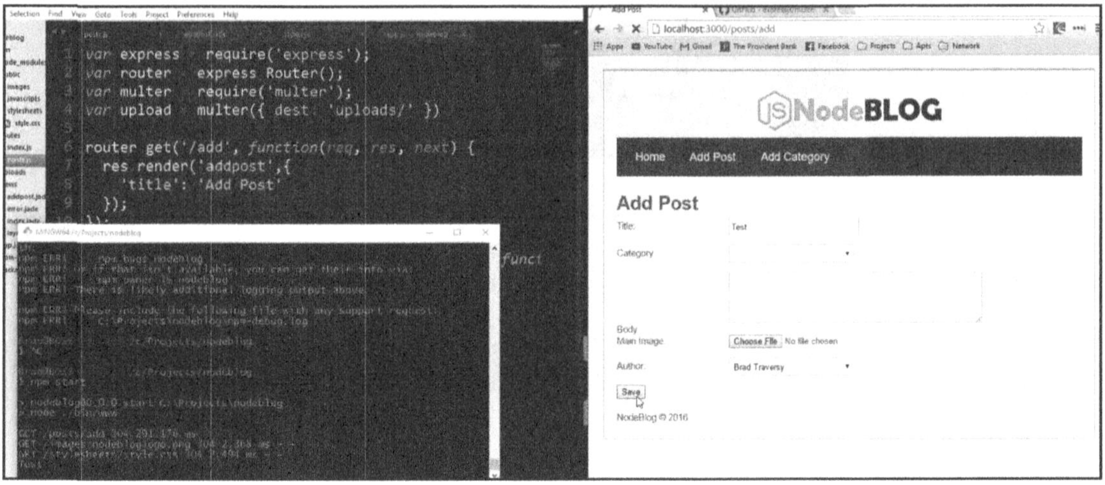

Now we want to check to see whether a file was actually uploaded, if the main image was uploaded. To do this, we will say `if(req.file.mainimage)` and just to do a test with, say, `console.log('YES')`, else, `NO`:

```
if(req.file.mainimage){
  console.log('YES');
} else {
  console.log('NO');
}
```

Let's go ahead and restart, and not submit. Now what's this? **Cannot read property 'mainimage' of undefined**, `req.file.mainimage`. Actually, we just want to say `req.file`. We'll save this and you can see over here that we're getting `NO`:

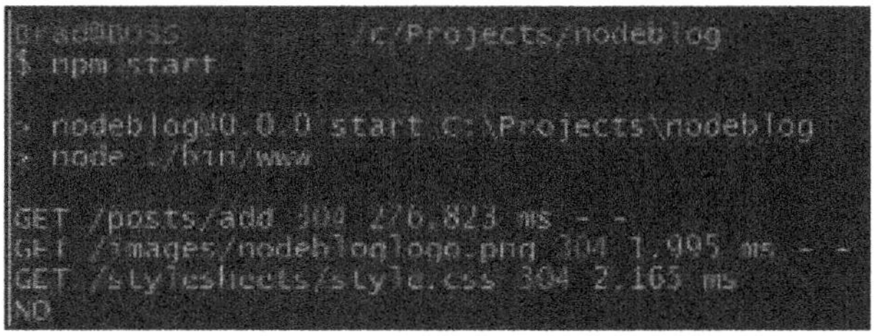

Now, let's choose a file; let's grab a sample image from Google. Lets grab an image of a bird. We'll grab this bird, save it in `Downloads` folder. Now in the command prompt, you can see we're getting `YES`; this is checking to see whether there's a file upload.

Then we will create a variable called `mainimage` and set it to `req.file.filename`, if not, we'll still set `mainimage`, but we will set it to a string of `noimage.jpg`:

```
} else {
  var mainimage = 'noimage.jpg';
}
```

Now we need to validate all of our fields; all we will validate is the title and the body, so I'll paste the below code in. We'll just say `req.checkBody 'title'`, and then at the end we have `notEmpty` and then, `body`; we should also have `notEmpty`. Now we need to set the errors. If there are any, we have to check them. So I'll just paste the below code in. If there are errors, then we will just render `'addpost'` again. We'll do this and then we need to say `else`. If there are no errors, we need to do an insert, so we'll say `posts.insert`. Let's also say `"title"` and set that to title; we also want `body`, `date`, `author`, and the `mainimage`. Then, after this ending curly brace, we'll put a comma and then `function`. This will take in the errors and post.

I want to say `if(err)`, then let's use `res.send`. Then, we'll say `else` we want to set a message, so `req.flash`; this will be a success message, so we'll just say `Post Added`, and then we just want to redirect, so we will say `res.location` and `res.redirect`.

```
// Check Errors
var errors = req.validationErrors();
if(errors){
  res.render('addpost',{
    "errors": errors
  });
  } else {
    var posts = db.get('posts');
    posts.insert({
    "title": title,
    "body": body,
    "category": category,
    "date": date,
    "author": author,
    "mainimage": mainimage
  }, function(err, post){
    if(err){
      res.send(err);
    } else {
      req.flash('success','Post Added');
      res.location('/');
      res.redirect('/');
    }
  });
}});
```

I didn't set this post variable yet, so we will go over here and create a variable called `posts`, set it to `db.get`, and then pass in the collection posts. Since we don't have db yet, let's go to `app.js` and enter these two lines:

```
var mongo = require('mongodb');
var db = require('monk')('localhost/nodeblog');
```

Let's save this and now restart the server. Go to **Add Post** and let's say `Test Post`. Category is blank because we don't have anything yet; we're not fetching them, so I'll leave it for now. We'll choose an image.

So now you can see that we have our **Test Post** down here with the author, date, and body:

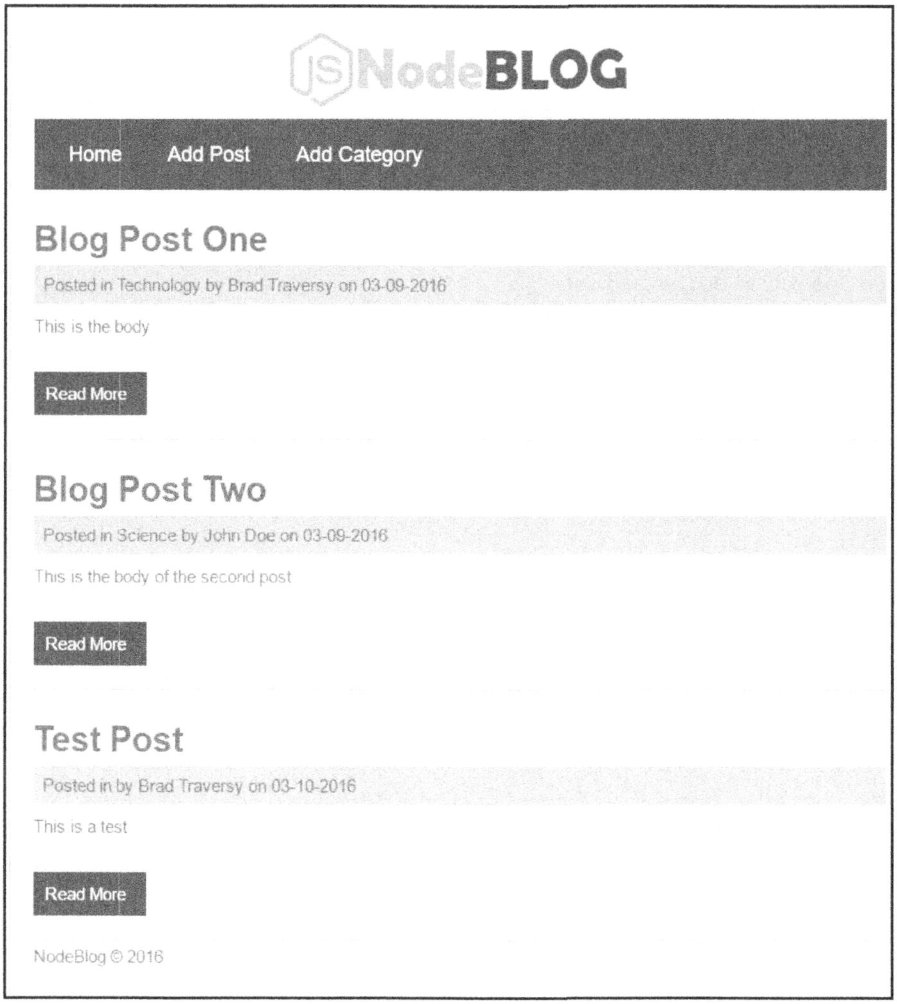

Now the last thing I want to do in this section is that I want to be able to see our categories here. So, I'll quickly add some through the Mongo shell. Since we have categories, let's say `db.categories.insert`, and for a name, we'll say `name: 'Technology'`. We'll more, let's say `Science` and `Business`.

To check the result, we can say `db.categories.find`:

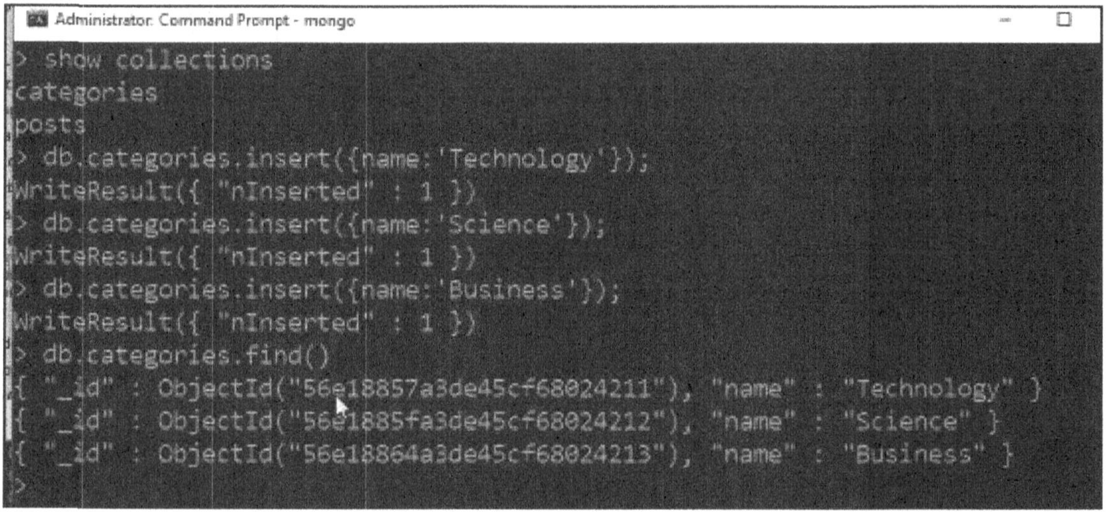

Now let's go back to `posts` route, and we want to put the code in the get method we're getting the add form. So let's go in the `router.get` method and create a variable called `categories`. We'll set that to `db.get('categories')`, and then, we'll do a `find` on these `categories`. We will pass in empty curly braces, and the third parameter will be `function`. We'll take this render, cut it, and put it inside the `categories`; this way we can actually include our `categories`:

```
router.get('/add', function(req, res, next) {
  var categories = db.get('categories');
  categories.find({},{},function(err, categories){
    res.render('addpost',{
      'title': 'Add Post',
      'categories': categories
    });
  });
});
```

Let's save this and go to our add form. We'll go down to where we have our select box for category, so we'll say `each category, i in categories`. Then we need `option(value= '#{cat}')`, and then, we want the title, so we will go and say `category`:

```
.form-group
    label Category
    select.form-control(name='category')
```

```
        each category, i in categories
         option(value='#{category.name}') #{category.name}
    .form-group
         label Body
         textarea.form-control(name='body', id='body')
```

Then we want the actual text, so this will go outside the parentheses. Also, we want the same thing, `category.name`, so let's save it and restart.

Looks like we have an issue here, **Invalid indentation**. You can use tabs or spaces, but not both. Since I used a tab, we need to make sure that we do spaces here. Now we have a choice for our categories.

Text editor and adding categories

Now we can add posts to our applications, so next we'll make the application in such a way that we can add categories; however, before we do this, I want to implement an editor so that when we enter, when we create a post, we can have this little text editor enabling us to make the text bold, change the font size and do things like that. There are a lot of different options you can use, but `CKEditor` is a really good one of them all; it has a lot of features and it's really simple to set up. So we will go to `ckeditor.com` and click on **Download**:

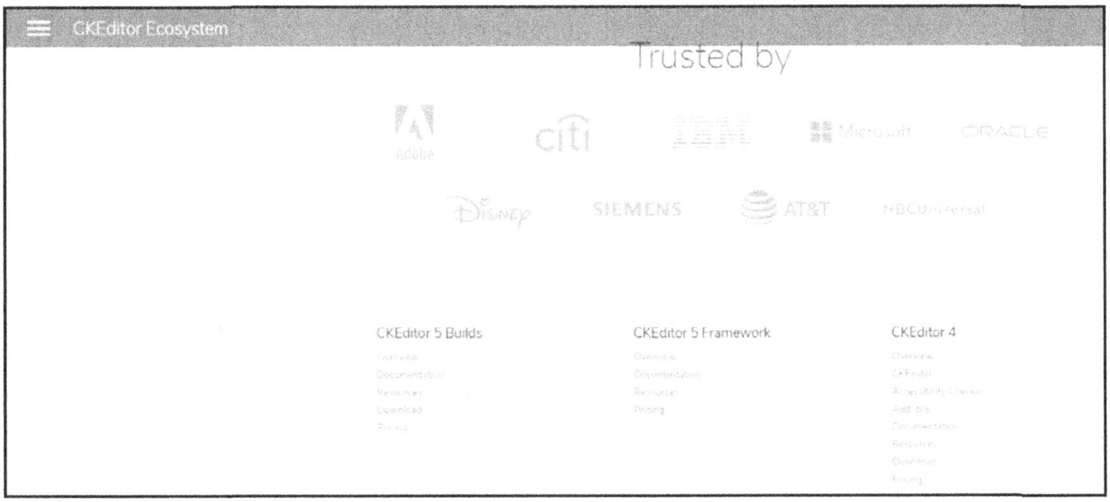

We need the standard version, not the basic one. So let's save it, then open it up, and take the whole folder and put it into our application. We'll take `projects` and `nodeblog` and will paste them inside the `public` folder. Next we'll go to `add`, which is in `views` and then `addpost.jade`. We need to include the script at the bottom, so let's go down and enter `script(src='/ckeditor/ckeditor.js')`:

```
.form-group
    label Author:
    select.form-control(name='author')
        option(value='Brad Traversy') Brad Traversy
        option(value='John Doe') John Doe
input.btn.btn-default(name='submit',type='submit',value='Save')
script(src='/ckeditor/ckeditor.js')
```

so we're including the script and then we need another `script` tag, and then down here we will have a pipe character (`|`) and then `CKEDITOR.replace` and we need to let it know what we, where we want to implement this, and that's will be inside of the `body` field. so let's save that:

```
option(value='John Doe') John Doe
input.btn.btn-default(name='submit',type='submit',value='Save')
script(src='/ckeditor/ckeditor.js')
script
    | CKEDITOR.replace('body');
```

Make sure that's saved and let's restart the server, and go back to our app and go to **Add Post**:

Now you can see we have a text editor we can bold text, we can make it italic, change the size, headings, cut, we can look at the source, it's a really nice editor, and you can see how simple it was to implement.

So next thing I want to do is we want to be able to add a category just like we can add a post, so let's do that. Now we will copy a lot of the functionality from our `Add Post` First thing we want to do here is in our routes, create a new file and let's save it as `categories.js`, and I will copy everything we have in `post.js`. We're just will change a couple of things, let's see we don't need `multer`, `add` is will stay so this will actually be `category/add`. So we want to render `addcategory`. Change the title and get the `add`.

```
router.get('/add', function(req, res, next) {
  res.render('addcategory',{
      'title': 'Add Category'
  });
});
```

So what we can do is create the view, so in our views let's create a file called `addcategory.jade`, and I will paste the below code in.

```
h1=title
ul.errors
    if errors
        each error, i in errors
            li.alert.alert-danger #{error.msg}
form(method='post', action='/categories/add')
    .form-group
        label Name:
        input.form-control(name='name', type='text')
    input.btn.btn-default(name='submit',type='submit',value='Save')
```

So very simple we just have title, we have our errors `ul`, a form that goes to `categories/add` and a title, actually I will change that to name. So that should be good, we don't need the `enctype` though, so we can remove it:

```
each error, i in errors
li.alert.alert-danger #{error.msg}
form(method='post', action='/categories/add', enctype="multipart/form-
data"))
.form-group
label Name:
input.form-control(name='name', type='text')
input.btn.btn-default(name='submit',type='submit',value='Save')
```

So let's see if it renders, we will have to restart. One thing that we did forget is in `app.js`, we need to add `categories`:

```
var routes = require('./routes/index');
var posts = require('./routes/posts');
var categories = require('./routes/categories');
```

So we'll restart one more time. What's this? `upload.single('mainimage')` I will just get rid of that post, so if we say `Add Category`, it looks like we have a Jade error. It looks like there's no ending parenthesis in this form, so we'll add that, there we go. So there's our form. Now it not will do anything yet we have to add the post. So let's go back to `categories.js` and I want to add `router.post('/add')`, we can then get rid of the middle functions and then all we need to get is the name:

```
router.post('/add', function(req, res, next) {
  // Get Form Values
  var name = req.body.name;
  var category= req.body.category;
  var body = req.body.body;
  var author = req.body.author;
  var date = new Date();
```

For validation, let's do the name, get rid of the rest, and let's change that to `categories` and all we have is a name, we'll change this to `Category Added` and that's it:

```
      } else {
          req.flash('success','Post Added');
          res.location('/');
          res.redirect('/');
      }
    });
  }
});
```

So save it, let's go add, what happened? **Not Found**:

Let's go to our `layout.jade` and we want to put a / right there:

```
a(href='/categories/add') Add Category
```

So let's add a category we'll say, I'll just say `Family`, **Save**:

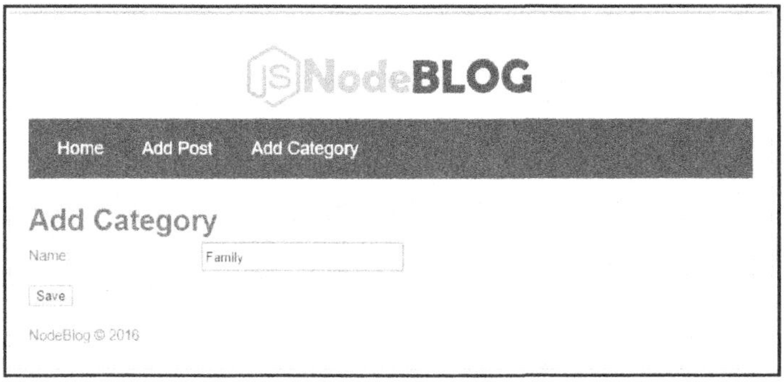

Now to confirm if it was added, if we go to `Add Post` now you can see **Family** is in the choice, in the options:

So in the next section what we will do is make the app such that we can click on one of these category links and it'll take us to a page that's will list all the posts only in that category, and then we also need to deal with our image, we want to be able to show an image for the post. Post that, we'll move on to our single posts and comments.

Truncating text and categories view

In this section, we will be doing a couple of different things. One we want to make it so that the images show if there is an image on the post:

We also want to truncate the text because right now if we have a long post it's will show the whole body and we don't want that we want to just show a portion of it and then click **Read More**, that'll go to a single post page. We also want to make it so that when we click on **Category** it'll show all the posts in that category.

So what I'm will do first is I'm will get rid of all these posts and we will start fresh. So I'm in the Mongo shell and I'm will say `db.posts.remove` and then we're just will pass in some empty curly braces, so that's will remove everything:

```
> db.categories.find()
{ "_id" : ObjectId("56e18857a3de45cf68024211"), "name" : "Technology
{ "_id" : ObjectId("56e1885fa3de45cf68024212"), "name" : "Science" }
{ "_id" : ObjectId("56e18864a3de45cf68024213"), "name" : "Business"
```

So if we reload we have nothing here, so let's go ahead and since we not we don't have our messages set up so we can do that:

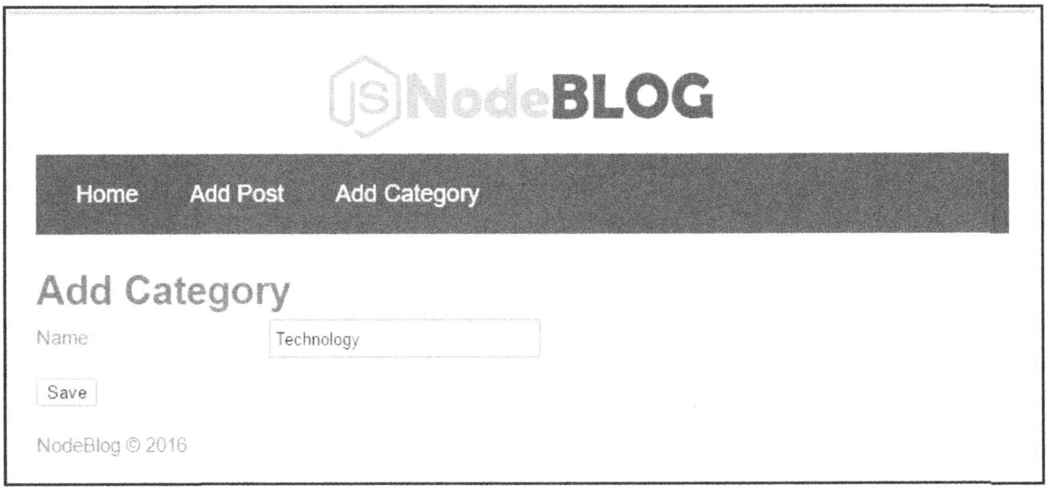

After we add a category we want to have a message, let's see, which it should be doing because we have this:

```
req.flash('success', 'Category Added');
```

So if we go to layout we want to go right above block content and we will say `!= messages` just like that:

```
a(href='/categories/add') Add Category
!= messages()
```

So now I just want to add a little bit of CSS to our style sheet:

```
ul.success li{
    padding: 15px;
    margin-top:10px;
    margin-bottom: 20px;
    border: 1px solid transparent;
    border-radius: 4px;
    color: #3c763d;
    background-color: #dff0d8;
    border-color: #d6e9c6;
    list-style:none;
}
```

I will paste that in, that's just will make the success message, give it some padding and background and so forth. So let's save that and we'll add a new category, let's say `Business`, **Save**, and we get **Category Added**:

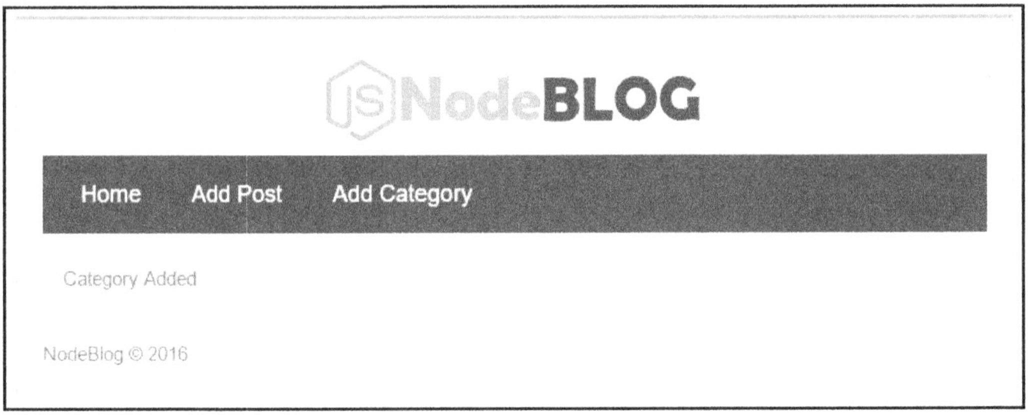

Now let's go to **Add Post**, you can see we have our two categories say a `Blog Post One`. For the body I will grab some sample text from **Lorem Ipsum** and let's go ahead and paste that in:

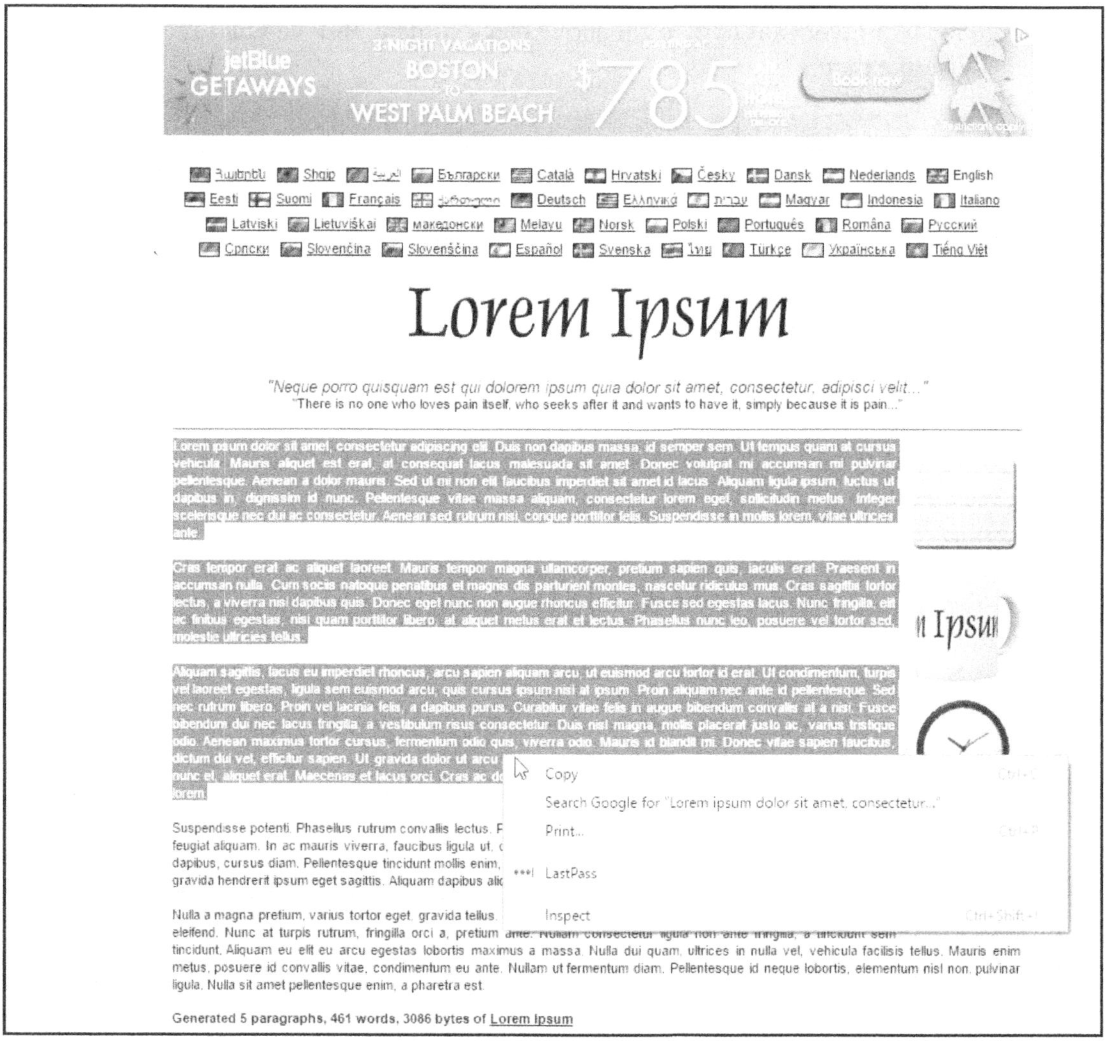

For an image I will grab that bird picture we have and save. Now notice that you can actually see the paragraph tags and it's not giving us any style as if it was a paragraph, so what we can do is let's go into `index.jade` and where we have the body I will add an `!` to the front of it, and that's will make it so that it will parse the HTML:

```
extends layout

block content
  if posts
   each post, i in posts
    .post
    h1
     a(href='/posts/show/#{post._id}')
      =post.title
    p.meta Posted in
     a(href='/categories/show/#{post.category}') #{post.category}
     by #{post.author}
     on #{moment(post.date).format("MM-DD-YYYY")}
    img(src='/images/#{post.mainimage}')
    !=truncateText(post.body,400)
    a.more(href='/posts/show/#{post._id}') Read More
```

Now what we actually want to happen is we want to truncate the text to make it smaller, so what we'll do is go to `app.js` and we will create a global function, we will put this function right under the moment and we will say `app.locals.truncateText` and we'll set that to a `function`. and that's will take in `text` and `length`, and then we will create a variable called `truncatedText` and let's set that to `text.substring` and we want to pass in `0`, we want to start at `0`, and then `length`, and then we just want to return that:

```
app.locals.truncateText = function(text, length){
  var truncatedText = text.substring(0);
}
```

Now we'll go into `index` file and instead of just having `post.body` we will say `truncateText` and then we will pass in `post.body` and then however long you want it to be lets say `400`:

```
!=truncateText(post.body,400)
 a.more(href='/posts/show/#{post._id}') Read More
```

So let's save that and we will have to restart and reload, and now you can see we're only getting 400.

Let's create one more post, we'll grab this:

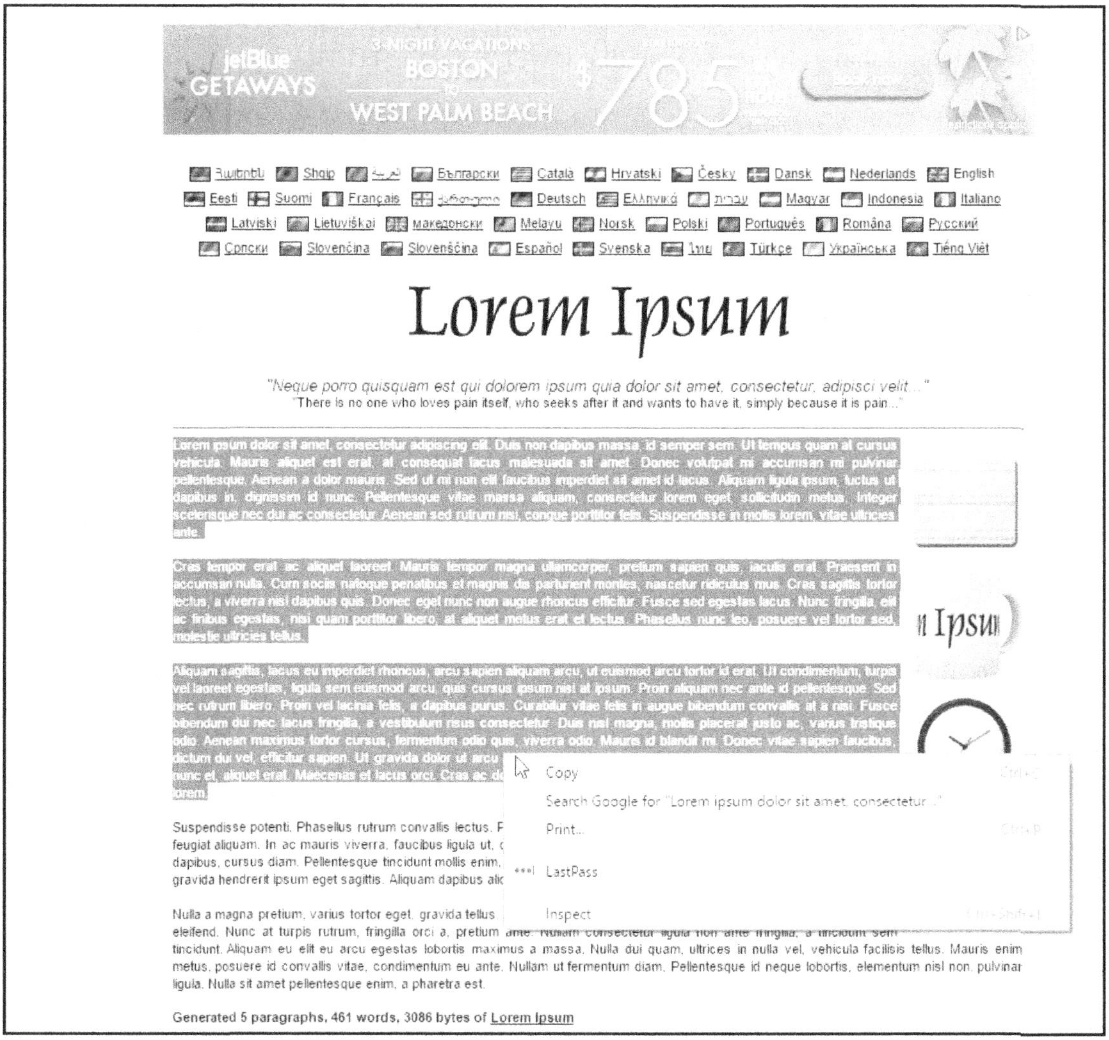

Now f you look at the source I guess you can paste the same content in, so this will be `Blog Post Two` and let's choose a different category, I'm will choose another image and **Save**:

So now we have two blog posts. Now we want to take care of the images so we will put this above the `truncateText` and if you don't like how it's laid out you can of course change it. You could put the image smaller on the side if you want but I'm just will put it right above the text. So this is will go to `/images` I think we did just uploads right in the root, we might actually have to change that location, but let's try `uploads/` and then we want to say `post.mainimage`. Yeah it's not loading from the right place:

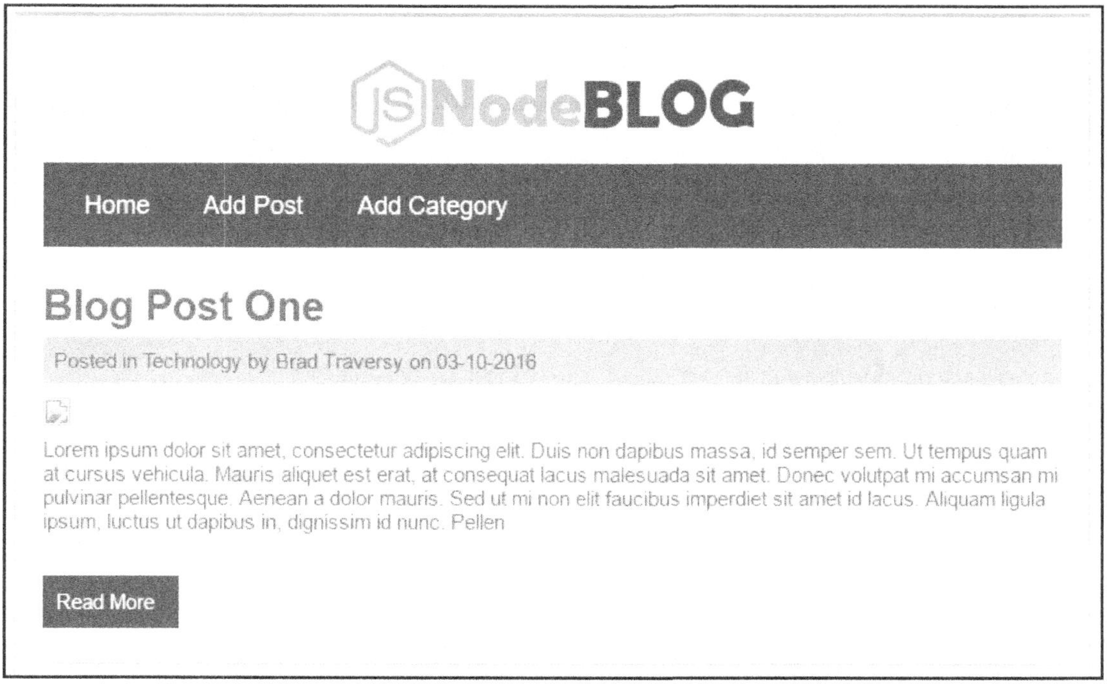

Now what we'll do is let's change the location, if we go to post, we will go to our post route and then change this right here. We want it to go to `./public/images`, actually yeah I'll just do public images:

```
var upload= multer({ dest: './public/images' })
```

So lets restart and there we go:

Now the image is will show on the `index` page, and you can mess with the size or whatever if you'd like, I will just leave it like that.

So we'll add one more, let's change this to **Business** and there we go there's our next post:

What I do want to do is make the width a hundred percent because they should all be the same.

So let's go into our style sheet and I will say `img`, `width:100%`:

```
img{
    width:100%;
}
```

I will actually move this up to the top. So we don't want that to be bigger, I think that these have a class of `posts` so let's do that, see if that works. There we go.

```
.post img{
    width:100%;
}
```

Now for the categories we want to be able to click on the categories and then show just the categories, I mean just the post from those categories:

So we want to add a new route to our categories page. Let's do this at the top. I'm just will copy this:

```
router.get('/add', function(req, res, next) {
    res.render('addcategory',{
        'title': 'Add Category'
    });
});
```

So this is will be `show/` and then we will do `:category` because that's will be dynamic, this is will be the ID of the category:

```
router.get('/show/:category', function(req, res, next) {
    res.render('addcategory',{
        'title': 'Add Category'
    });
```

I will actually copy from the code from our `posts.js` and then we'll paste that in `categories. js`

```
categories.find({},{},function(err, categories){
  res.render('addpost',{
    'title': 'Add Post',
    'categories': categories
  });
});
```

We want to change `categories` to `posts` and then what we want to do is say `post.find`, the view is will be `index` and `title` is will be the `category` So we can actually we can say `req.params.category`, and then we want to pass along the `posts` like this:

```
posts.find({},{},function(err, posts){
    res.render('index',{
        'title': req.params.category,
        'posts': posts
    });
```

Right now this is will get all posts, so we need to limit it, so we will go into this first parameter here and we will say `category: req.params.category`. Now this `req.params` this is just how you can get values from the URL:

```
posts.find({category: req.params.category},{},function(err, posts){
    res.render('index',{
        'title': req.params.category,
        'posts': posts
    });
```

What we want to do now is in our `index.jade` we want to turn this category name into a link and go to that route.

Let's find it in the `post.category` What we'll do is put an `a` tag, we'll say `href=` and it's will go to `/categories/show/` and then `post.category`. We want to put the link on its own line and then indent it. So let's save that and reload:

```
a(href='/posts/show/#{post._id}')
 =post.title
 p.meta Posted in
 a(href='/categories/show/#{post.category}') #{post.category}
 by #{post.author}
 on #{moment(post.date).format("MM-DD-YYYY")}
 img(src='/images/#{post.mainimage}')
 !=truncateText(post.body,400)
 a.more(href='/posts/show/#{post._id}') Read More
```

Now if we click that it takes us to `categories/show/Technology` and you'll see that only this post is showing. If we go back to index and I click on **Business** only the **Business** posts are showing. So that's working. So that's will be it for this section.

In the next section we will take care of our single page, which is the `posts/show` page. So we'll get into that next.

Single post and comments

In this section we will make it so that we can go to the **Read More** link, click on it, it'll show us the entire post and we'll also have comment functionality:

We want to do first is go in to route and then `post.js` and let's copy this:

```
router.get('/add', function(req, res, next) {
```

```
    var categories = db.get('categories');
    categories.find({},{},function(err, categories){
        res.render('addpost',{
            'title': 'Add Post',
            'categories': categories
        });
    });
});
```

And what we will do is say `get/show/:id` and then what we want to do is change this to `posts, get('posts')` and then change that to `posts`. And next we will pass functions to `findById` where we can actually get rid of these two and then we just want to pass in `req.params.id`:

```
router.get('/show/:id', function(req, res, next) {
  var posts = db.get('posts');
  posts.findById(req.params.id,function(err, post){
    res.render('show',{
      'post': post
    });
  });
});
```

Then we will render `'show'` and we need to pass along the post. So that should do it for the route, let's save it and let's go to our `views` folder.

Now I will create a new page called as `show.jade`. This will be similar to the index page, so I'm will go to the index view and copy all the code and paste it in here. We're not will need a loop because we're passing in the post itself, so let's get rid of the `if` and `each`, We don't need the `Read More` and `truncate`, all we want is `post.body`. so we can get rid of this and image, that's good. We also don't need the link for the `post.title` so remove that as well. The code that we need is:

```
extends layout

block content
    .post
    h1=post.title
    p.meta Posted in
     a(href='/categories/show/#{post.category}')
     #{post.category}
     by #{post.author}
     on #{moment(post.date).format("MM-DD-YYYY")}
     img(src='/images/#{post.mainimage}')
     !=post.body
```

Let's save that and let's go and restart.

If we go when we click on this title it brings us to the full view.

So what we will want now is under the post, we will have a list of comments and also a comment form. Now remember we don't have a special collection for comments it's just they will be embedded inside of the `post` object. We're just will add some stuff to this view, first of all let's put in a line break and then we'll do a horizontal rule, and then we will test for comments, so we'll say `if post.comments` and then under that let's put an `h3`, we'll say `comments` and then we need to loop through them, we'll use `each` comment, `i in post.comments`, add a class of `comment` and then a paragraph, this will be `comment-name` Then we'll have `body`:

```
hr
if post.comments
 h3 Comments
 each comment, i in post.comments
  .comment
   p.comment-name #{comment.name}
   p.comment-body #{comment.body}
```

Put a line break, and then we will have an `h3` that will say `Add Comment`. We will check for errors because we will do this just like any other form. so we'll say `each error, i in errors`. Then we'll have an `li`, let's give it a class of `alert.alert-danger`:

```
br
h3 Add Comment
if errors
ul.errors
each error, i in errors
li.alert.alert-danger #{error.msg}
```

I know we're not using Bootstrap but sometimes I like to just use the same class names. This will be `error.msg`. Now for the form itself, we will go in the code and say `form.comment-form`, give it a method of `post`, we will give it an `action`, `action` is will be `post/addcomment`. Then the `input` will have a `name` of `postid`, and this is actually will be hidden because we need a way to pass the ID along. So `name` is `postid`, `type` is `hidden`, and let's do `value`, `value` is will be the actual post ID so we can get that like this `post._id`. so next we need a `form-group` div, so this will be the name field.

```
h3 Add Comment
 if errors
 ul.errors
 each error, i in errors
 li.alert.alert-danger #{error.msg}
 form.comment-form(method='post', action='/posts/addcomment')
 input(name='postid', type='hidden', value='#{post._id}')
 .form-group
```

So we will say `label Name`, `input(type=)`, type is text, actually let's give this input a class of `form-control`, `type=('text')` and `name` is will equal `name`, so we can copy this:

```
.form-group
 label Name
 input.form-control(type='text', name='name')
```

the next one here is will be `Email`, change the `name` to `email` and then the next one will be the `Body` and this is will be a `textarea`, change the `name` to `body`. So after that let's put a `br` and then we need an `input`, we need a submit button, so `input.btn.btn-default` and let's see, we will say `type='submit'`, `name` will also be `submit` and then we need a `value`. For the value we're just will say `Add Comment`:

```
input(name='postid', type='hidden', value='#{post._id}')
.form-group
label Name
input.form-control(type='text', name='name')
.form-group
label Email
input.form-control(type='text', name='email')
.form-group
label Body
textarea.form-control(type='text', name='body')
br
input.btn.btn-default(type='submit', name='submit',value='Add Comment')
```

Let's save that, and let's see if we reload, now we have this **Add Comment** form:

There's no comments showing because we don't have any. What we want to do is make it so that we can add a comment through that form. You can see that that's will `posts/addcomment` so we want to go create that in our post file. So we'll go all the way to the bottom here and I'm actually will copy what we have here in this post:

```
// Form Validation
req.checkBody('title','Title field is required').notEmpty();
req.checkBody('body', 'Body field is required').notEmpty();
// Check Errors
var errors = req.validationErrors();
if(errors){
  res.render('addpost',{
```

```
      "errors": errors
    });
  } else {
    var posts = db.get('posts');
    posts.insert({
    "title": title,
    "body": body,
    "category": category,
    "date": date,
    "author": author,
    "mainimage": mainimage
  }, function(err, post){
    if(err){
      res.send(err);
    } else {
      req.flash('success','Post Added');
      res.location('/');
      res.redirect('/');
    }
```

Because it's will be very similar so we'll change this to `addcomment` and we'll remove the upload thing. Now for the values we know we have a `name`, we have `email`, and we know we already have a `body` so we can leave that. Actually I want the date, so this will be called `commentdate`:

```
router.post('/addcomment', function(req, res, next) {
  // Get Form Values
  var name = req.body.name;
  var email= req.body.email;
  var body = req.body.body;
  var commentdate = new Date();
```

Form `Validation`, `name`, `Name will be required`, we also want to require email. We'll say `Email field is required but never displayed`. We also want email validation so let's copy `checkbody`, and let's see we will change it from `notEmpty` to `isEmail` and we'll change the message as well, we'll say `Email is not formatted properly`, so that's the validation, then we will want to check errors just like any other form. If there are errors we want to re-render the show form but in order to do that we will have to also get the post, so we will say `var posts = db.get('posts')` and then we'll say `posts.findById`, in here we will pass in `postid` which I don't think we actually added up here, no we didn't. So let's go back to the top and add the following code:

```
var post id = req.body.postid;
```

Remember the postid is the hidden field. So now back down here findById(postid) then function will be error and post and then what we'll do is put the render method and put it inside the post method, so then we want to render show, pass in errors and we also want to pass in post.

```
if(errors){
  var posts = db.get('posts');
  posts.findById(postid, function(err, post){
    res.render('show',{
      "errors": errors,
      "post": post
    });
  });
```

Then in the else what we will do is create a variable called comment and this is will be an object, so first thing we want is a name, email, body, and commentdate, so that's our new comment object. Now what we want to do is get the posts. and then we want to do an update, so we'll say post.update and we will pass in the _id to postid, actually that's it for that. In the next parameter this is, we will say push, comments, and then after that we want function, we'll say error and doc for a document, check for the error. If there is one let's just throw, if there's not then we're just will set a message so req.flash, this is will be a success message, and we're just will say Comment Added and then we just want to redirect. Actually you know what we want to redirect to the same page to the post, so what we'll have to do is say posts/show/ and then we need to concatenate on postid:

```
if(errors){
  var posts = db.get('posts');
  posts.findById(postid, function(err, post){
    res.render('show',{
      "errors": errors,
      "post": post
    });
  });
  } else {
    var comment = {
      "name": name,
      "email": email,
      "body": body,
      "commentdate": commentdate
    }
    var posts = db.get('posts');
    posts.update({
      "_id": postid
    },{
      $push:{
```

```
        "comments": comment
      }
    }, function(err, doc){
      if(err){
        throw err;
      } else {
        req.flash('success', 'Comment Added');
        res.location('/posts/show/'+postid);
        res.redirect('/posts/show/'+postid);
      }
    });
```

So let's save that and let's try to restart the server. we're getting an error `Unexpected token,` after `body`:

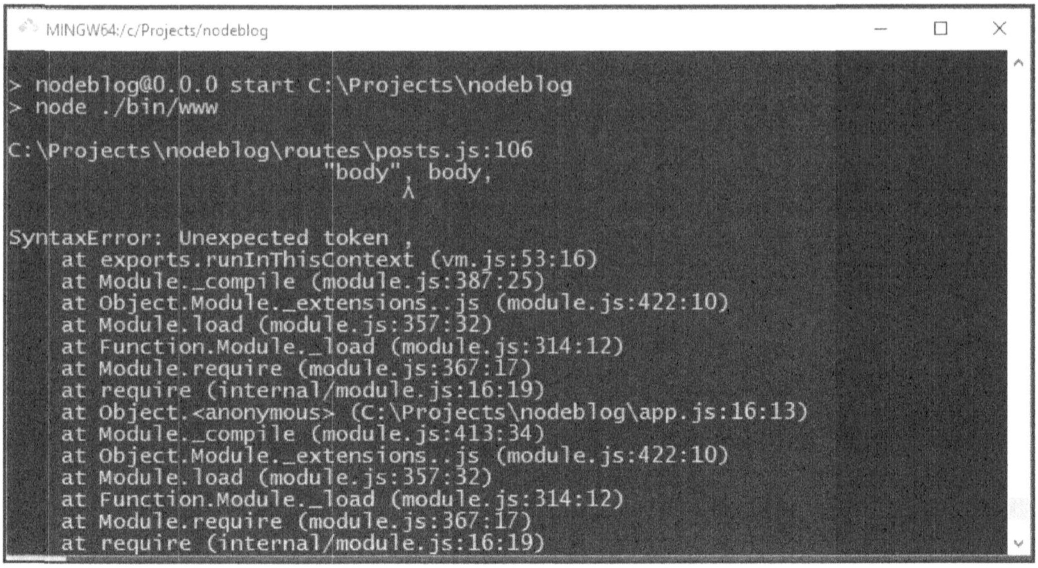

Let's see where is that, we missed on adding : after body:

```
var comment = {
  "name": name,
  "email": email,
  "body": body,
  "commentdate": commentdate
}
```

So now let's reload this page and let's try to add a comment. We'll say `Thanks for the post`:

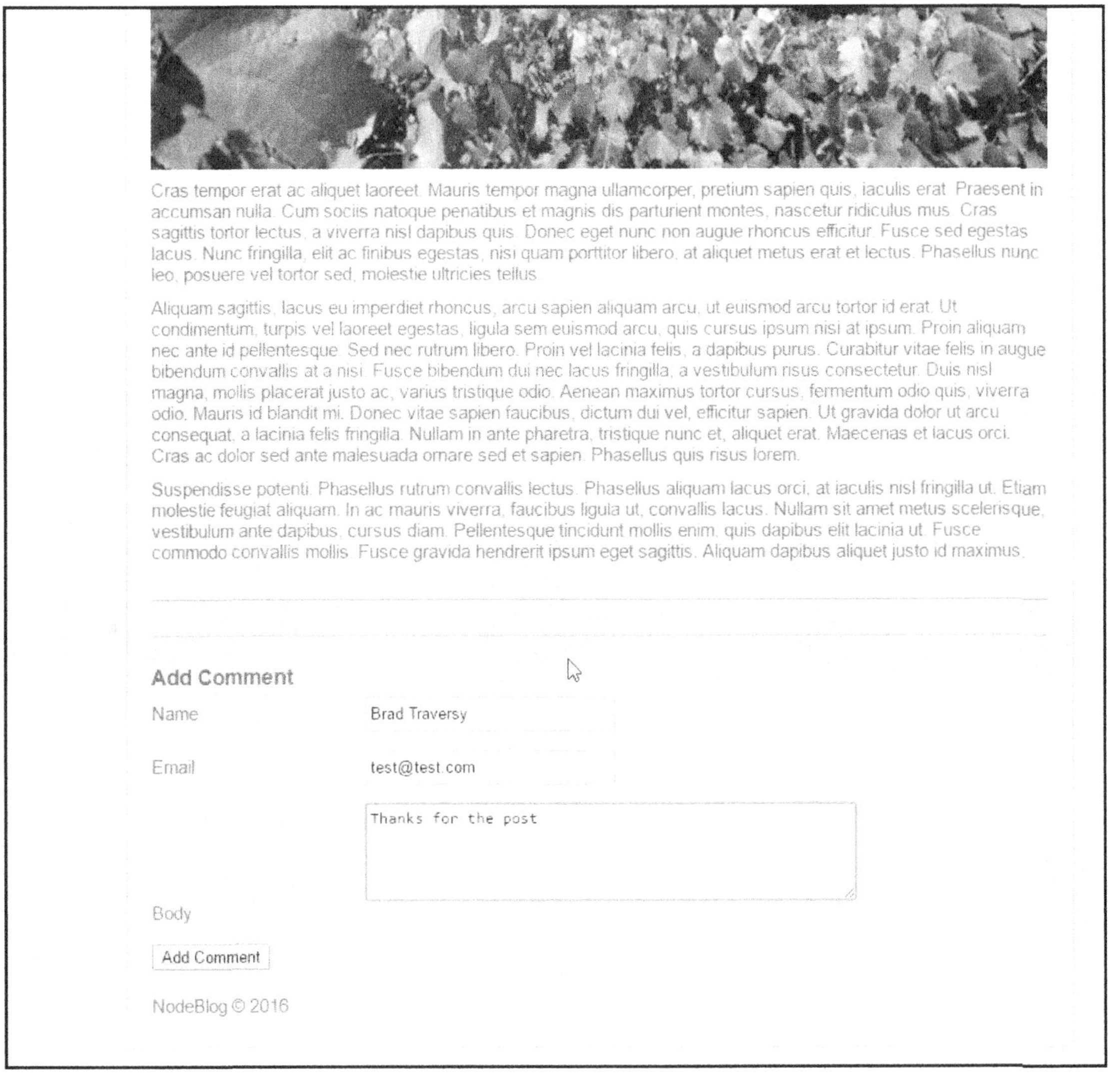

Actually we'll change the name let's say `Jeff Smith`. Comment added and there it is:

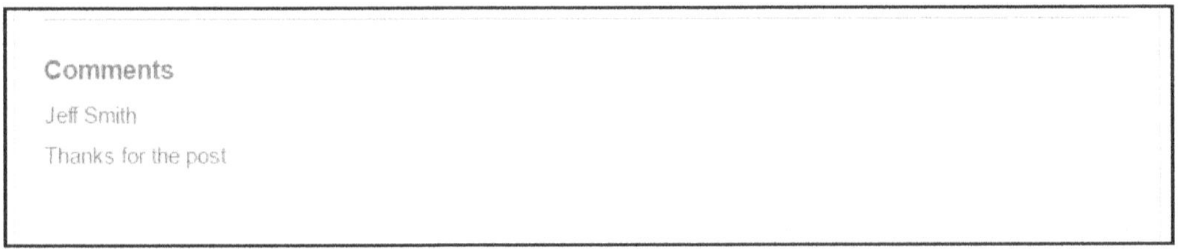

So we now have a blog application with categories and comments. Hopefully, you guys liked this project and you learned something from it.

Summary

In this chapter, we started with understanding the app and module setup. Once thorough with the setups, we further learnt about designing a template using custom layouts. We then added some posts and categories through the Mongo shell after which we created the functionality to get some posts displayed on the Home page. Along with adding posts, we further added categories and text editors. After truncating views we finally took care of our single page, which is the posts/show page.

In the next chapter, we will get into the details of ChatIO.

5
ChatIO

In this project, we're going to build a chat application that uses Node.js along with socket.io and WebSockets.

Basically, we come to the page and we get a prompt for a username. We put a username in and submit. Then it takes us to the main chat interface, which is very simple. We didn't use Bootstrap or anything, it's just completely custom. On the right-hand side, you can see the list of users and on the left-hand side, the main area, we have the chat box. If we put something here, let's say `Hello World`, and click on **Submit**, you can see it says the text that I typed along with my username.

What's really cool is that we can actually connect through another socket, just by opening another tab. If we go in, let's say my name is Mike, and I click on **Submit**, you can see that Brad's already in the chat room.

So, if I type `Hi Brad`, click on **Submit**, and go back to Brad's tab, you can see we have Mike's message:

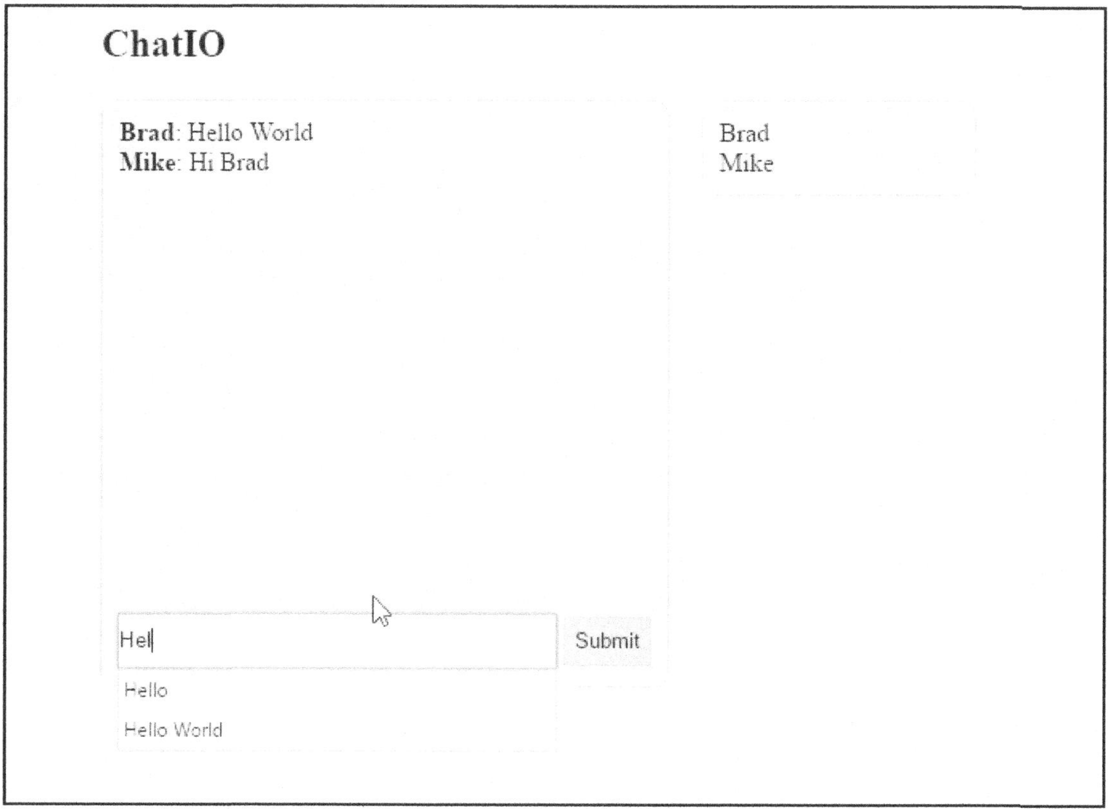

I'll reply back with `Hello Mike`, and Mike sees that. So, using WebSockets is perfect for something like a chat application, something that needs to be loaded in real time. You'd have noticed that we don't have to refresh the page, or anything like that. Let's get started.

In this chapter, we will learn:

- The ChatIO user interface
- Sending Chat Messages
- User Functionality
- Deploying an App with Heroku

The ChatIO user interface

In this project, we'll create a chat application. This is going to be a little different than what we than we've done in any of the previous projects, and that's because we'll be using WebSockets, more specifically we'll be using socket.io. WebSockets allows us to communicate have the client and server in a different way.

There will be an open connection between the client and server. Instead of just making request-response, there will be an open connection, and that makes everything completely instant. So we can send messages to the server, and it'll update all the other clients that are connected. We'll also be able to open a tab and write a message, and open another tab and be viewing the application as a different user. Then if one user replies or writes in a message, the other one will update automatically without even having to reload.

WebSockets is a really nice technology to learn, and it's actually really easy; it's basically just events. You call separate events on through the socket. Go to `socket.io`:

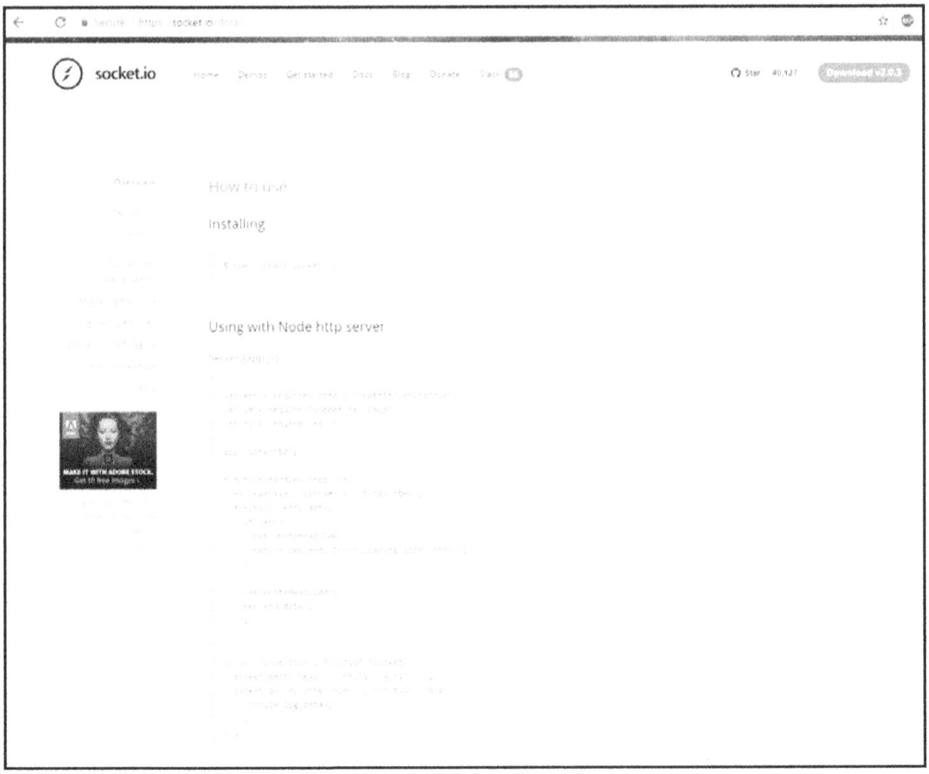

If we go to **Docs**, it will give you a really nice example on how to use socket.io with a Node HTTP server, as well as using Node with Express, which is what we'll be doing:

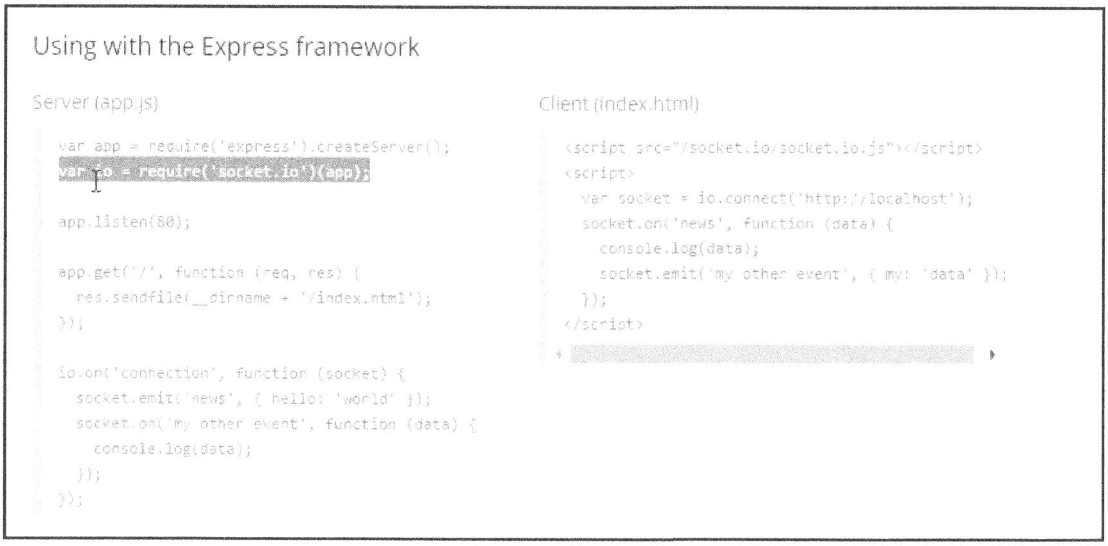

If we take a look here, we have a server file, `app.js`, and a client, `index.html`. On our server, we'll include socket.io, we'll create one route that's going to be `/`, which is just the home view, and we'll send the `index.html` file, that's the only route we need. Then under that, we can do our connection, we can our socket connection here - and then we can emit events. So, right here, we're saying `socket.emit ('news'`, and we're passing along `hello world`. Well, we're sending the string `world` inside `hello`.

Then on the client, we can actually say `socket.on('news'`, and that's going to connect it with `socket.emit('news'`. We have a callback function, and we'll able to access the data that's being sent, which in this case is the string `world`. It'll be a lot easier to understand when we actually do it.

Setting up the ChatIO UI

The first thing we're going to do here is go to the `Projects` folder.

> The file structure is going to be very, very simple; it's not going to be even near as many files and folders as we've been using.

Let's create a new folder here, and call this application `chatio`. We then create our `index.html`; that's going to have our interface. We want to create the interface first, and then we'll create our server. So, let's create `index.html` and open this with Sublime Text. We'll put in some base HTML code lines; and what we're going to do is put a title in the `title` tag, say `ChatIO`. In the `body`, we'll create a div; give it an ID of `container`. We're creating a very simple user interface, and we won't be using Bootstrap etc.; instead, we'll just have some custom CSS.

In the `container`, we'll have a few different areas. The first one will be the names wrapper, and this is going to be where our username form goes. So, let's create a `div` with the ID of `namesWrapper`. Inside there, let's put an `h2` that will say `ChatIO`. And then, we'll have a paragraph, and we're just going to say `Create Username`. Under that, we'll have our form. This will have an ID of `usernameForm`. In there, let's put an input with a size of `35`, and an ID of `username`. Let's also specify the input type, `type="text"`. Then under that, we'll have input type is going to be `submit`, and the `value` will be `Submit`:

```
<!DOCTYPE html>
<html>
<head>
  <title>ChatIO</title>
</head>
<body>
  <div id="container">
    <div id="namesWrapper">
      <h2>ChatIO</h2>
      <p>Create Username:</p>
      <form id="usernameForm">
        <input type="text" size="35" id="username">
        <input type="submit" value="Submit">
      </form>
    </div>
```

So that's the form and that's the `namesWrapper`. We'll go under `namesWrapper` and create the `mainWrapper`. So, we'll type in `div id="mainWrapper"`. In the `mainWrapper` let's do an `h2` with X. The `usernameForm` and `mainWrapper` are never going to show up at the same time; once the user enters the username, that will disappear and the `mainWrapper` will show up:

```
<div id="mainWrapper">
  <h2>ChatIO</h2>
```

We want `div id=chatWrapper`, and then in there, we're going to have an ID of `chatWindow`. That's not going to have anything inside it, because that's going to be generated through our JavaScript. Below that, we'll have the actual `messageForm`. Notice none of these forms will be submitted to an action; we'll just grab them using their ID. Now, in here, so we have a `text` input. Let's change this ID to `message` and add a `placeholder`. So that's the `mainWrapper`:

```
      <input type="text" size="35" id="message" placeholder="Say
      Something...">
    </form>
  </div>
```

Now, we go under the `chatWrapper`, and this will have an ID of `userWrapper`. This is where all the usernames will be, and we're not going to put anything in this. In this `div`, it'll be generated through JavaScript. So, we'll give it an ID of `users`.

```
<div id="userWrapper">
  <div id="users"></div>
</div>
```

That should be it! We save that and check out the result; it's not going to look like much, just two forms:

What we'll do now is just add some CSS, and I'll put it inside the `head`. I will give the `body` a light grey background. Then we'll add `container` with a `width` of `700` and a `margin` of `0 auto`, pushing everything to the middle. Now, for the `chatWindow`, we will have a fixed height of `300` pixels:

```
<head>
  <title>ChatIO</title>
  <style>
    body{
      background:#f9f9f9;
    }
    #container{
      width:700px;
      margin:0 auto;
    }
    #chatWindow{
      height:300px;
    }
    #mainWrapper{
      display:none;
    }
```

Then we have the `mainWrapper`, which kind of wraps around everything except the username form. To begin with, we want this to display none. After that, let's put in our `chatWrapper`; and I'll put some code in. Then we need our `userWrapper`, and let's paste some code lines in (which is shown next):

```
#chatWrapper{
  float:left;
  border:1px #ccc solid;
  border-radius: 10px;
  background:#f4f4f4;
  padding:10px;
}

#userWrapper{
  float:left;
  border:1px #ccc solid;
  border-radius: 10px;
  background:#f4f4f4;
  padding:10px;
  margin-Left:20px;
  width:150px;
  max-height:200px;
}
```

Then we need our `namesWrapper`, and for that we're actually going to have a lot of the same stuff as well as the `chatWrapper` and `userWrapper`. One last thing: I just want to make the inputs a little higher; height will be `30` pixels. Have a look at the code lines we just added:

```
#namesWrapper{
  float:left;
  border:1px #ccc solid;
  border-radius: 10px;
  background:#f4f4f4;
  padding:10px;
  margin-Left:20px;
}
input{
    height:30px;
    }
```

Alright, so let's save that and reload. We have our username form:

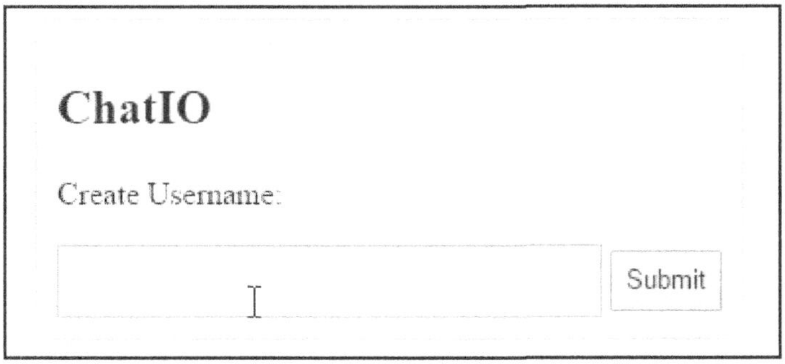

We show the `mainWrapper` and then we don't display the `namesWrapper`. That will give us the following screen, where we can add chats in the left page and then the users will be on the right:

I'll revert the `namesWrapper` change, which. That's our interface!

In the next section, we'll make it so that we can send chat messages. We'll do the usernames later in the chapter. For now, I just want to be able to send messages.

Sending chat messages

In the last section, we created our user interface in `index.html`; that's the only file we created. Now, we want to start to create our server, the Node.js server.

Creating the Node.js server

The first thing I will do is create a `package.json` file. We could manually create it, but I'll to open a command line into our `projects` folder and run `npm init`, and of course you have to have Node.js installed.

So, the name will be `chatio`, `version` will be `1.0.0`, and `description` will be `simple chat app`. We'll change `entry point` to `server.js`. That's good and then put your own name so that should go ahead and create it:

```
$ npm init
This utility will walk you through creating a package.json file.
It only covers the most common items, and tries to guess sensible defaults.

See `npm help json` for definitive documentation on these fields
and exactly what they do.

Use `npm install <pkg>` afterwards to install a package and
save it as a dependency in the package.json file.

Press ^C at any time to quit.
package name: (chatio)
version: (1.0.0)
description: Simple chat app
entry point: (index.js) server.js
test command:
git repository:
keywords:
author: Brad Traversy
license: (ISC)
About to write to C:\Projects\chatio\package.json:

{
  "name": "chatio",
  "version": "1.0.0",
  "description": "Simple chat app",
  "main": "server.js",
  "scripts": {
    "test": "echo \"Error: no test specified\" && exit 1"
  },
  "author": "Brad Traversy",
  "license": "ISC"
}


Is this ok? (yes)
```

I will add it to Sublime Text. Let's go to the `C:\Projects\chatio`. There's our `package.json` file. Now, we want to go in the code and add a couple dependencies. So, we'll say `dependencies` and add `socket.io` and `express` (latest versions) as shown in the following code snippet:

```
"dependencies": {
  "socket.io": "*",
  "express": "*"
}
```

Let's save that and we'll go back to our command line and run `npm install`. This will install socket.io and Express. Now that those are installed, we'll create our `server.js` file. Let's open that up, and the first thing we'll do is include Express and continue on with the things we need to initialize. So, `app` will take in `express` and `server` will take in `require ('http')`. Here, we'll say `.createServer` and pass in `app`. We then include `socket.io`, and call `.listen` and put in `server`. The next thing we do is ask it to listen on whatever port we want to use, so, we'll say `server.listen` and pass in `process.env.port` or, let's just say `PORT 3000`, but you could put anything really. So we need one route, just for the `index.html` file. Let's say `app.get` and this will have `/`. Then this will take in request-response, and then say `res.sendfile` . We'll then say `dirname`, and let's concatenate onto that `/ index.html`. In essence, we're saying that when you go to the home screen, or `/`, we want to load this file, simple:

```
var express = require('express'),
  app = express(),
  server = require('http').createServer(app),
  io = require('socket.io').listen(server);

server.listen(process.env.PORT || 3000);

app.get('/', function(req, res){
  res.sendFile(__dirname + '/index.html');
});
```

Let's actually test that out. So, we'll save and then go into our command line and run `node server`. Let's put a console log, just so we can tell if we're actually running the server. Let's say, `console.log ('Server Running...')`. Now, let's go to localhost port 3000. So it loads, and that's exactly what we want. I just want to fix the indent. To fix that, let's go to our HTML and edit the CSS.

We'll just say `border:solid 1px, gray`:

```
input{
  height:30px;
  border:solid 1px #ccc;
}
```

Reload, and that fixes the indent.

Back to `server.js`; what we want to do here is connect to our socket. So we're going to say `io.sockets.on`, and say on `connection` run a function pass `socket`. Firstly, let's just use `console.log`; we'll say `Socket Connected`. We'll make it so we can send a message. To do that, I'll use `socket.on`. In here, we could pretty much put whatever we like. I'll put `Send Message`, that's the name of the event. We'll then have a `function` to pass in data, put `io.sockets.emit` as we want to emit new message, and pass along the data, so put `msg: data`:

```
io.sockets.on('connection', function(socket){
  console.log('Socket Connected..');

  // Send Message
  socket.on('send message', function(data){
    io.sockets.emit( 'new message', {msg: data});
  });
});
```

Now we want to go on to the client side. We'll go back to `index.html` and we go down to the bottom, right above the ending `body` tag. We'll include two things here: two scripts. The first one is jQuery, we'll use the CDN; and then the second one is going to be the `socket.io.js` file so that we can actually interact with the server. We'll be using jQuery. Let's open up the script tag:

```
io.sockets.on('connection', function(socket)
  console.log('Socket Connected...');

  // Send Message
  socket.on('send message', function(data){
    io.sockets.emit('new message', {msg: data});
  });
});
```

The first thing we'll do is open up the dollar sign and parentheses. In there, we'll put a function and create a variable called `socket` and set that to `io.connect`. This will connect using this connection, and then we should see this in the console. Let's give that a shot. We'll stop this, and run `node server`. I can see socket connected:

```
gauravg@PPMUMCPU0268 MINGW64 /c/Projects/chatio
$ node server
Server Running...
Socket Connected...
```

That's what we want. Going back to `index.html`, what we want to do is not show the user form yet because we don't have that functionality. So, I'll remove the `display : none` from the `mainWrapper`, and I'll put that into the `namesWrapper`:

```
#namesWrapper{
  display:none;
  float:left;
  border:1px #ccc solid;
  border-radius: 10px;
  padding:10px;
  margin-Left:20px;
}
```

Let's reload, and now we have our chat window:

Now, this is where the users will go; just don't pay attention to the rest. When we submit this form, we need to catch the input:

```
<scripts>
$(function(){
  var socket = io.connect();
  var $messageForm = $('messageForm');
  var $message = $(#message);
  var $chat = $('#chatWindow');

  $messageForm.submit(function(e){
    e.preventDefault();
    console.log('Submitted');
  });
});
</script>
```

For this, we'll use jQuery;

```
var socket = io.connect();
var $messageForm = $('#messageForm');
var $message = $('#message');
var $chat = $('#chatWindow');

$messageForm.submit(function(e){
  e.preventDefault();
});
```

I'll create a variable called `messageForm`. Notice `$` in front of it, we don't need to do that, but since it's a variable that is referencing jQuery, I'll use the `$`. We'll set that to jQuery, and we want the ID of `messageform`. We also want a variable called `message`, and we'll set that to the ID of `message`. Let's create a variable called `$chat`, and we'll set that to the chat window. So we have those variables; we want to get the message form and say `.submit`. We have a `submit` event, then in there, we'll create a function. We'll pass in an event, and then just to prevent the act of the form from actually submitting, we'll say `preventDefault`. To test things, we'll say `console.log` and use `submitted`. We'll save that and restart the server.

I'll also open the console in Chrome. If we say something and submit, you can see that we get submitted. We know that's connected and working. Now, we want to emit the send message event when we submit. So, we'll say `socket.emit` and we want send message. This is going to emit `new message` to the client along with the data.

```
io.sockets.emit('new message', {msg: data});
```

Let's go back to `index.html`. In addition to this, we want to send along whatever is passed in the form. So, as a second parameter, we'll use `message.val`. That will send the message, and then we clear the form. We'll use `message.val` and pass in empty quotes. We still have to add the message to the chat window. Under this whole thing, we'll use `socket.on`. This time, it will be `new message`. We sent the message to the server, the server gets it, and then it sends new message back along with the data. We can do what we want with that data. We'll use `chat.append`,, append `data.message`, and put a line break after that:

```
  socket.emit('send message', $message.val());
  $message.val('');
});
socket.on('new message', function(data){
  $chat.append(data.msg+ '<br>');
});
```

Let's save that; reload the server, refresh the page, and let's say **Hello**.

So now we can send messages. So, in the next section, we're going to want to implement username functionality, so that we could login; we'll see the names, and we'll also see a name next to each message, so we know who sent it.

User functionality

In this section, we will learn to implement username functionality so that we can distinguish what messages are from whom. The first thing we'll do is in the HTML, in `namesWrapper`, we have `display : none`. So, we're going to actually cut that, and put it back to where we originally had it, in the main wrapper.

```
#mainWrapper{
  display:none;
}
```

That way, when we go to the application, we just see the username form. We'll go into `server.js`, and down to where we have our connection. Let's type in `socket.on`, and we want to pass in `new user`. Then we have a function and it's going to take a `data`, `callback`, and check the username, because we don't want to have double usernames. If there's already one taken, then the user's not going to be able to use that one. So, let's say `usernames` that actually needs to be initialized. `usernames` is going to be an array that holds all the usernames.

```
socket.on('new user', function(data, callback){
  usernames
});
```

I'll simply initialize it with an empty array:

```
usernames = []
```

We'll say if `usernames.indexOf`, pass in `data`, and say not equal to `-1` then `callback (false)`. So we'll check if the username is there. Then we'll do an `else` and we'll set `callback (true)`. We'll say `socket.username` will be equal to the data that gets passed in. We'll add it to the `usernames` array: `usernames.push (socket.username)`. Then we'll call a function called `updateUsernames`. We'll create that. Let's go under the above code and let's say `updateUsernames`. What we want to do here is emit an event; so use `io.sockets.emit`, we want to emit `usernames`, and we also want to pass along the `usernames`:

```
    if(usernames.indexOf(data) != -1){
      callback(false);
    } else {
      callback(true);
      socket.username = data;
      usernames.push(socket.username);
      updateUsernames();
    }
  });

  // Update Usernames
  function updateUsernames(){
    io.sockets.emit('usernames', usernames);
  }
```

We'll pass that so that we can actually list them on the sidebar in the app. So this is the server and it's looking good. The last thing I want to do here is write a disconnect event. So we'll say `socket.on 'disconnect'`, and pass in data. Then we'll say if not `socket.username`, then we want to `return`. We'll use `usernames.splice` because we want to take that user out of the `usernames` array. So we use `splice usernames.indexOf(socket.username)`, and then we pass in the second parameter of `1`. Post that we'll call `updateUsernames` again, so let's grab that:

```
  // Disconnect
  socket.on('disconnect', function(data){
    if(!socket.username){
    }
    usernames.splice(usernames.indexOf(socket.username), 1);
    updateUsernames();
  });
```

So, let's save it and go back to `index.html`; Go down to the bottom and we're going to add a couple more variables. Let's say `var $usernameform`, we'll say `var $users`, set that to jQuery users, `username` is going to equal jQuery user name, and we also want an error because we want to be able to show error:

```
var $usernameForm = $('#usernameForm');
var $users = $('#users');
var $username = $('#username');
var $error = $('#error');
```

Let's go to make a copy of `$messageForm.submit` and then we'll change this to username `form.submit`, and let's just do a simple test and observe the unexpected token:

```
$usernameForm.submit(function(e){
  e.preventDefault();
  console.log('Submitted');
});
```

The following code needs to have an equals sign:

```
if(usernames.indexOf(data) != -1)
```

So let's submit, we submit that and we're catching that.

Let's go back to `index.html` and we want to use `socket.emit('new user'`, and then we want a second parameter of the value of the username; finally, we want a function, and that will to take data. Let's check for the data and that will take an `else`, as well. What we do next is hide the username form, and show the `mainWrapper`. So, we can do that with jQuery. We'll say `namesWrapper.hide`, and we'll say `mainWrapper.show`:

```
socket.emit('new user', $username.val(), function(
  data){
  if(data){
    $('#namesWrapper').hide();
    $('#mainWrapper').show();
  } else{
  }
});
```

Let's test that so far. We'll save it, restart, reload, and if we put something in **ChatIO**, it hides the username form and shows us the `mainWrapper`. That's good!

Now, it will say else and error variable and say `.html`. Then take whatever error we want to say, for example, `username is taken`:

```
} else{
  $error.html('Username is taken');
}
```

Now we need to actually create a div with the ID of error in our HTML. So let's go right above the username form, and we'll say `div id ="error"`. Go back down.

We'll submit that new user that's going to go to the server. Then if you look down, we'll call `updateUsernames`, which emits an event called `Usernames` to the client. So, we have to catch that on the client. You can see all this is basically passing stuff back and forth from the server to the client. We now need to say `socket.on` with `usernames, function`. I'll initialize a variable called `html`, set it to just an empty string, and then loop through the usernames. So, we'll use a `for` loop and say `i = 0`, as long as `i` is less than `data.length`. We then need to increment by `1`—so, `i++`. So for every username that we scroll through, we'll add to the `html`; we'll append using `+/=`. Then whatever iteration it's on, we'll just concatenate a line break. Next, outside the for loop, we'll say `users.html` and pass in that `HTML` variable. That should do it; let's go ahead and restart:

```
socket.on('usernames', function(data){
  var html = '';
  for(i = 0;i < data.length;i++){
    html += data[i] + '<br>';
  }
  $users.html(html);
});
```

Let's refresh this page, enter the username and click on **Submit**. Now you can see that the name is over on the side. If I say `Hello`, you will notice that we are yet to make the name show up there as well. So, we need to go to `new message`, let's put it in some `strong` tags, and then inside the tag put `concatenate data.user`:

```
socket.on('new message', function(data){
  $chat.append('<strong>'+data.user+'</strong>'+data.
    msg+'<br>');
});
```

Now I don't think we actually sent the user. So we need to save that and go back to the server, and see where we sent the message. We also want to send the user, so we'll say `user : socket.username`:

```
socket.on('send message', function(data){
  io.sockets.emit('new message', {msg: data, user: socket.username});
});
```

That should do it!

Now if I say `Hello`, we get **Brad Hello**. So if I open another tab, go to the same localhost port 3000, and sign in as John, you can see that Brad is there. If I go back to Brad's tab, John is there. So, as John, if I say **Hi Brad** and we go back, you can see that I can see John's message. I say **Hello John**, he gets that as well. That's exactly what we want. Now if I close John's tab, you can see that on Brad's tab John is now gone. So, it's working perfectly. That's how we can create a chat application. Now in the next section, I'll show you how we can actually deploy a Node.js application.

Deploying an app with Heroku

Now that our local application is complete, I want to do something that we haven't really done—make our application live on the web. There are a few different ways you can do it, a few different services. I want to use Heroku, which is an application-hosting provider, among other things, and it's used commonly for Node.js as well as Ruby on Rails, Python, and a whole bunch of other programming languages.

Now, there are a few different packages. We want the free package, which is mostly used for development, maybe some small production apps. But you can see, if we go to **Pricing** and go down, you can see that packages for enterprise-level businesses can go up to $30,000. So, it can be very expensive; but that's if you have a site like Instagram or Twitter where there's just loads of data. This is an excellent solution, because it's really easy to scale.

First, sign up! I already have an account so I'll not go through that here, but fill in your information. Once you do that, we can log in and you should see your dashboard. You can see that we have a bunch of different selections for different programming languages and platforms:

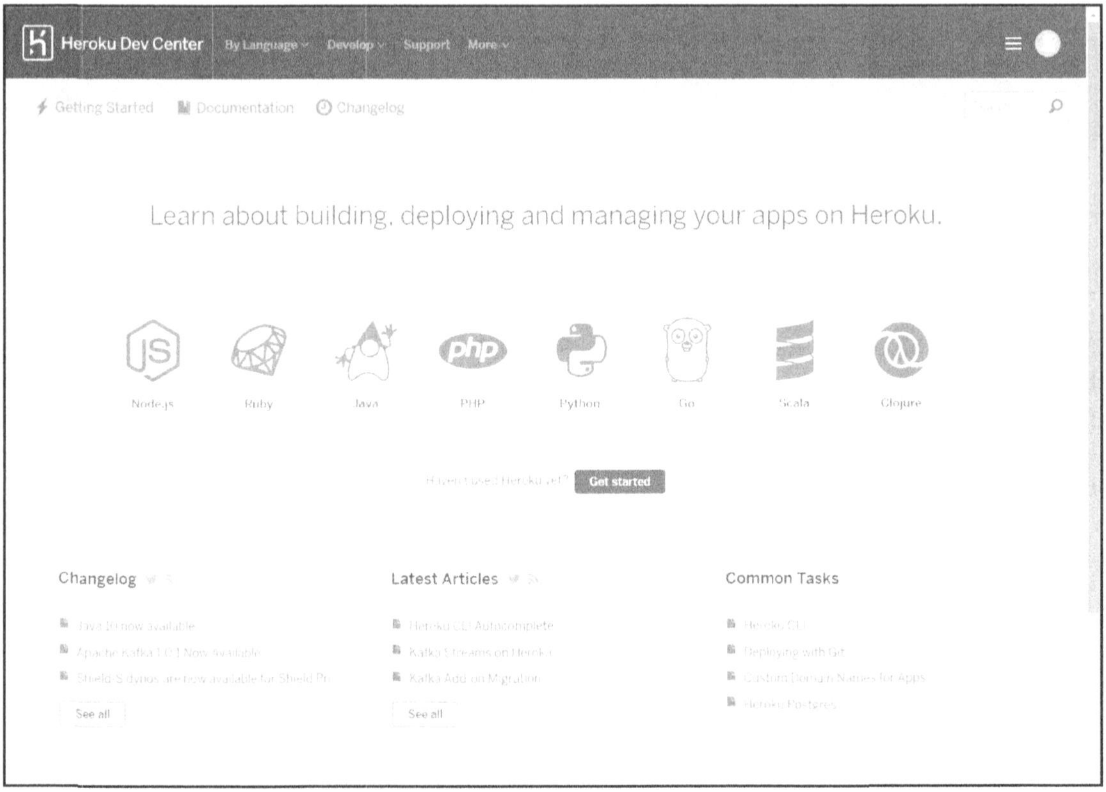

Obviously, we want Node.js. If we click on **Node.js**, it's going to take us to a little guide to get started. We'll go ahead and click on **I'm ready to start**. You can see it says that **This tutorial assumes that you have an account, as well as Node.js and npm, installed**, which we do.

The first thing we do is click on **Download Heroku Toolbelt for Windows**. You can choose your OS if you're using a different system. We are using Windows. Download it and run that. It's just a Windows software installation; just go through it. I'll use the default directory, `Program Files`, and it already exists. I'll override it and choose full installation. I'll also install the Ruby programming language as well:

Now, if we scroll down, we want to log in with the command prompt. I'll not use the Git Bash because it has had issues. Instead, we'll use just the standard Windows command prompt and go to the application directory (mine is in `projects/chatio`). Let's do Heroku login, and you're just going to put in your `email` and `password`. You'll see the message **authentication successful**:

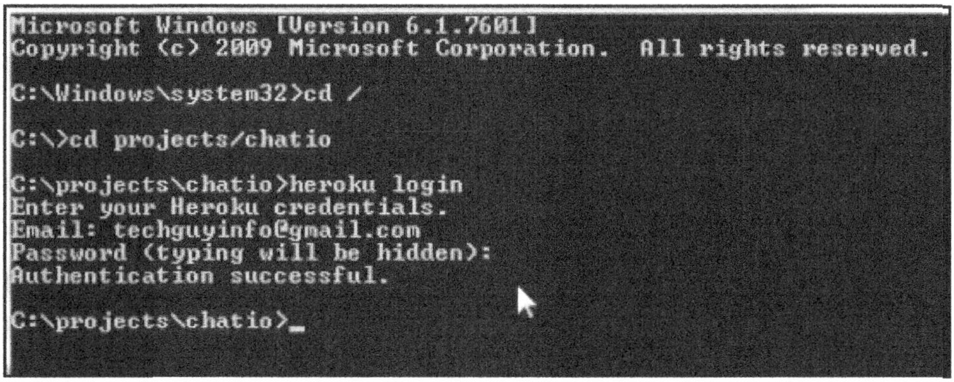

Now we need to create the app. So let's click on **I have installed Toolbelt**. We now need to create a Git repository. So, I'll go into the Windows command prompt. We'll run `git init`. We'll create a `.git` folder in your project folder by default, it's going to be hidden. If you want to unhide folders in Windows, you'll see the `.git` folder. Next, let's add everything to the Git repository.

We run `git add`, and then a `.`. This just means add everything that's in the folder. We should now be able to commit locally; so we'll run `git commit`, and I'll add the `m` tag and then a comment:

```
git commit -m 'Initial Commit'
```

It's committed locally. Let's go to the next page to deploy the app.

We run `heroku create`, and that should give us a random name: `still-castle-3340.herokuapp.com`:

Now, if we go back to the panel and reload, we can see that we have an app now. There's not much we can look at yet, but let's go ahead and push it by running `git push heroku master`. That will push to the remote repository. That's complete! Now, to test your app, you can actually have the command line open it and run `heroku open`. It's probably going to give us an error:

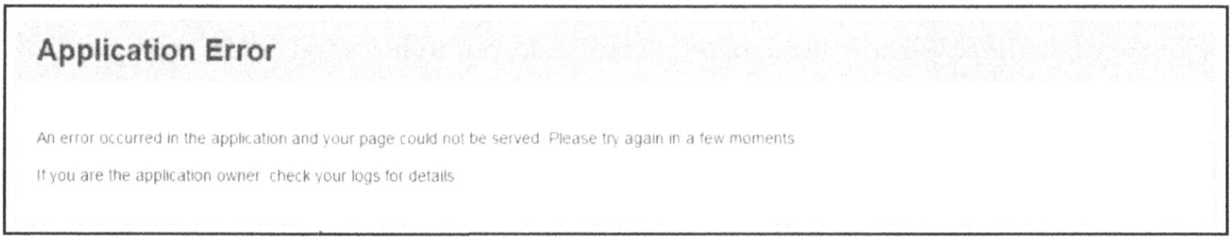

Let's continue with the guide, because there are some things we didn't do. The application is deployed; we need to ensure that at least one instance of the app is running. Let's go ahead and copy this command in the command prompt:

```
Scaling dynos... Failed
No such process type web defined in Procfile.
```

We now need to define a Procfile. Basically, we need to create a file called `Procfile` with no extension, and we just need to include the main file that we want them to open, which is `app.js`:

```
node index.js
```

This example says index, I'll copy the above code, and then we want to go to our project folder and create a new document, `Procfile`. It should have a capital P. We'll open that up, and I'll paste the above code in it, and change `index.js` to `app.js` and save that. Now, we have to make the changes in the prompt. We'll add `git add`, then commit using `git commit -m`, and we'll say `"Added Procfile"`. Now we should be able to run `git push heroku master`:

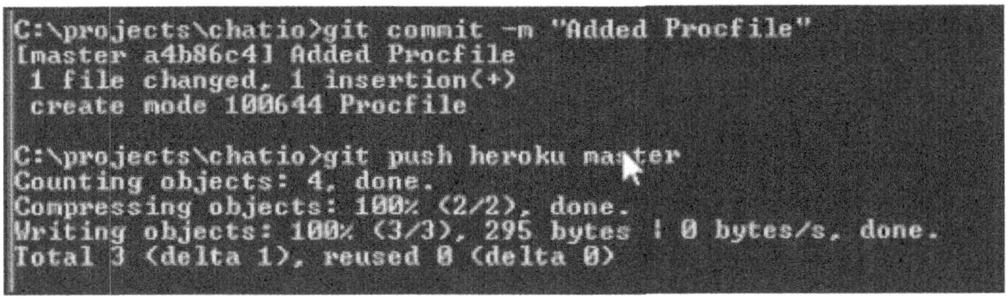

Let's go ahead and see if that worked. We're still getting the error. We can show our log with `heroku logs`. We now need to define our scale, our dynos scale, in the code:

```
heroku ps:scale web=1
```

So basically, we need to just copy the preceding code from the documentation and paste. Then we should just scale your dynos at `1` and now it's running. So, now we can go ahead and reload, and there's our app.

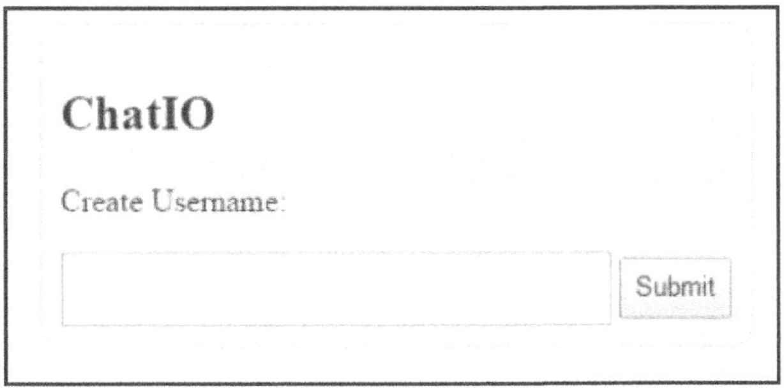

This is now live on the internet; you can get to this from anywhere, using this subdomain; of course, you can add your own domain, but let's just make sure that this works.

> Remember to get rid of that **S** in that **HTTPS** and then submit.

So that's working and we should be able to connect to another browser tab. Let's say, **Mike**. You can see **Brad** and **Mike**. We'll say `Hi Brad`, and we can see that. Then we'll say `Hi Mike`. It's working! Now, to get your own domain (because, obviously, if this was a production app, you don't want this as your domain) - you can do that from the panel. Go to **Settings** | **Domains** | **Add your custom domain here** | **Point your DMS to Heroku**. Then click on **Edit**; you could type in your domain, and then you just need to point your DNS. You can then just click on the link **Point your DMS to Heroku** that will take you to the page that explains all that. That's how you can get your Node.js app live on the web using Heroku.

Summary

In this chapter, we started with learning the ChatIO interface. Along with adding more features to the interface, we learned about how to send chat messages. To further improve the app, we added user functionality to it. And lastly, we designed an app using Heroku.

In the next chapter, we will start with e-learning.

6
E-Learning Systems

In this project, we're going to build an online learning application. It's going to be relatively simple compared to some of the production applications but it's a good foundation.

Here's our landing page:

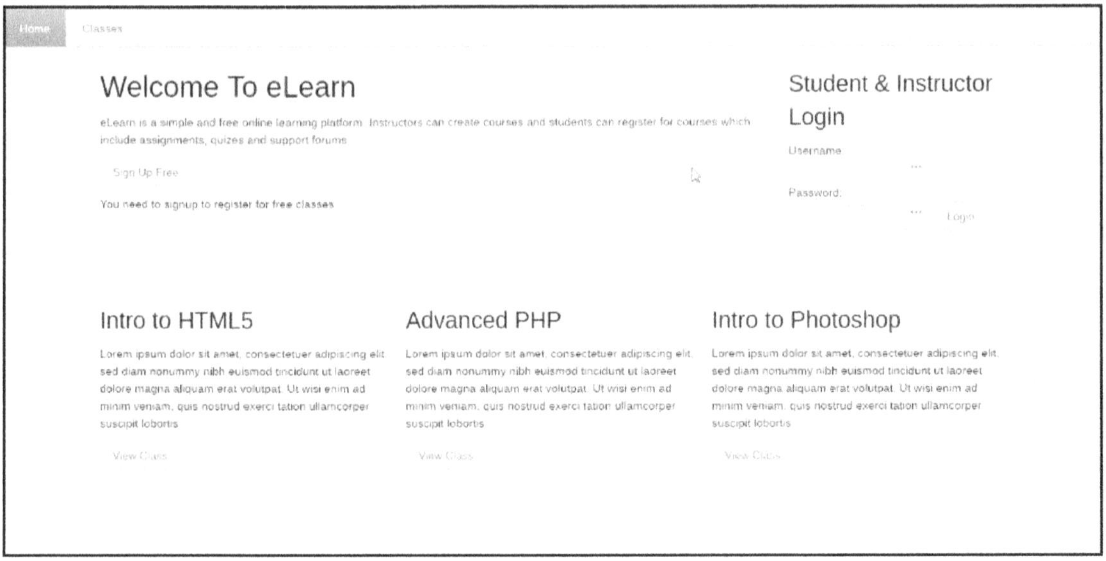

Here, we have a **Classes** link. If we click on it, we can see all the different classes. We can click on **Class Details** there. The **Class Details** button is going to show us the class description, the instructor, and also any lessons.

Now, we have to be registered to register for this class or logged-in to register for this class. So at the top-right side corner, we have our login area. I'll show you how we can register first, then we'll go ahead with the project. We'll click on **Sign Up Free**. You can choose either **Student** or **Instructor** in the **Account Type** option; let's choose **Student**.

Next, we can fill up the different sections given on the **Create An Account** page:

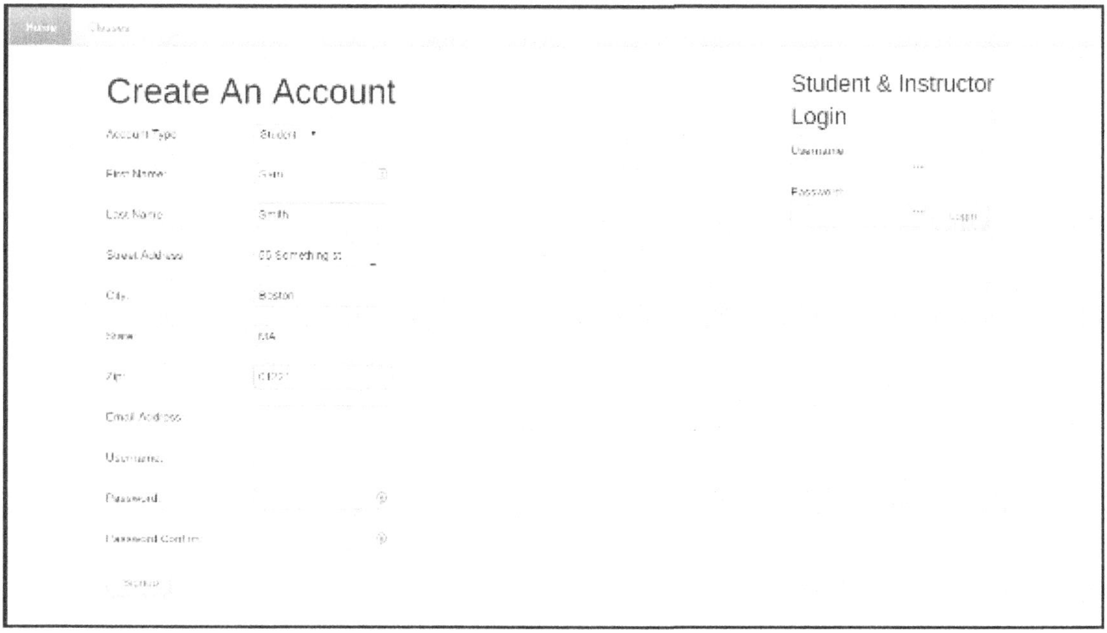

Creating an account

We can set the **First Name** field to `Sam`, **Last Name** to `Smith`, **Street Address** to `Something St`, **City** to `Boston MA 01221`, and **Email Address** can be `something.com`. Then, we can add the **Username** and the **Password**. The Username will be `sam`. We can put the **Password** we like and click on **Signup**. So, now we have the user. Let's try logging in with the set credentials. We'll add the **Username**, `sam`, and its password:

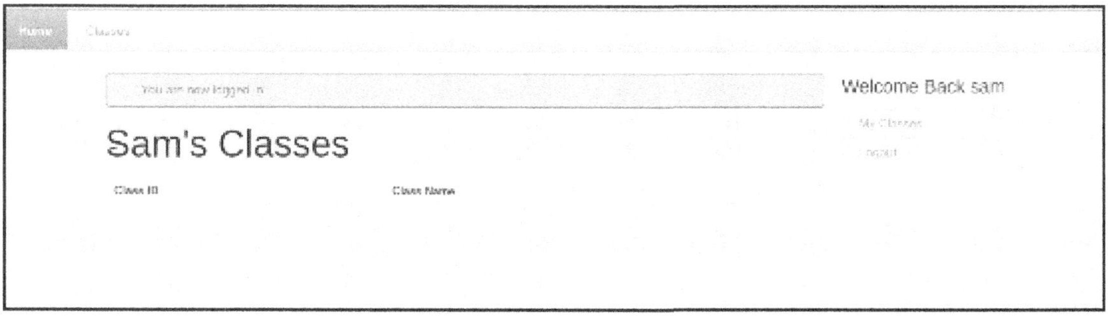

Logged in as Sam

So, now we're logged in as Sam. At present we don't have any classes, so we can go ahead and register for some classes. For this, we can go to our **Classes**.

Let's say we want HTML5 and we can go ahead and register for the class:

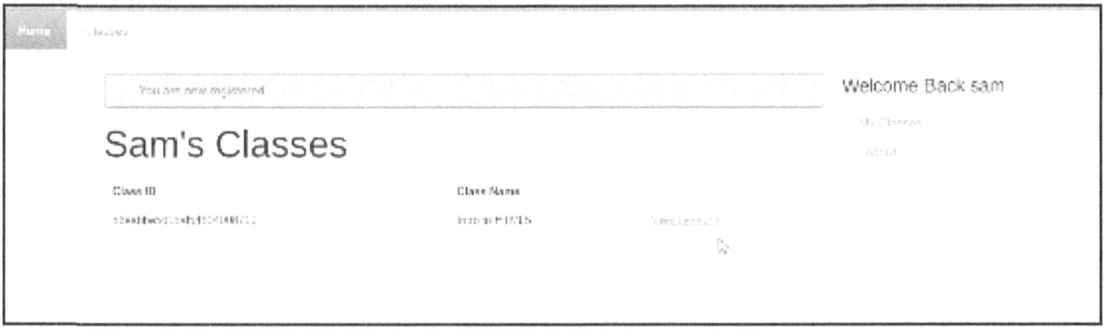

Sam's classes

Now it's added in our **Classes**. If there are lessons, we can view those by clicking on the **View Lessons** button. So, this is how we can register of the classes and explore them.

Now, let's log out and then log in as an instructor, Brad:

Brad's classes

These are classes that I'm registered to teach. Now, we can view the lessons just like we could with the students, but we can also add a lesson by clicking on the **Add Lesson** button. Let's say we want to add a lesson under the name **Another Lesson**.

For this, we'll fill the following form and add the lesson:

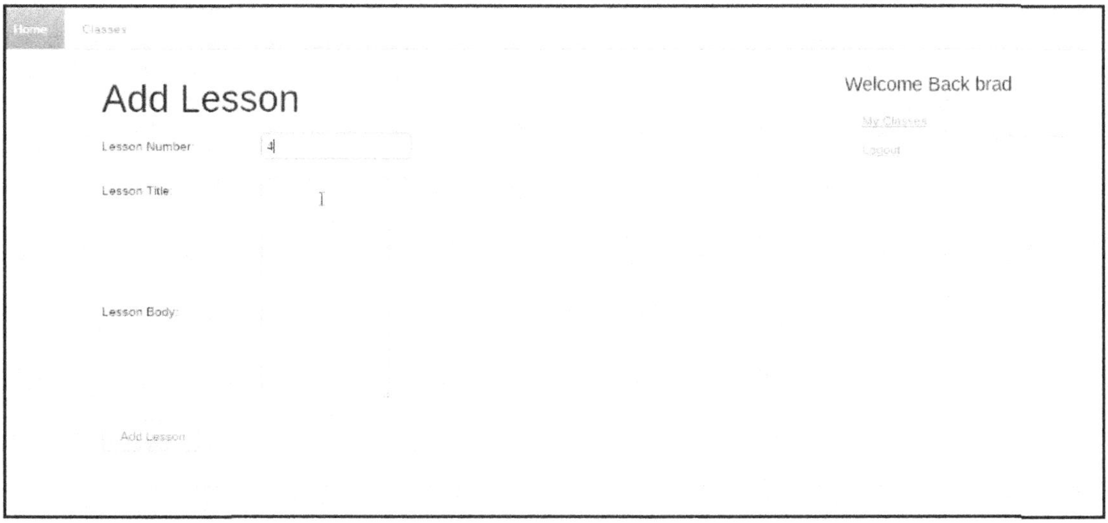

We'll add the lesson number, let's say `4`, then lesson title, `Another Lesson`, and we can set the lesson body to, `Test` and we'll add this lesson.Now if we go to HTML5, **View Lessons**, you can see we have **Another Lesson**:

Now, we can log out. So, the registering and exploring the classes is very simple. As far as technologies are concerned, we'll be using Passport and bcrypt for login. We'll also be using Mongoose and MongoDB. We're going to use Express validator and Express handlebars for our templating engine, which is a nice break from Pug. Let's get started!

The app and HTML Kickstart setup

In this section, we'll build a fairly simple online learning system. So we'll use obviously Node.js along with some other technologies. We have used some of them (not all). We are going to use Passport and use an authentication system. We're also going to use HTML KickStart for our frontend, which is just something that's similar to Bootstrap. I just wanted to kind of change it up a little bit. Now I want to be able to have students and instructors both come and register and login. Instructors will be able to create classes and lessons within those classes, and then students will be able to register for those classes.

Setting up an application using Express Generator

First, we'll set up our application using Express Generator. So let's go to the `Projects` folder and open up a command line in `Projects`. I'm using my Git Bash tool and we're going to run our Express Generator. If you don't have this, then you want to install it using the `npm install -g express` command. That will install Express, and then run the following command, if you want the generator:

```
$ npm install -g express-generator
```

I already have it installed so I'm not going to do that. Once you've done that, you will enter `express` and then the name of your application; I'm going to call it `elearn`:

```
$ express elearn
```

Now we're going to go `cd elearn`:

```
$ cd elearn
```

I'll also open it up inside of my Sublime Text. We want go to `Projects | elearn`. In the `elearn` folder, let's open up `package.json` and you can see it's included a bunch of dependencies here:

```
{
  "name": "elearn",
  "version": "0.0.0",
  "private": true,
  "scripts": {
  "start": "node ./bin/www"
  }
  "dependencies": {
```

```
        "body-parser" : "~1.13.2"
        "cookie-parser": "~1.3.5",
        "debug": "~2.2.0",
        "express": "~4.13.1",
        "jade": "~1.11.0",
        "morgan": "~1.6.1",
        "serve-favicon": "~2.3.0"
      }
    }
```

But we're going to add some to this. We're not going to be using Pug, but Express Handlebars. So I'll replace that and we'll just say the latest version:

```
      "dependencies": {
        "body-parser" : "~1.13.2"
        "cookie-parser": "~1.3.5",
        "debug": "~2.2.0",
        "express": "~4.13.1",
        "express-handlebars": "*",
        "morgan": "~1.6.1",
        "serve-favicon": "~2.3.0"
      }
```

Then we have a bunch of other stuff to put in here and I'm just going to paste that in:

```
      "dependencies": {
        "body-parser" : "~1.13.2"
        "cookie-parser": "~1.3.5",
        "debug": "~2.2.0",
        "express": "~4.13.1",
        "express-handlebars": "*",
        "morgan": "~1.6.1",
        "serve-favicon": "~2.3.0"
        "bcryptjs": "*",
        "passport": "*",
        "passport-http": "*",
        "passport-local": "*",
        "mongodb": "*",
        "mongoose": "*",
        "express-session": "*"
        "connect-flash": "*"
        "express-messages": "*"
        "express-validator": "*"
      }
    }
```

We have bcryptjs, which is just a simpler version of bcrypt, taking two hashed passwords. We're using Passport for our login authentication. We're using MongoDB along with Mongoose. `express-session`, `connect -flash`, and `express-messages` are all for flash messaging, and then we have our `express-validator` to validate forms. So let's save that and then we're going to go back and we're going to type `npm install`:

```
$ npm install
```

Configuring the app.js file

Now what we'll do is open `app.js` and there's a bunch of stuff that we have to include up there. So, I'll paste some code in here, like this:

```
var express = require('express');
var path = require('path');
var favicon = require('serve-favicon');
var logger = require('morgan');
var cookieParser = require('cookie-parser');
var bodyParser = require('body-parser');
var exphbs = require('express-handlebars');
var expressValidator = require('express-validator');
var flash = require('connect-flash');
var session = require('express-session');
var passport = require('passport');
var LocalStrategy = require('passport-local'),Strategy;
var mongo = require('mongodb');
var mongoose = require('mongoose');
```

First thing, we're including Express Handlebars. Then we have the Validator flash, session, passport. Then we have the passport `LocalStrategy` and then our Mongo stuff. Next, we have some default routes:

```
var routes = require('./routes/index');
var users = require('./routes/users');
```

We're going to keep both of these. The index route is just for the main dashboard area. The users will be the registration and so forth. So we'll leave that as is. Now the view engine setup is going to be a little different:

```
// view engine setup
app.set('views', path.join(__dirname, 'views'));
app.set('view engine', 'jade')
```

We're going to keep the first line of the two, because it's just telling us to use the folder called `views`. But for the second one, we're going to change `pug` to `handlebars` and then there's one additional line that we need to include here, which is `app.engine`, and we're going to pass in handlebars. Then we want to take that variable that we created above `exphbs` and just pass in an object. We want to define the default layout. This will be the name of the file that you want to use for your layout. We're just going to call it `layout`. The view engine setup is going to look like this:

```
// view engine setup
app.set('views', path.join(__dirname, 'view'));
app.engine('handlebars', exphbs({defaultLayout:'layout'}));
app.set('view engine', 'handlebars');
```

That's all we have to do to set up Express Handlebars.

Now there's some other middleware that we need to add. So we're going to the `app.use` statements, and the first thing we're going to add is for the Express session:

```
app.use(express.static(path.join(__dirname, 'public')));

// Express Session
app.use(session({
    secret: 'secret',
    saveUninitialized: true,
    resave: true
}));
```

It's just providing a secret. You can change this if you'd like.

The next thing is going to be for our Passport. We're going to want to call initialize as well as session:

```
// Passport
app.use(passport.initialize());
app.use(passport.session());
```

The next thing is for Express Validator, and this is right from the GitHub page. I haven't changed anything:

```
//Express Validator
app.use(expressValidator({
  errorFormatter: function(param, msg, value) {
      var namespace = param.split('.')
      , root = namespace.shift()
      , formParam = root;
```

```
    while(namespace.length) {
      formParam += '[' + namespace.shift() + ']';
    }
    return {
      param : formParam,
      msg : msg,
      value : value
    };
  }
}));
```

Finally, we have our `connect-flash` and `express-messages`:

```
// Connect-Flash
app.use(flash());

// Global Vars
app.use(function(req, res, next) {
  res.locals.messages = require('express-messages')(req, res);
  next();
});
```

We want to add `app.use(flash())` and then in Global vars, we're going to set a global variable called messages if there's anything we want to put out there. That should do it. Let's save that.

Configuring the views directory

We'll now go to our views file and we have three files there: `error.pug`, `index.pug`, and `layout.pug`. We'll configure them using handlebars.

First, we're going to rename the `error.pug` file to `error.handlebars`. For the content, we can get that out and we're just going to paste in an `h1` in the paragraph like this:

```
<h1>Error</h1>
<p>You are in the wrong place</p>
```

Then for `index.pug`, we're going to rename that as well to `index.handlebars`. For that, we're just going to put in an `h1` and we'll just say `Welcome`:

```
<h1>Welcome</h1>
```

Then we delete the `layout.pug` file and create a folder called `layouts` because that's where Express Handlebars is going to look. Next, we're going to create a file called `layout.handlebars` in that folder:

Folder structure

In `layout.handlebars`, let's put our base HTML and we'll add the title as `Elearn`. Then, in the `body`, we just want to add triple curly braces `{{{}}}` and then add `body`:

```
<!DOCTYPE html>
<html>
<head>
    <title>Elearn</title>
</head>
<body>
    {{{body}}}
</body>
</html>
```

That will output whatever view we're at, at the current time. Let's save that.

Running the setup in the browser

Now, let's test out our setup and run the `npm start` command:

```
$ npm start
```

Then, we'll go to `localhost:3000`, and we get **Welcome** as shown here:

Next, let's start implementing our layout.

Implementing our layout

We're going to use HTML KickStart for implementing the layout:

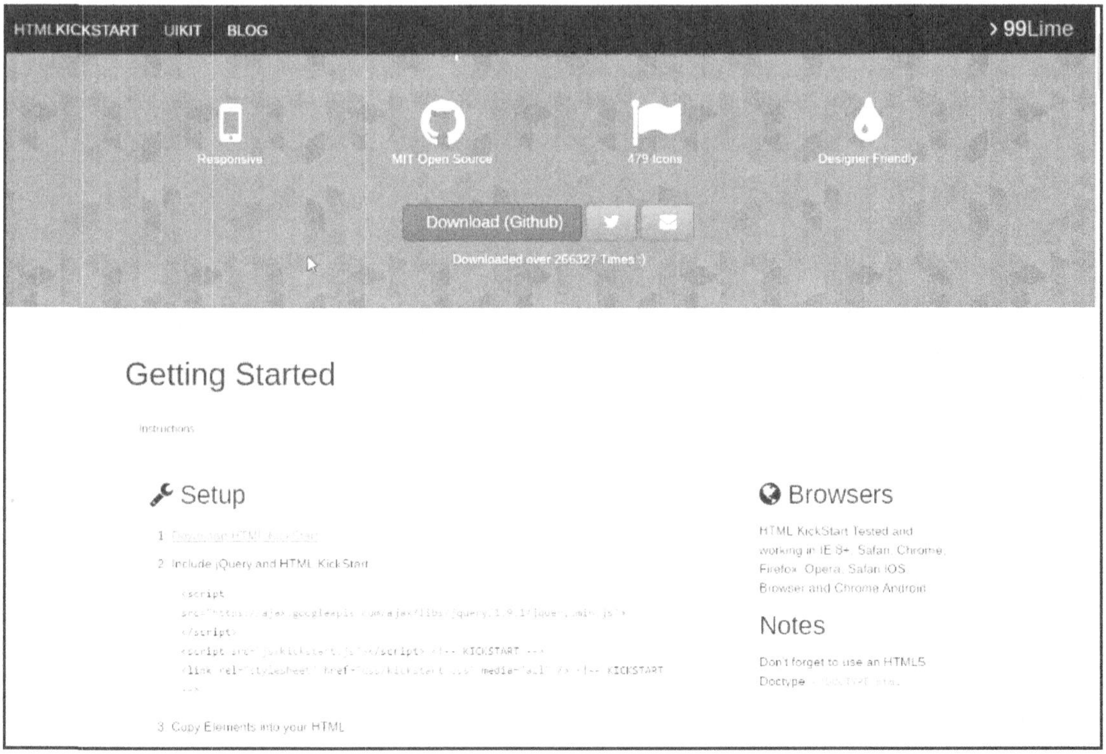

I'm going to click on the **Download** button shown in the preceding screenshot and that should start to download. We'll open that up and what we're going to do first is bring over the CSS stuff:

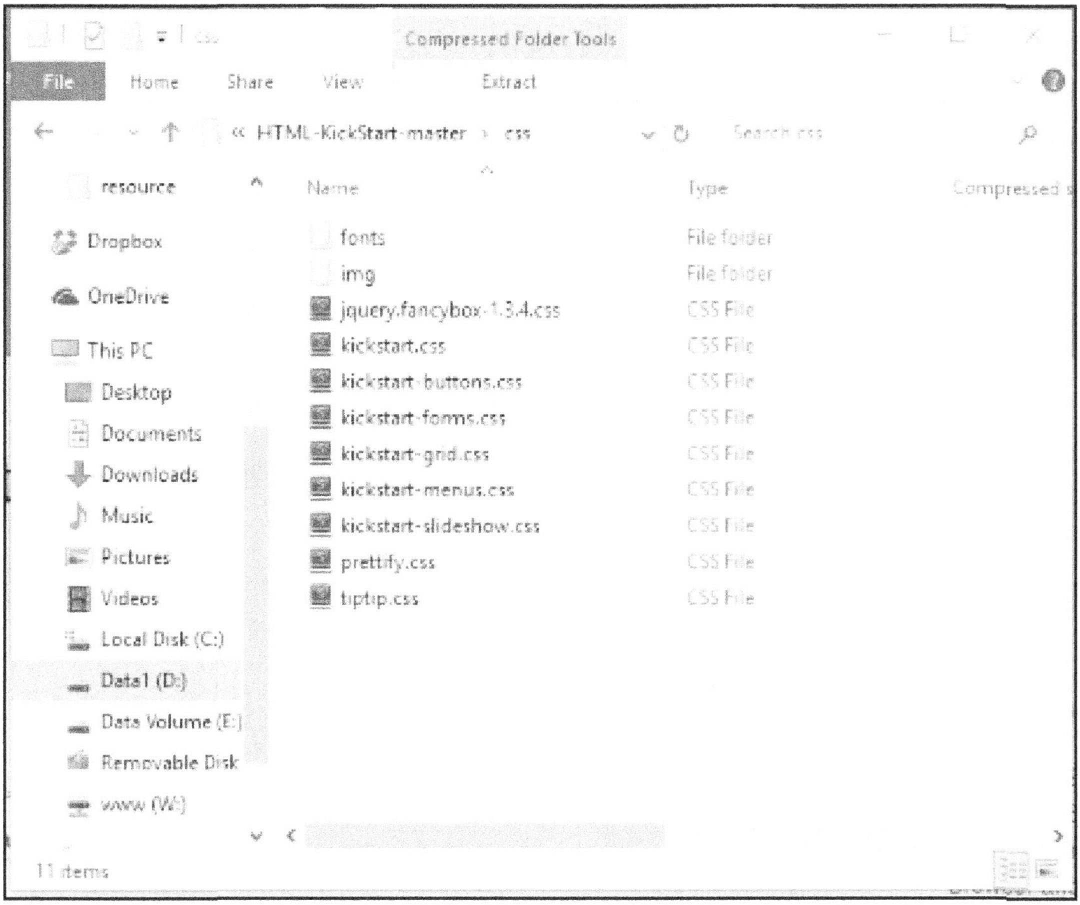

The css folder

I'm just going to copy everything that's shown in the preceding folder and paste it into the `Projects | public | stylesheets` folder. Then inside `js`, we're going to bring `kickstart.js` over to our `JavaScripts` folder. I think that's good.

Now let's open this `example.html` provided in the `HTML-kickstart-master` and this is what it looks like:

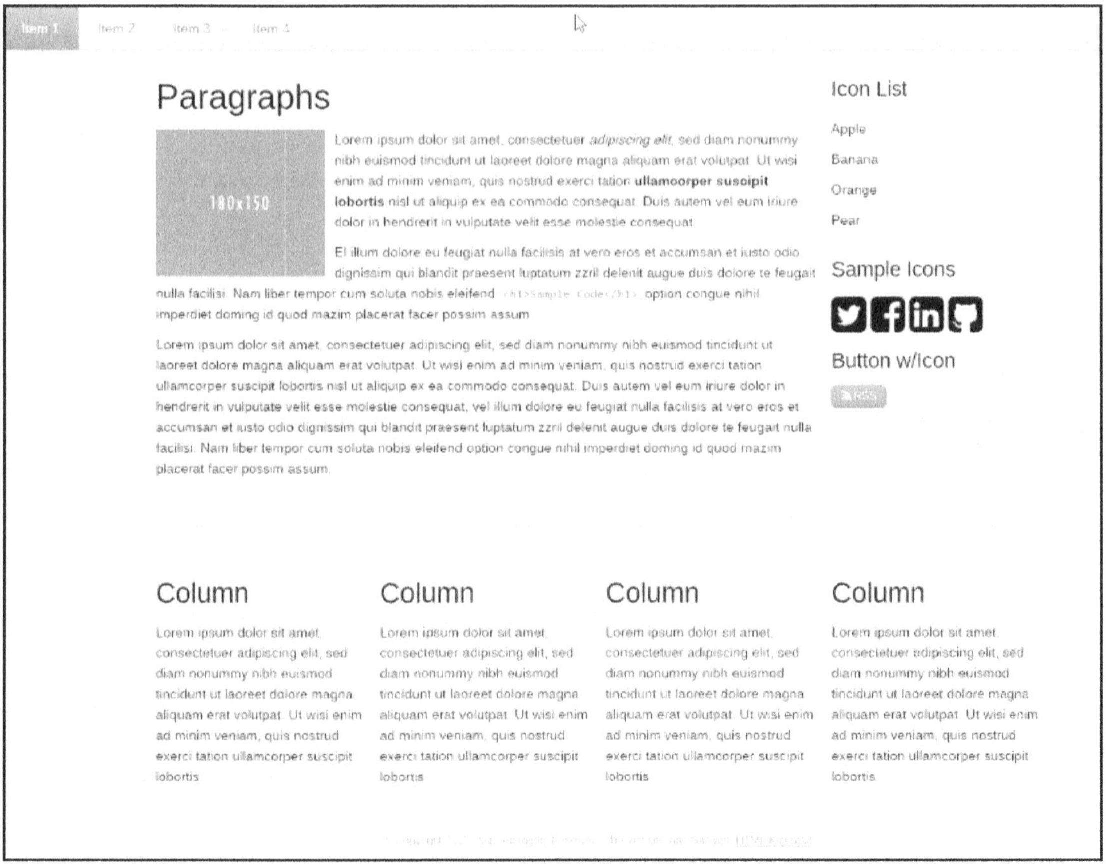

What we'll do is we'll open that `example.html` with Sublime Text. We'll grab the code that's in here, copy it, and bring it over to our `layout.handlers`. I'm just going to overwrite this for now, but we'll fix it:

```
<!DOCTYPE html>
<html><head>
<title>HTML KickStart Elements</title>
<meta charset="UTF-8">
<meta name="viewport" content="width=device-width, initial-scale=1.0"/>
<meta name="description" content="" />
<meta name="copyright" content="" />
<link rel="stylesheet" type="text/css" href="css/kickstart.css" media="all"
```

```
/> <!-- KICKSTART -->
<link rel="stylesheet" type="text/css" href="style.css" media="all" /> <!--
CUSTOM STYLES -->
<script type="text/javascript"
src="https://ajax.googleapis.com/ajax/libs/jquery/1.9.1/jquery.min.js"></sc
ript>
<script type="text/javascript" src="js/kickstart.js"></script> <!--
KICKSTART -->
</head><body>

<!-- Menu Horizontal -->
<ul class="menu">
<li class="current"><a href="">Item 1</a></li>
<li><a href="">Item 2</a></li>
<li><a href=""><span class="icon" data-icon="R"></span>Item 3</a>
 <ul>
 <li><a href=""><i class="fa fa-car"></i> Sub Item</a></li>
 <li><a href=""><i class="fa fa-arrow-circle-right"></i> Sub Item</a>
 <ul>
 <li><a href=""><i class="fa fa-comments"></i> Sub Item</a></li>
 <li><a href=""><i class="fa fa-check"></i> Sub Item</a></li>
 <li><a href=""><i class="fa fa-cutlery"></i> Sub Item</a></li>
```

Configuring the title and header in the layout

Starting at the top, let's take the title out and add `Elearn`. Then, we don't need the meta stuff present in the code, so we'll remove this. Then, we'll move on to the link to the stylesheets. We know that we don't have a `css` folder; it's actually called `stylesheets`. You want to have / at the beginning of the `stylesheets` as well. We want it for the scripts as well. We want it for this one. That stylesheet was actually in the root of the framework, so we might have to bring that over. Then, we'll change the script type, `javascript`, to `/javascripts` like this:

```
<!DOCTYPE html>
<html><head>
<title>Elearn</title>
<link rel="stylesheet" type="text/css" href="/stylesheets/kickstart.css"
media="all" />
<link rel="stylesheet" type="text/css" href="/stylesheets/style.css"
media="all"
  />
```

```
<script type="text/javascript"
src="https://ajax.googleapis.com/ajax/libs/jquery/1.9.1/jquery.min.js"></sc
ript>
<script type="text/javascript" src="/javascripts/kickstart.js"></script>
```

That's the head area!

Configuring the body in the layout

This menu here is going to get much, much simpler. I will get rid of all the `<li>` below the first row `<li>`s:

```
<body>

<!-- Menu Horizontal -->
<ul class="menu">
<li class="current"><a href="">Item 1</a></li>
<li><a href="">Item 2</a></li>
</ul>
```

Then we're going to edit the `Item 1` to `Home`. In the `href`, we'll add `/`, item 2 will be `Classes`, and the `href` will go to `/classes`:

```
<body>

<!-- Menu Horizontal -->
<ul class="menu">
<li class="current"><a href="/">Home</a></li>
<li><a href="/classes">Classes</a></li>
</ul>
```

Next to it we have our grid, we'll keep it as it is.

Configuring the paragraph

In the paragraph, I'm going to get rid of the image. In this `h3`, we'll just add `Welcome To Elearn`. Then, we'll leave the content just so it's not completely empty, but I'm only going to keep the top paragraph:

```
<div class="col_12">
     <div class="col_9">
     <h3>Welcome To Elearn</h3>
     <p>
     Lorem ipsum dolor sit amet, consectetuer, <em>adipiscing elit</em>,
sed diam
```

```
        nonummy nibh euismod
        tincidunt ut laoreet dolore magna aliquam erat volutpat. Ut wisi enim
ad
        minim veniam, quis
        nostrud exerci tation <strong>ullamcorper suscipit lobortis</strong>
nisl ut
        aliquip ex ea commodo consequat.
        Duis autem vel eum iriure dolor in hendrerit in vulputate velit esse
        molestie consequat
        </p>
```

Configuring the sidebar

Then for the sidebar, let's change the heading. We're going to add `Student & Instructor Login`. We're going to get rid of the `ul` and let's put a form. In the form, we're going to have a label. So this label will be `Username` and then we'll have an input with a type of text. Then we'll have another label `Password`. Let's give these inputs a name as well. Let's put a `Submit` button and give this a `class="button"`:

```
<div class="col_3">
<h5>Student & Instructor Login</h5>
<form>
<label>Username: </label>
<input type="text" name="username">
<label>Password: <label>
<input type="password" name="password">
<input class="button" type="submit" value="submit">
</form>
```

We can then get rid of the stuff in the `h5`.

Configuring hr

Now, under `hr`, I don't want four columns. I want three of them, and they're going to be classes. Let's get rid of this last one and then change the classes to a 4-column one. Then, we'll have our classes. Let's say `HTML 101`, `Intro To PHP`, and then let's say `Learn Node.js`:

```
</hr>

<div class="col_4">
<h4>HTML 101</h4>
<p>Lorem ipsum dolor sit amet, consectetuer, adipiscing elit, sed diam
nonummy
   nibh euismod tincidunt ut laoreet dolore
```

```
   magna aliquam erat volutpat. Ut wisi enim ad minim veniam, quis nostrud
exerci
   tation ullamcorper suscipit lobortis</p>
</div>

<div class="col_4">
<h4>Intro To PHP</h4>
<p>Lorem ipsum dolor sit amet, consectetuer, adipiscing elit, sed diam
nonummy
   nibh euismod tincidunt ut laoreet dolore
   magna aliquam erat volutpat. Ut wisi enim ad minim veniam, quis nostrud
exerci
   tation ullamcorper suscipit lobortis</p>
</div>

<div class="col_4">
<h4>Learn Node.js</h4>
<p>Lorem ipsum dolor sit amet, consectetuer, adipiscing elit, sed diam
nonummy
   nibh euismod tincidunt ut laoreet dolore
   magna aliquam erat volutpat. Ut wisi enim ad minim veniam, quis nostrud
exerci
   tation ullamcorper suscipit lobortis</p>
</div>
```

Configuring the footer in the layout

In the footer, we will change the `HTML Kickstart` to `Elearn` and we'll add `Copyright 2016` like this:

```
 <!-- ================================= START FOOTER
================================= -->
 <div class="clear"></div>
 <div id="footer">
 &copy; Copyright 2018 All Rights Reserved. Elearn</a>
 </div>
```

Let's save that and go to our app.

The final application

If we go to the app, this is how it is going to look:

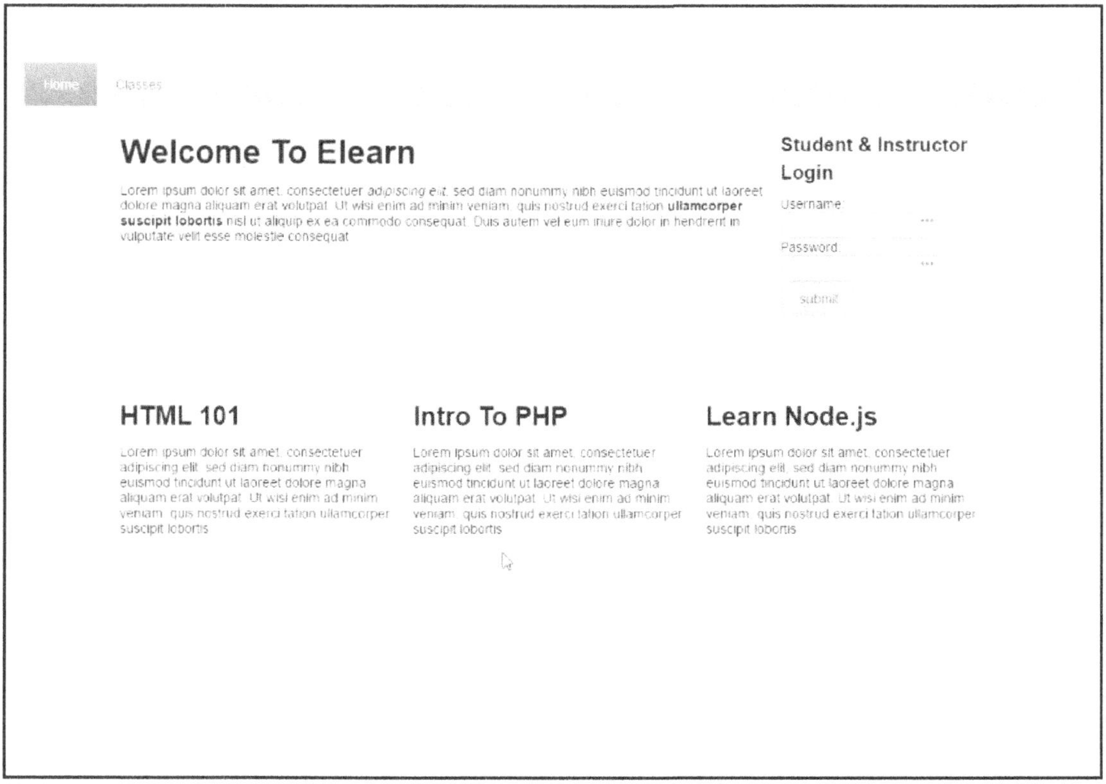

Now you'll notice that this looks a little weird considering the padding and background colors, and all that grey. The reason for that is because if we look at the HTML template that we have, there's a `style.css` file that's outside of the `css` folder for some reason. So what we're going to do is just copy that and then bring that over to our `Projects` | `public` | `stylesheets` folder and then we'll paste it there. There might be already a `style.css` file in this folder. In that case, we'll replace that file. Now, if we go back to our app, it looks a lot better:

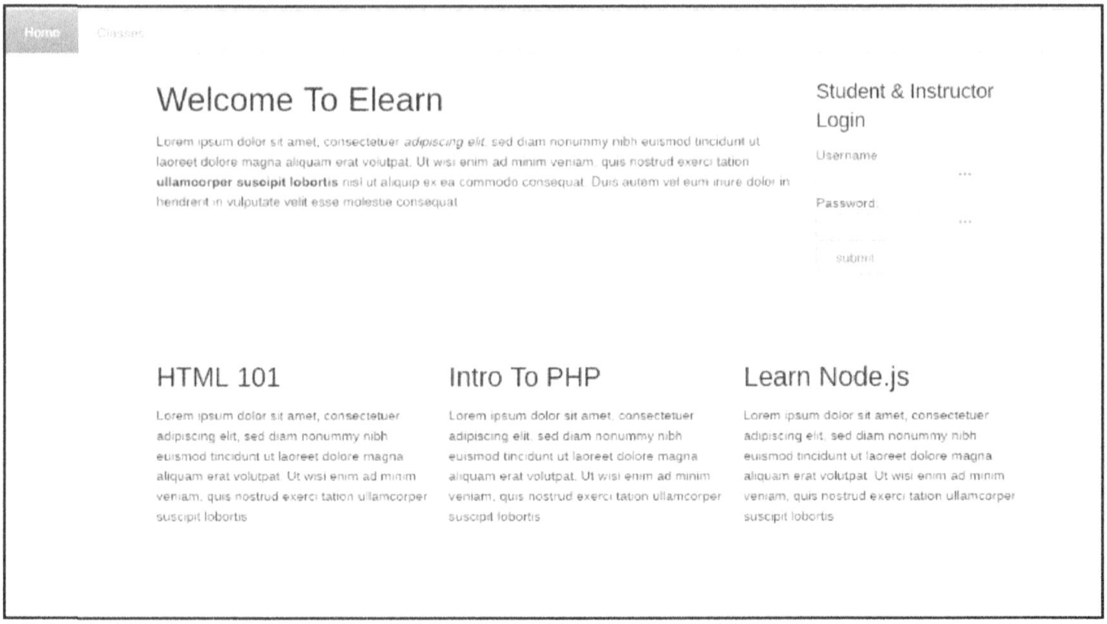

Now, I do want to add some buttons to the classes in `<hr>`. So if we go in each of these columns in the HTML file, we're going to put a link with a class of `button`, and for now, we'll just set this to go nowhere and then that'll just say `View Class`:

```
<div class="col_4">
<h4>HTML 101</h4>
<p>Lorem ipsum dolor sit amet, consectetuer, adipiscing elit, sed diam
nonummy
  nibh euismod tincidunt ut laoreet dolore
  magna aliquam erat volutpat. Ut wisi enim ad minim veniam, quis nostrud
exerci
  tation ullamcorper suscipit lobortis</p>
<a class="button" href="#">View Class</a>
</div>
```

```
<div class="col_4">
<h4>Intro To PHP</h4>
<p>Lorem ipsum dolor sit amet, consectetuer, adipiscing elit, sed diam
nonummy
  nibh euismod tincidunt ut laoreet dolore
  magna aliquam erat volutpat. Ut wisi enim ad minim veniam, quis nostrud
exerci
  tation ullamcorper suscipit lobortis</p>
<a class="button" href="#">View Class</a>
</div>

<div class="col_4">
<h4>Learn Node.js</h4>
<p>Lorem ipsum dolor sit amet, consectetuer, adipiscing elit, sed diam
nonummy
  nibh euismod tincidunt ut laoreet dolore
  magna aliquam erat volutpat. Ut wisi enim ad minim veniam, quis nostrud
exerci
  tation ullamcorper suscipit lobortis</p>
<a class="button" href="#">View Class</a>
</div>
```

Now, we can also put the paragraph part into into the `index` template. Let's grab everything that's in the `col_9` div, cut that, and then we're going to put our `{{{}}}` tag thing in there:

```
<div class="col_12">
    <div class="col_9">
    {{{body}}}
    </div>
```

Then let's go to `index` and we'll paste this in:

```
<h3>Welcome To Elearn</h3>
   <p>
   Lorem ipsum dolor sit amet, consectetuer, <em>adipiscing elit</em>, sed
diam
   nonummy nibh euismod
   tincidunt ut laoreet dolore magna aliquam erat volutpat. Ut wisi enim ad
minim
   veniam, quis
   nostrud exerci tation <strong>ullamcorper suscipit lobortis</strong>
nisl ut
   aliquip ex ea commodo consequat.
   Duis autem vel eum iriure dolor in hendrerit in vulputate velit esse
molestie
   consequat</p>
```

If we reload the app, it should look like this:

In the next section, we're going to start to add some dynamic functionality `fetch` classes, things like that.

Fetching classes – part A

In the last section, we went ahead and set up our application and we integrated Kickstart on the frontend. So we have a basic layout. What I want to do now is start to focus on getting classes from the database, and we want to fix the homepage so that the Login part is coming from its own file as well as the classes. These are going to be what's called **partials**.

Setting up partials

We're going to create a folder called partials. For now, we're going to have two files in here. We'll create one and let's save it as `classes.handlebars`. We also want one called `login.handlebars`.

Let's start with the login. What we'll do is go to our layout and we're going to grab from the heading down to where the form ends, cut that out, paste it in the `login.handlebars`:

```
<h5>Student & Instructor Login</h5>
   <form>
   <label>Username: </label>
   <input type="text" name="username">
   <label>Password: </label>
   <input type="password" name="password">
   <input class="button" type="submit" value="submit">
   </form>
```

Then in place of that in `layout.handlebars`, we're going to use a `{{>login}}`:

```
<div class="col_3">
{{>login}}
<div>
```

That's how you can include a partial. So let's go ahead and save that. Then, we'll restart our app, and it should look like this:

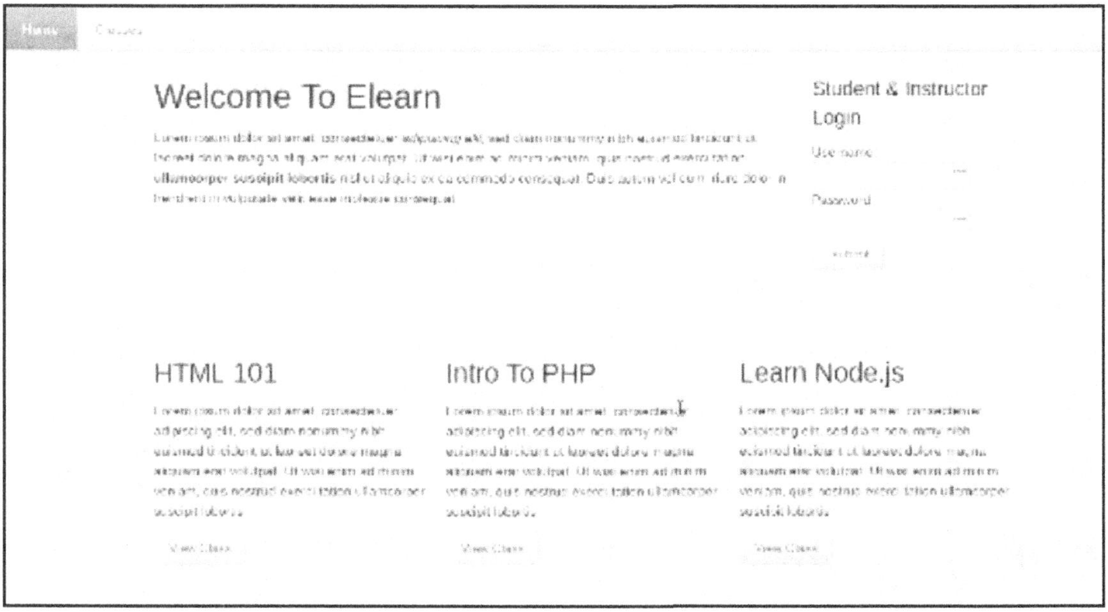

Our eLearn page

Now we want to do the same for classes. So we're going to go back to our layout and grab all of the `col_4` divs, cut that, and then in place of it we're going to say `classes` and we'll save that:

```
     <hr />
         {{>classes}}
</div>
```

Now let's go into `classes.handlebars`, paste the column classes, and I'm also going to put a heading here, so we'll put an `h4` and we'll say `Latest Classes`:

```
<h4>Latest Classes</h4>
<div class="col_4">
   <h4>HTML 101</h4>
   <p>Lorem ipsum dolor sit amet, consectetuer, adipiscing elit, sed diam
nonummy
      nibh euismod tincidunt ut laoreet dolore
      magna aliquam erat volutpat. Ut wisi enim ad minim veniam, quis
nostrud
      exerci tation ullamcorper suscipit lobortis</p>
   <a class="button" href="#">View Class</a>
   </div>

   <div class="col_4">
   <h4>Intro To PHP</h4>
   <p>Lorem ipsum dolor sit amet, consectetuer, adipiscing elit, sed diam
nonummy
      nibh euismod tincidunt ut laoreet dolore
      magna aliquam erat volutpat. Ut wisi enim ad minim veniam, quis
nostrud
      exerci tation ullamcorper suscipit lobortis</p>
   <a class="button" href="#">View Class</a>
   </div>

   <div class="col_4">
   <h4>Learn Node.js</h4>
   <p>Lorem ipsum dolor sit amet, consectetuer, adipiscing elit, sed diam
nonummy
      nibh euismod tincidunt ut laoreet dolore
      magna aliquam erat volutpat. Ut wisi enim ad minim veniam, quis
nostrud
      exerci tation ullamcorper suscipit lobortis</p>
   <a class="button" href="#">View Class</a>
   </div>
```

Let's save that and now we have our classes in a partial.

Now I just want to change the **Welcome To eLearn** area a little bit and put some content in there and also a button to signup. Let's go to `index.handlebars` and paste some relevant content. So we just have a simple paragraph with some real text and then we have a **Sign Up Free** button, and then just a paragraph letting them know they need to sign up to register for classes:

```
<h3>Welcome To eLearn</h3>
   <p>
   eLearn is a simple and free online learning platform. Instructors can
create
   courses and students can register for courses which include assignments,
   quizzes and support forums.
   </p>

   <a class="button" href="/users/signup">Sign Up Free</a>
   <p>You need to signup to register for free classes</p>
```

Let's reload the app:

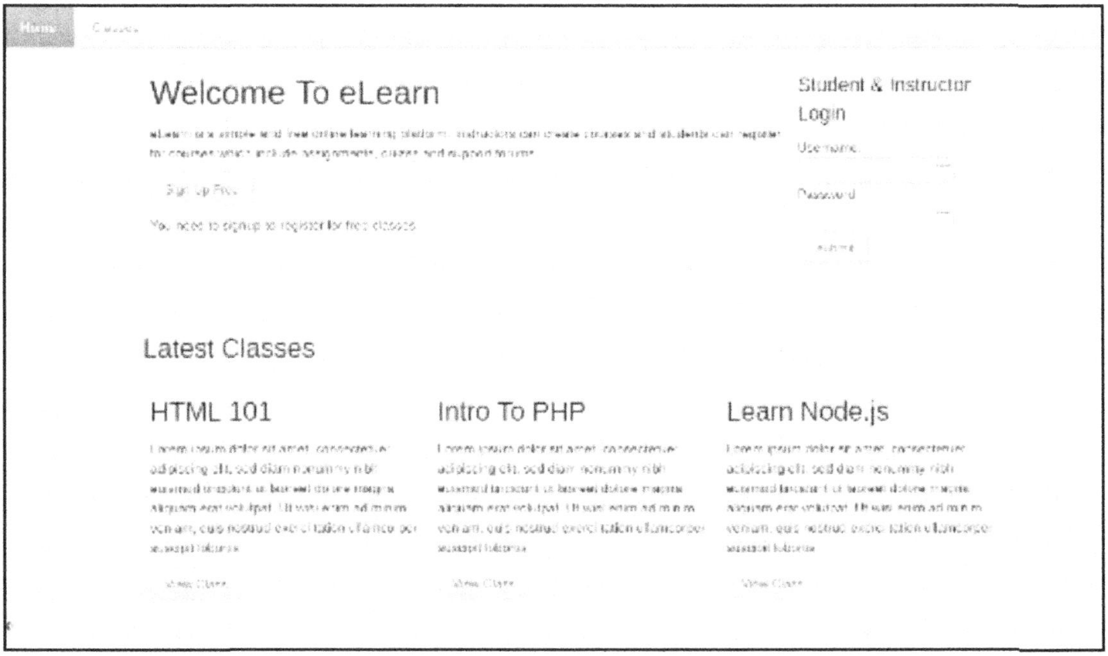

That looks a little better. Now what we want to do is we need to add some classes. So we'll open a Mongo shell.

Adding some classes

I'm going to run the Command Prompt as an administrator and we'll go to your MongoDB `bin` directory. In my case, it's in my `C:` drive, so I'll run the `mongodbbin` command. Then, I'm going to run `mongo`:

```
C:\Windows\system32>cd/
C:\>cd mongodb/bin
C:\mongodb\bin>mongo
...
```

Now, we're going to create a database by saying `use elearn`, and we're going to create a couple of collections. We'll say `db.createCollection`. We want one called users and then we want one for our students, instructors, and classes:

```
> use learn
switched to db elearn
> db.createCollection('users');
{ "ok" : 1}
> db.createCollection('students');
{ "ok" : 1}
> db.createCollection('instructors');
{ "ok" : 1}
> db.createCollection('classes');
{ "ok" : 1}
>
```

Now we want to add a couple of classes. To do that, we'll add the `db.classes.insert`. We now need a title. Let's say `'Intro to HTML5', description:'');`. I'm just going to grab the text we have in the HTML 101 column in the app and paste that in and then an instructor:

```
> db.classes.insert({title:'Intro to HTML 5', description: 'Lorem ipsum
dolor sit amet, consectetuer, adipiscing elit, sed diam nonummy nibh
euismod tincidunt ut laoreet dolore magna aliquam erat volutpat. Ut wisi
enim ad minim veniam, quis nostrud exerci tation ullamcorper suscipit
lobortis', instructor: 'Brad Traversy'});
WriteResult({ "nInserted" : 1 })
```

Now we have one class, let's go ahead and add another one. I'm going to change the name to John Doe and then we'll also change the title. [Silence] Alright, so this one let's say Advanced PHP:

```
sses.insert({title:'Advanced PHP', description: 'Lorem ipsum dolor sit
amet, consectetuer, adipiscing elit, sed diam nonummy nibh euismod
tincidunt ut laoreet dolore magna aliquam erat volutpat. Ut wisi enim ad
minim veniam, quis nostrud exerci tation ullamcorper suscipit lobortis',
instructor: 'John Doe'});
WriteResult({ "nInserted" : 1 })
```

Then we'll do one more. So this one let's call `Intro to Photoshop`:

```
insert({title:'Intro to Photoshop', description: 'Lorem ipsum dolor sit
amet, consectetuer, adipiscing elit, sed diam nonummy nibh euismod
tincidunt ut laoreet dolore magna aliquam erat volutpat. Ut wisi enim ad
minim veniam, quis nostrud exerci tation ullamcorper suscipit lobortis',
instructor: 'John Doe'});
WriteResult({ "nInserted" : 1 })
```

Now we should have three classes. So we can close out of that and what we need to do now is we need to create a class model.

Creating a class model

So let's create a new folder called `models` and then inside there, we'll create a file called `class.js`. Let's include `mongoose`, and then we need a schema for our class, which I'm going to paste in:

```
var mongoose = require('mongoose');

// Class Schema
var ClassSchema = mongoose.Schema({
    title: {
        type: String
    },
    description: {
        type: String
    },
    instructor: {
        type: String
    },
    lessons:[{
        lesson_number: {type: Number},
        lesson_title: {type: String},
```

```
        lesson_body: {type: String}
    }]
});
```

We have a title description and instructor, and then we're also going to have lessons and this is going to be an array of objects and the object will have lesson number `title` and `body`.

Then what we need to do is make this available outside, so I'm going to paste this in:

```
var Class = module.exports = mongoose.model('Class', ClassSchema);
```

Now we're going to have a couple functions in our model.

Fetch all classes

We're going to have one that's going to fetch all classes. So this one will say `module.exports.getClasses`. We want to set that equal to a `function`, and that's going to take `callback` and then also `limit` and then in the function what we'll do is say `Class.find` and we'll pass in callback and say `.limit`, whatever the limit that's passed in:

```
// Fetch All Classes
module.exports.getClasses = function(callback, limit){
    Class.find(callback).limit(limit);
}
```

Fetch single classes

Then we need one to fetch single classes, so use `module.exports.getClassById`. That's obviously going to take an `id` and then a `callback`. Then in the function what we'll do is say `Class.findById` and pass in the `id` and the callback. So that's it for that:

```
// Fetch Single Class
module.exports.getClassById - function(id, callback){
   Class.findById(id, callback);
}
```

Let's save it and now we need to go to our route.

Working on the GET home page route

So we're going to go to routes and then `index.js` and we want to work on this GET home page route. What we want to do is use the `class` model and then get all the classes and then pass to our view. So before we can do that, we have to create our class object here. We're going to set this to require, and we want to say `../` to go up one and then `models/class`:

```
var Class = require('../models/class');
```

Then in the `router.get` function, we can say `class.getClasses` and we want our function. That will take the error and classes, and then what we want to do is grab the `res.render` statement and put that below the `Class.getClasses` statement:

```
/* GET home page. */
router.get('/', function(req, res, next) {
   Class.getClasses(function(err, classes){
       res.render('index', { title: 'Express' });
   });
});
```

Then we just want to pass along the classes. Now, remember we have a limit we can set, so we're going to 3, like this:

```
        res.render('index', { classes: classes });
    },3);
```

Alright so now the index view should have access to our classes.

We want to go to the partial `classes.handlebars` and we're going to get rid of two out of three of these divs. We just want to wrap this, say `{{#each classes}}`. Then, we want the title. We want the description and then for the link it's going to go `/classes/_id}}/details`:

```
{{#each classes}}
    <div class="col_4">
        <h4>{{title}}</h4>
        <p>{{description}}</p>
        <a class="button" href="/classes/{{_id}}/details">View Class</a>
   </div>
{{/each}}
```

Let's go to `apps.js` and right under the `mongoose` variable, we're going to say `mongoose.connect`. Then in here, we'll say `mongodb://localhost/elearn` and then right under it, we're going to just say `var db = mongoose.connection`:

```
var mongoose = require('mongoose');
mongoose.connect('mongodb://localhost/elearn');
var db = mongoose.connection;
```

So let's save that and let's restart. There we go:

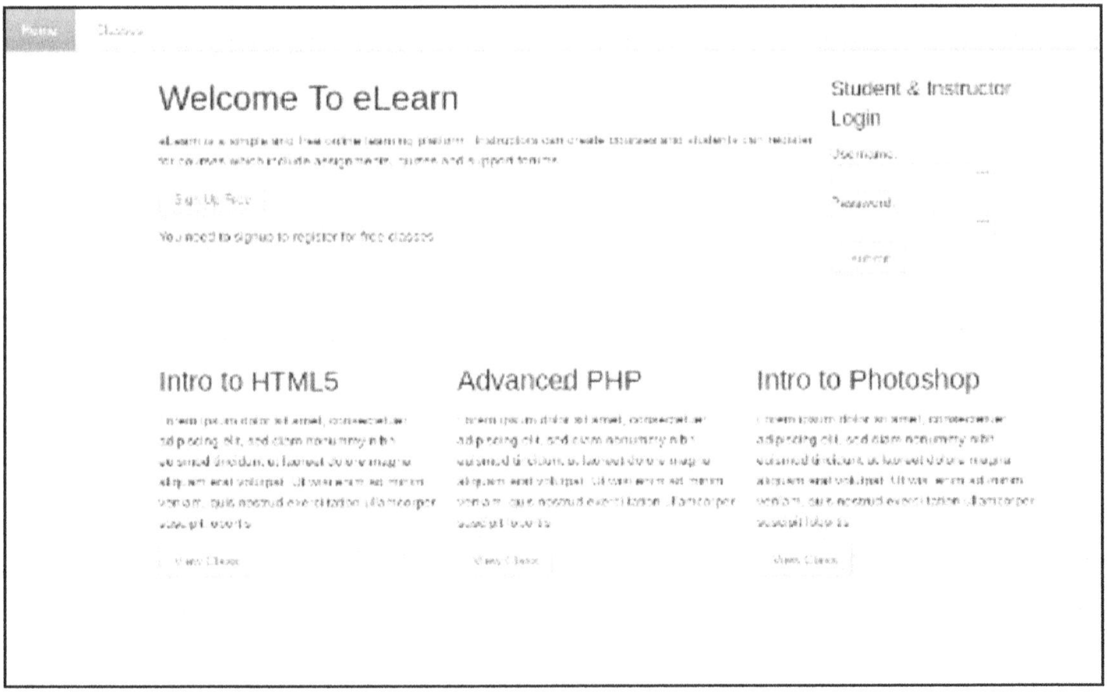

Our eLearn page now

So it's getting the classes. Now these classes are being fetched from the database. Now in the next part of this section, what I want to do is take care of the details page so we have a single class view. And then when we click on **Classes**, I want to list all the classes, just like we do on the index but without a limit. We'll do that in the next part.

Fetching classes – part B

In this section, we're going to set up the **Classes** page:

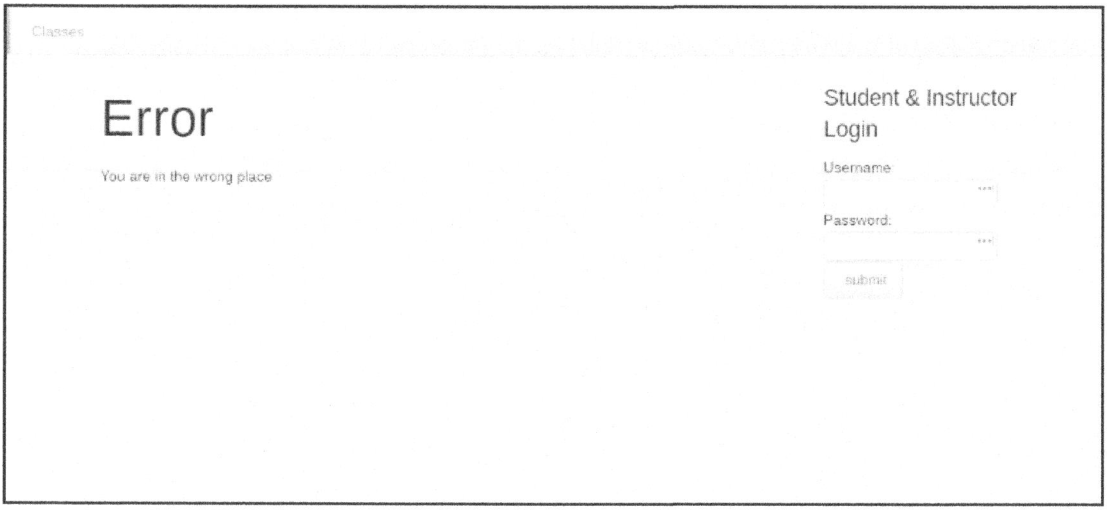

The error page

Here's so the details page. OK, so what we need to do is we need to create a new routes file

Setting up new route file – classes.js

We're going to call this new routes file `classes.js`. Then what we'll do is copy everything from `index.js` and paste that in:

```
var express = require('express');
var router = express.Router();

var Class = require('../models/class');

/* Get home page */
router.get('/', function(req, res, next) {
   Class.getClasses(function(err, classes){
       res.render('index', { classes: classes });
   },3);
});

module.exports = router;
```

This is pretty much going to stay the same except we want to change the render to `classes/index`:

```
var express = require('express');
var router = express.Router();

var Class = require('../models/class');

// Classes Page
router.get('/', function(req, res, next) {
   Class.getClasses(function(err, classes){
       res.render('classes/index', { classes: classes });
   },3);
});

module.exports = router;
```

Let's save this file. Next, we're going to include the routes file in `app.js`. So what we need to do is add a classes variable and require it like this:

```
var users = require('./routess/users');
var classes = require('./routes/classes');
```

Then down below to `app.use`, we also need to add it below the `/users` statement:

```
app.use('/', routes);
app.use('/users', users);
app.use('/classes', classes);
```

Creating the index.handlebars file for the classes page

Next, in our `views` folder we're going to create a new folder called `classes`. Then in here, we're going to create a new file called `index.handlebars`. We'll open that up and I'm going to paste this in:

```
<h2>Classes</h2>
{{#each classes}}
    <div class="block">
        <h3>{{title}}</h3>
        <p>
            {{description}}
        </p>
        <p>Instructor: <strong>{{instructor}}</strong></p>
        <a class="button" href="/classes/{{_id}}/details">Class Details</a>
    </div>
{{/each}}
```

Here, we're just looping through the classes. We're displaying a `div` with the class of `block`. We have a title description. We have the instructor and then a link to the details. Let's save that and then we'll go ahead and restart the server. Then click on **Classes**:

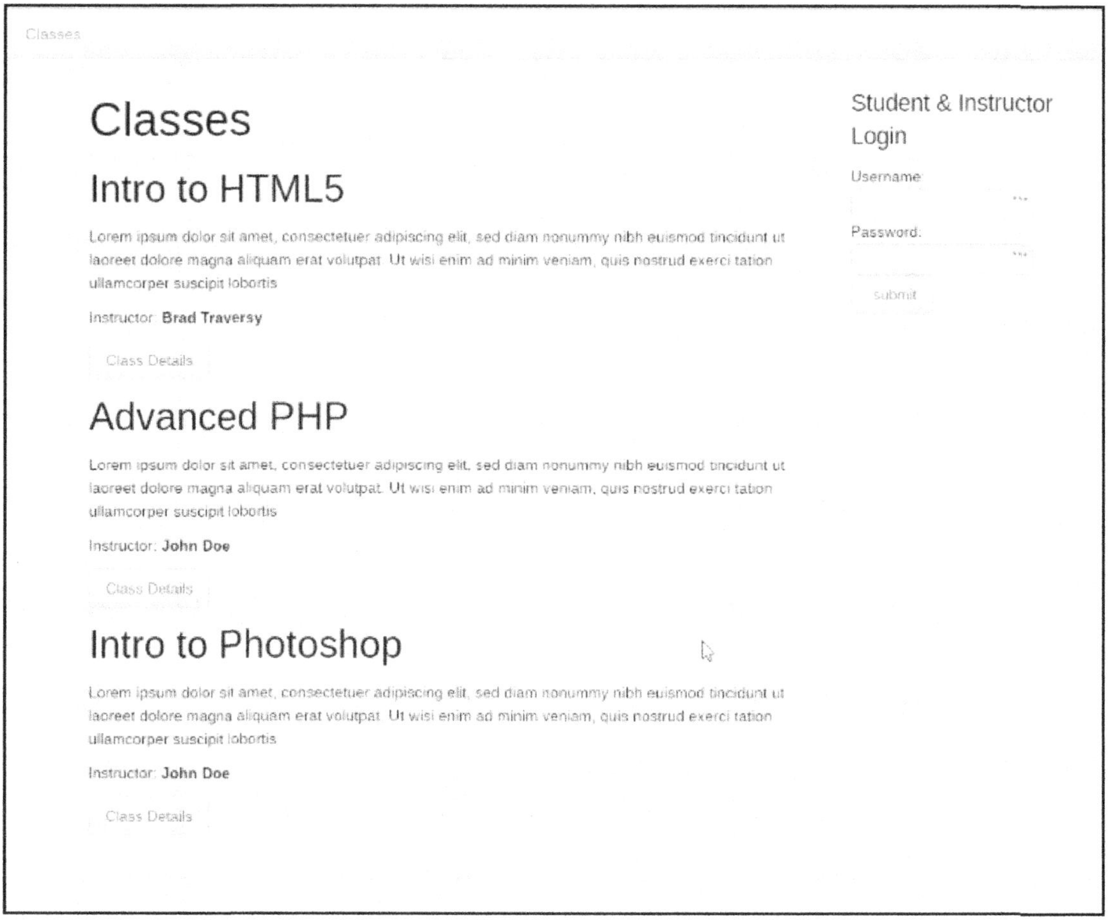

Page with classes

Now we have a page with classes.

Configuring classes.js for the class details page

For the details, what we'll do is go back to our `routes` and then `classes.js` and let's copy the **Class Page** code snippet and this will be **Class Details**:

```
// Class Details
router.get('/:id/details', function(req, res, next) {
    Class.getClassById([req.params.id],function(err, classes){
        res.render('classes/details', { class: classes });
    });
});
```

The route is going to go to `/:id/details`. Then in the `getClasses` object will be `getClassById` method. Then let's change this to `classname`. Then we also need to pass in a parameter just before the function object, which will be the `id`. We're going to use some brackets and then we're going to say `req.params.id`. Then in the render statement, we're just going to render classes/details. We'll then pass in `classname`. Now, we don't need the limit 3 so we can get rid of that. The resultant code should look like this:

```
// Class Details
router.get('/:id/details', function(req, res, next) {
    Class.getClassById([req.params.id],function(err, classes){
        res.render('classes/details', { class: classes });
    });
});
```

We can check for an error in both of the **Class Details** and **Class Page**. So let's just say `if(err) throw err` like this:

```
//Classes Page
router.get('/', function(req, res, next) {
    Class.getClasses(function(err, classes){
        if(err) throw err;
        res.render('classes/index', { classes: classes });
    },3);
});

// Class Details
router.get('/:id/details', function(req, res, next) {
    Class.getClassById([req.params.id],function(err, classname){
```

```
            if(err) throw err;
            res.render('classes/details', { class: classname });
        });
    });
```

So we'll save that.

Creating details.handlebars for the class details page

Now what we need to do is go to our views classes and then create a new file, save it as `details.handlebars`. We'll put in an `h2` and this is going to be the `class.title`:

```
<h2>{{class.title}}</h2>
```

That's our `h2`. Now let's put in a paragraph and then this is going to be the instructor. Let's put a `<strong>` tag and say `Instructor` and then we can say `class.instructor`. Under that, let's put in the description:

```
<h2>{{class.title}}</h2>
<p>
    <strong>Instructor: </strong> {{class.instructor}}
</p>
<p>
    {{class.description}}
</p>
```

Under the description, we're going to take the lessons and spit them out in a list, so we'll say `ul`. I'm going to give this a class of `"alt"` and then what we want to do is say `#each class.lessons`, which we don't have any now. The instructors will be able to add the lessons later. So let's end the `each` and in the `each` object, we want just list items. We should be able to `get lesson_title`:

```
<ul class="alt">
    {{#each class.lessons}}
        <li>{{lesson_title}}</li>
    {{/each}}
</ul>
```

Under the lesson, we're going to want a form to register for the class. But in order to do that, we need the user to be logged in. Now, we don't have the login functionality yet but we will later. So, we'll add `if user`, then let's create a form, like this:

```
{{#if user}}
    <form id="classRegForm" method="post" action="/students/classes/register">
        <input type="hidden" name="student_id" value="{{user._id}}">
        <input type="hidden" name="class_id" value="{{class._id}}">
        <input type="hidden" name="class_title" value="{{class.title}}">
        <input type="submit" class="button" value="Register For This Class">
    </form>
{{/if}}
```

`form id="classRegForm"` will go to `students/classes/register`. We have some hidden inputs. This is going to be the student `id`, which we will be able to get with this once they're logged in. We have access to the class ID, the class title, and then a Submit button.

I'll now add an else statement. So just move this down and we'll say `{{else}}` and then we'll put a paragraph, `"You must be logged in to register for this class"`:

```
{{#if user}}
    <form id="classRegForm" method="post" action="/students/classes/register">
        <input type="hidden" name="student_id" value="{{user._id}}">
        <input type="hidden" name="class_id" value="{{class._id}}">
        <input type="hidden" name="class_title" value="{{class.title}}">
        <input type="submit" class="button" value="Register For This Class">
    </form>
{{else}}
    <p>You must be logged in to register for this class</p>
{{/if}}
```

Let's save that and restart the server. If I click on **View Class**, it takes us to the details page:

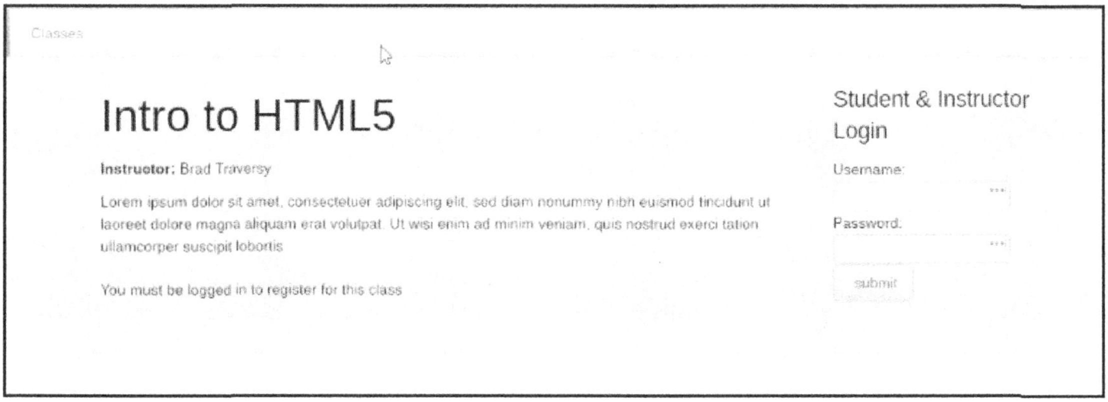

The Intro to HTML5 page

We have the title, the instructor, and it's telling us we have to be logged in to register. That's exactly what we want. So in the next section, what we'll do is we'll start to work on the user registration and login.

Registering users

In the last section, we made it so that we could fetch classes from the database and display them. So now what we want to do is work on the login and registration. So before we can do anything with login and registration we need to create a user model.

Creating a user model

Under `models`, let's create a new file and save it as `user.js`. Now this is where we're going to keep the basic user information such as the username and password but we will also be creating a student model and then an instructor model that will hold things like their address and extended information. Let's just do this one really quick. I'm going to paste in some requirements. We need Mongoose. We need bcrypt for password encryption and then I'm going to paste in the User Schema:

```
var mongoose = require('mongoose');
var bcrypt = require('bcryptjs');

// User Schema
```

```
var UserSchema = mongoose.Schema({
    username: {
        type: String
    },
    email: {
        type: String
    },
    password:{
        type:String,
    bcrypt: true
    },
    type:{
        type:String
    }

});
```

This is very simple, we have username, email password, and then we also have a type, so the type is going to be whether they're an instructor or a student. The next line is we're going to assign the model to a variable and also make it available outside of this file:

```
var User = module.exports = mongoose.model('User', UserSchema);
```

So the next thing we want some functions for the user model.

Get User by Id

We want to get a single user. So, we're going to paste that in `getUserById`. It's going to take in an id and a callback and then we're just going to call `User.findById`:

```
// Get User By Id
module.exports.getUserById = function(id, callback){
   User.findById(id, callback);
}
```

Get User by Username

The next function we want to add is `Get User by Username`. This is going to be the same thing, except we need to just have a query saying we want a certain username and then we're just using `findOne`:

```
// Get User by Username
module.exports.getUserByUsername = function(username, callback){
   var query = {username: username};
```

```
    User.findOne(query, callback);
}
```

We'll have two different ones. One is going to be to create the instructor and one is going to be to create the student account.

Create Student User

So the first one will say `Create Student User`. I'm going to paste the code for this:

```
// Create Student User
module.exports.saveStudent = function(newUser, newStudent, callback){
    bcrypt.hash(newUser.password, 10, function(err, hash){
        if(err) throw err;
        // Set hash
        newUser.password = hash;
        console.log('Student is being saved');
        async.parallel([newUser.save, newStudent.save], callback);
    });
}
```

We're going to take the `bcrypt.hash` function and pass in the new user's password, which comes as the first argument in the function. You'll notice that we're also passing in `newStudent`. Then down here, we're setting the hash and then we're going to call this `async.parallel` because we want to save two different things. We want to save in the users table with `newUser.save` or the users collection and then also in the student collection with `newStudent.save`, and `async.parallel` allows us to do that.

Create Instructor User

So now we want to do the same thing for instructors. Let me just paste that in the code for instructor:

```
// Create Instructor User
module.exports.saveInstructor = function(newUser, newInstructor, callback){
    bcrypt.hash(newUser.password, 10, function(err, hash){
        if(err) throw errl
        // Set hash
        newUser.password = hash;
        console.log('Instructor is being saved');
        async.parallel([newUser.save, newInstructor.save], callback);
    });
}
```

This is literally the same exact thing except we're passing in a `newInstructor` here and we're saving it to the instructors collection.

Compare Password

Then the last function we need is the `Compare password`. I am going to put that just below the GET user by username function:

```
// Compare password
module.exports.comparePassword = function(candidatePassword, hash,
callback){
   bcrypt.compare(candidatePassword, hash, function(err, isMatch){
       if(err) throw err;
       callback(null, isMatch);
   });
}
```

That's just taking in a candidate password and it's going to hash it and it's going to check to see if it's a match. We'll save that and that should do it for the user model.

Configuring User Register

Now we want to go to `routes` and then `users.js` and we want to get rid of the `/*GET users listings*/` statement. This will be User Register. Then we want the `/ to` go to `/register`. We'll get rid of the res.send statement, and we just want this to render the template. So we're going to say res.render and we want to render `users/register`:

```
// User Register
router.get('/register', function(req, res, next) {
   res.render('users/register');
});

module.exports = router;
```

We'll save that.

Configuring the register.handlebars file

Now, down in views all we need to do is create a new folder called `users`. Inside there, we'll create a file called `register.handlebars`, and I'm going to paste the code in:

```
<h2>Create An Account</h2>
<form id="regForm" method="post" action="/users/register">
    <div>
        <label>Account Type</label>
        <select name="type">
            <option value="student">Student</option>
            <option value="instructor">Instructor</option>
        </select>
    </div>
    <br />
    <div>
```

Now, this code is kind of a lot. It's a lot of different fields. So it's a form. We have the `id` `regForm`. It's going to go to `users/register`:

```
<h2>Create An Account</h2>
<form id="regForm" method="post" action="/users/register">
```

Now, the first option is to create an account type. You want to give this the name of type and then we have a `Student` or `Instructor`:

```
    <div>
        <label>Account Type</label>
        <select name="type">
            <option value="student">Student</option>
            <option value="instructor">Instructor</option>
        </select>
    </div>
```

OK, then we have first name, last name, street address, city, state, zip, email, username, and password. So let's save that and now we should be able to at least see the form. So let's go ahead and restart our app:

```
$ npm start

elearn@0.0.0 start C:\Projects\elearn
> node ./bin/www
```

We'll go to `Sign Up Free`, which we have to change this. Right now, it's going to signup. I called it register, so let's go to let's see `index.handlebars` and just change the sign up to register there:

```
<h3>Welcome To eLearn</h3>
    <p>
    eLearn is a simple and free online learning platform. Instructors can
create
    courses and students can register for courses which include
assignments,
    quizzes and support forums.

    </p>
    <a class="button" href="/users/register">Sign Up Free</a>
    <P>You need to signup to register for free classes</p>
```

Now, restart the app and there's our form:

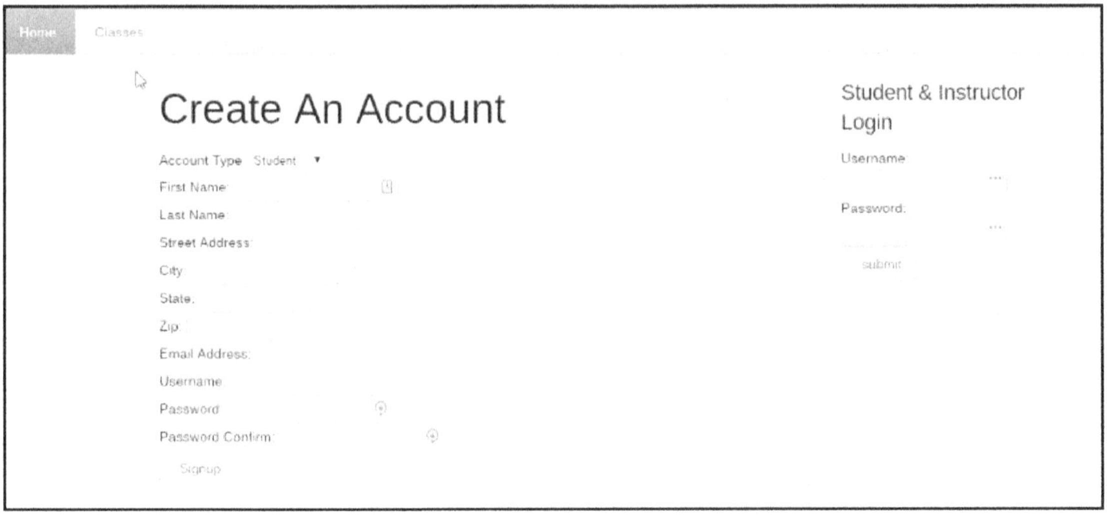

The Create An Account form

It doesn't look too good. I want to push all the inputs over a little bit, so what we can do is go to our public stylesheets and then `style.css` and we'll go all the way to the bottom. Let's just say form label. We want to display as an inline-block and let's set the width to 180:

```
form label{
    display:inline-block;
    width:180px;
}
```

We can close the `style.css` and I just want to put a line break in between each one of the divs in the `register.handlebars`.

Our app page looks a little better:

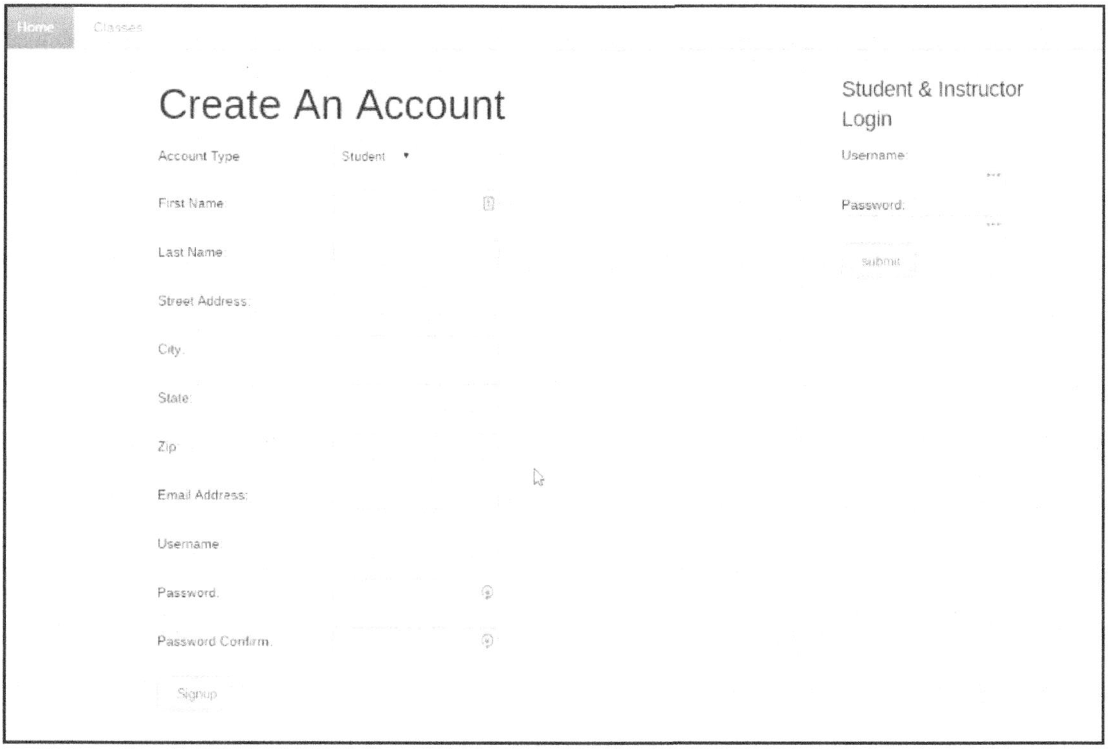

Laid out page

To create the account, first we need to create our student and instructor models. Under models, we'll save this as `student.js` and then we'll save one as `instructor.js`.

Creating the student model

Let's open up `student` and this is all stuff that we've done, so I'm going to just paste the code in. We'll create a schema here:

```
var mongoose = require('mongoose');

// Student Schema
var StudentSchema = mongoose.Schema({
    first_name: {
        type: String
    },
    last_name: {
        type: String
    },
    address: [{
        street_address:{type: String},
        city:{type: String},
        state:{type: String},
        zip:{type: String}
    }],
    username: {
        type: String
    },
    email: {
        type: String
    },
    classes:[{
        class_id:{type: [mongoose.Schema.Types.ObjectId]},
        class_title: {type:String}
    }]

});
```

So students are going to have a first name, last name, address, which is going to be an array, and it's going to have their own certain fields, username, email and then classes that they're registered to. Now what we're doing here is we're saying that the class id is going to map to the `ObjectId`. Then we're going to have a title and then here we're just basically creating the model and setting it to be available outside. Let's save that.

Creating the instructor model

Then we're going to go to the `instructor` model, and we're going to paste that in and the same thing we're doing all the the user information and also the classes that this instructor has created:

```
var mongoose = require('mongoose');

// Instrucor Schema
var InstructorSchema = mongoose.Schema({
    first_name: {
        type: String
    },
    last_name: {
        type: String
    },
    address: [{
        street_address:{type: String},
        city:{type: String},
        state:{type: String},
        zip:{type: String}
    }],
    username: {
        type: String
    },
    email: {
        type: String
    },
    classes:[{
        class_id:{type: [mongoose.Schema.Types.ObjectId]},
        class_title: {type:String}
    }]
});
```

Then we'll make it available here. So we'll save that. Now we're going to close these and we need to go back to our users route, in `routes` we want `users.js`.

Configuring the users.js file

We're going to have to include `passport` first of all, along with `LocalStrategy`:

```
var express = require('express');
var router = express.Router();
var passport = require('passport');
var LocalStrategy = require('passport-local').Strategy;
```

Then we need to include all the different models because we're working with all of them. So I'm going to paste this in and we'll `require User`, `Student`, and `Instructor` models:

```
// Include User Model
var User = require('../models/user');
// Include Student Model
var Student = require('../models/student');
// Include Instructor Model
var Instructor= require('../models/instructor');
```

Then we need to catch the form when it's submitted. We want to create a post request to register, like this:

```
// Register User
router.post('/register', function(req, res, next) {

});
```

Now we'll grab all the values and put them into variables. So, I'm going to paste this in. There are quite a few variable as shown here:

```
// Register User
router.post('/register', function(req, res, next) {
   // Get Form Values
   var first_name = req.body.first_name;
   var last_name = req.body.last_name;
   var street_address = req.body.street_address;
   var city = req.body.city;
   var state = req.body.state;
   var zip = req.body.zip;
   var email = req.body.email;
   var username = req.body.username;
   var password = req.body.password;
   var password2 = req.body.password2;
   var type = req.body.type;
});
```

We're getting the first name, last name, all the address info, email, username, password, and password2 because we're going to validate it and then the type. The next thing we want to do is our form validation. I'm going to paste this stuff in:

```
   // Form Validation
   req.checkBody('first_name', 'First name field is required').notEmpty();
   req.checkBody('last_name', 'Last name field is required').notEmpty();
   req.checkBody('email', 'Email field is required').notEmpty();
   req.checkBody('email', 'Email must be a valid email address').isEmail();
   req.checkBody('username', 'Username field is required').notEmpty();
```

```
    req.checkBody('password', 'Password field is required').notEmpty();
    req.checkBody('password2', 'Passwords do not
      match').equals(req.body.password);
```

These are all required, and then we do our password match here.

After that, we're going to say `errors = req.validationErrors` and then `if(errors)`. If there are errors, then we're going to `res.render`. We want the same form to be rendered, users/register, and then we just want to pass along the errors and check for these errors:

```
errors = req.validationErrors();
if(errors){
   res.render('users/register', {
   errors: errors
   });
   } else {

   }
});
```

So let's go to `views`, `users`, and then our register page, and we're going to go ahead and just paste in the code, checking for errors:

```
<h2>Create An Account</h2>
{{#if errors}}
            {{#each errors}}
                 <div class="notice error"><i class="icon-remove-sign icon-
                   large"></i> {{msg}}
                 <a href="#close" class="icon-remove"></a></div>
            {{/each}}
        {{/if}}
<form id="regForm" method="post" action="/users/register">
```

If there are errors, then we're going to loop through them and we're going to spit out a `div` and notice we have the class of error. So that's going to be kind of like a Bootstrap alert, and then we want to echo out the message. Let's save that and we'll test this out.

Testing the app for the errors

Now, we'll restart the app. Then go to the free signup. If I click on **Sign Up**, we get a bunch of different errors, like this:

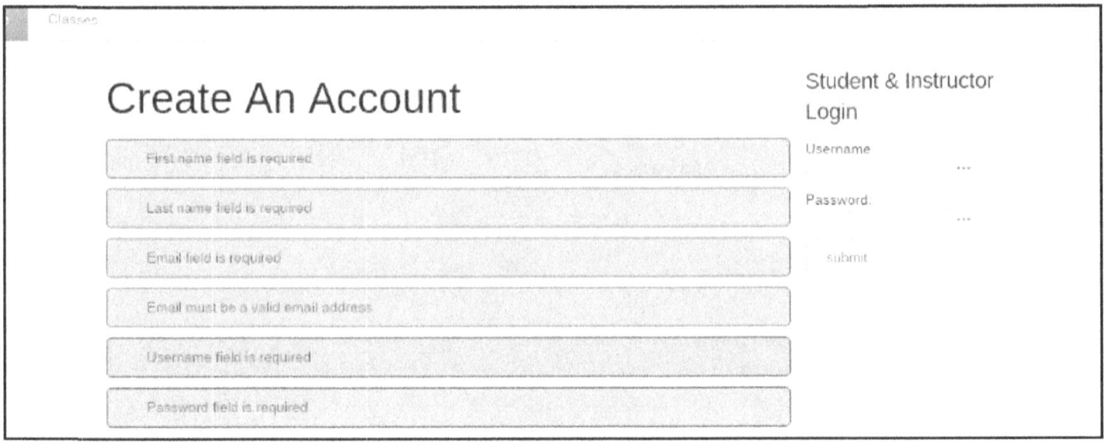

Error page 1

If I put in the first name and click on **Sign Up**, you can see that the error for the first name is not here anymore:

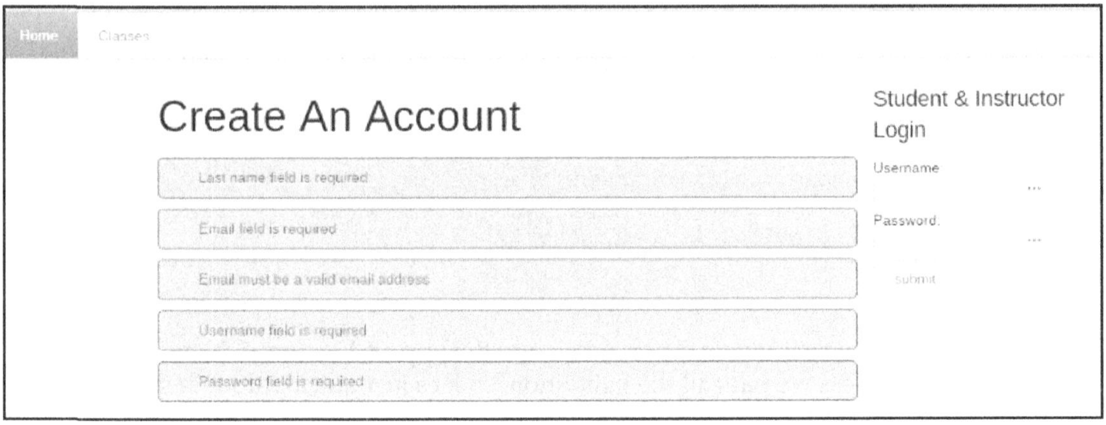

Error page 2

So the form validation is working. Now we want each option to do what it is supposed to do when the form actually passes.

Creating different objects in user.js for user collection

We need to create a couple of different objects in the `else` statement in `users.js`. So first we have the `newUser` object, which is going to go into the user collection:

```
    if(errors){
      res.render('users/register', {
          errors: errors
      });
    } else {
      var newUser = new User({
          email: email,
          username: username,
          password: password,
          type: type

      });
    }
  });
```

Then, we want to test to see if the type is a student or an instructor. For this, I'm going to add an `if` statement, `if(type)`, remember we put the type into a variable, so, we'll `add if(type) == 'student'`. Then, we'll do something else, then we'll do something else; for now let's just `console.log('is instructor');` and then the `if` statement one is `student`:

```
          if(type == 'student'){
              console.log('is student');
          } else {
              console.log('is instructor');
      }
  });
```

Let's give this a shot. We'll save it. Then, let's go to the app and restart it. Now it's not going to let us through unless we pass all the validation, so let's just quickly do that signup, and you can see student printing on the screen:

```
GET /stylesheets/css/img/gray_jean.png 404 6.28 ms - 1236
is student
```

For the instructor signup and we get is instructor:

```
POST /users/...
is instructor
```

Now let's actually just keep this `if else` statement and in the `console` statement, we'll say `Registering Student...` and `Registering Instructor....` like this:

```
        if(type == 'student'){
            console.log('Registering Student...');
        } else {
            console.log('Registering Instructor...');
    }
});
```

Creating the new student object

For the student, we're going to have to create a new `student` object, so I'm going to paste the code in, just like we did with the new user, except we have all the fields that will go in the student collection:

```
if(type == 'student'){
    console.log('Registering Student...');

    var newStudent = new Student({
        first_name: first_name,
        last_name: last_name,
        address: [{
            street_address: street_address,
            city: city,
            state: state,
            zip: zip
        }],
        email: email,
        username:username
});
```

After that, we're going to call `User.saveStudent`:

```
User.saveStudent(newUser, newStudent, function(err, user){
    console.log('Student created');
});
```

We're going to pass in the user and student object, and then just go ahead and create the student.

Creating the new instructor object

I'm going to just copy what we have in the `if` statement, paste that in the `else` statement, and change the `newStudent` to `newInstructor`. Then we change the `Student` object to `Instructor`. We'll also change the `saveStudent` to `saveInstructor`:

```
        } else {
            console.log('Registering Instructor...');
            var newInstructor = new Instructor({
                first_name: first_name,
                last_name: last_name,
                address: [{
                    street_address: street_address,
                    city: city,
                    state: state,
                    zip: zip
                }],
                email: email,
                    username:username
        });
```

Then outside this `if` statement, we'll just do `req.flash ('success'), '');` and then we'll redirect with `res.redirect('/')`:

```
        req.flash('success_msg', 'User Added');

        res.redirect('/');
    }
```

Let's save that and see what happens. Now, what I want to do is go to the `layout.handlebars`, go right above the `body`, and put in `messages`, like this:

```
<div class="grid">
<div class="col_12">
    <div class="col_9">
        {{{messages}}}
        {{{body}}}
    </div>
```

Let's go back to signup and register as an instructor.

Running the app for the instructor

We'll add first name and last name. Then, for **Street Address** I'm just going to put whatever. Then, we'll add **Email**, **Username**, let's just say `Brad`, enter the password, and we sign up:

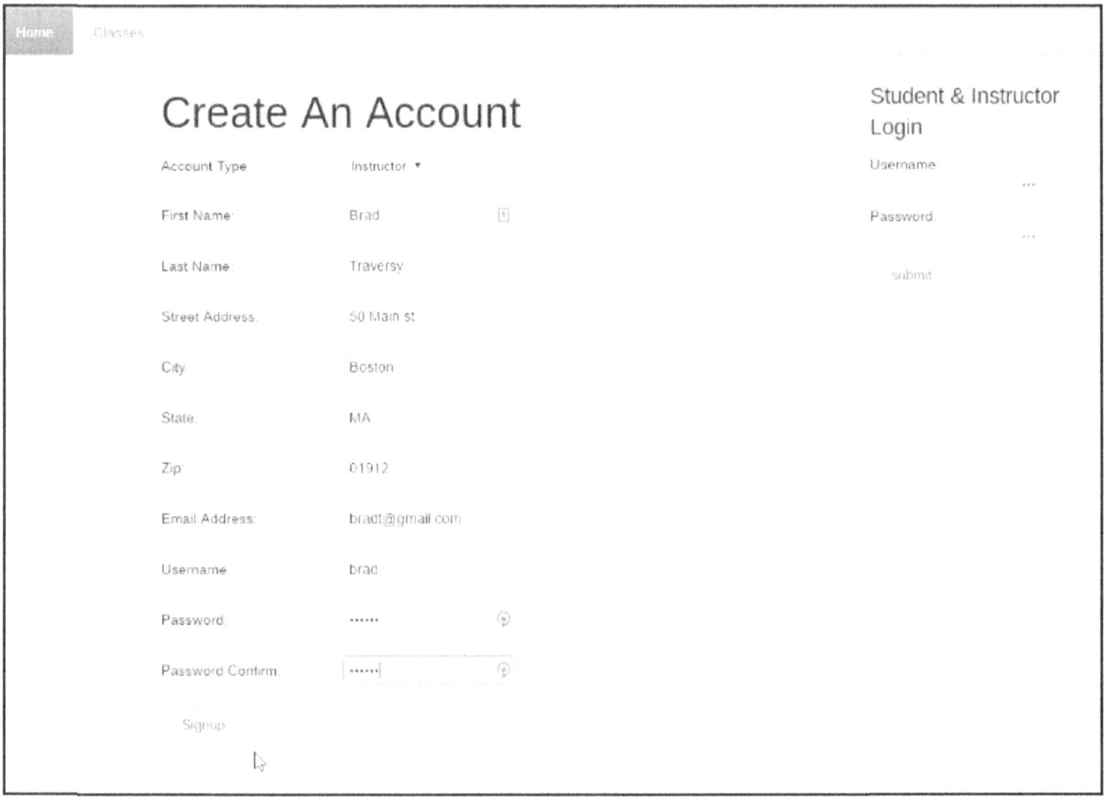

Instructor account page

So something happened:

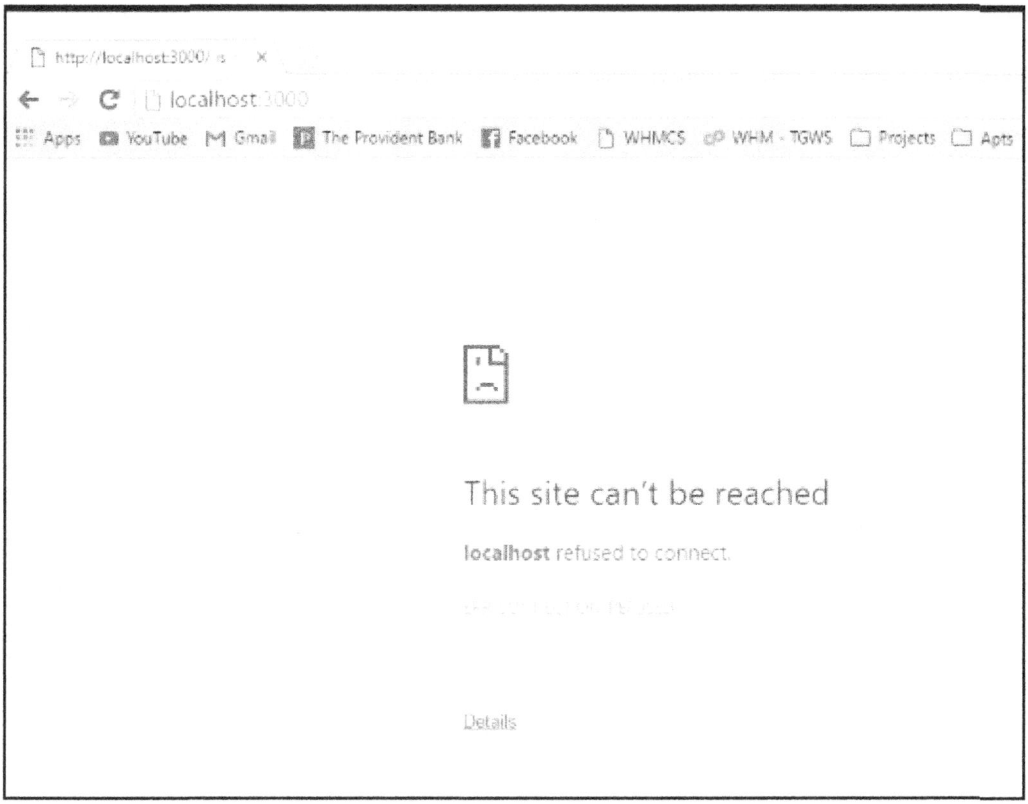

Page load error

Now, if we go and check the errors, we'll see that async is not defined. So we'll go to `app.js` and down at the bottom, below the `db` variable, we'll say `async = require('async')` like this:

```
var db = mongoose.connection;
async = require('async');
```

Let's try running the app again and restart it. Alright, so that redirected us to the eLearn page:

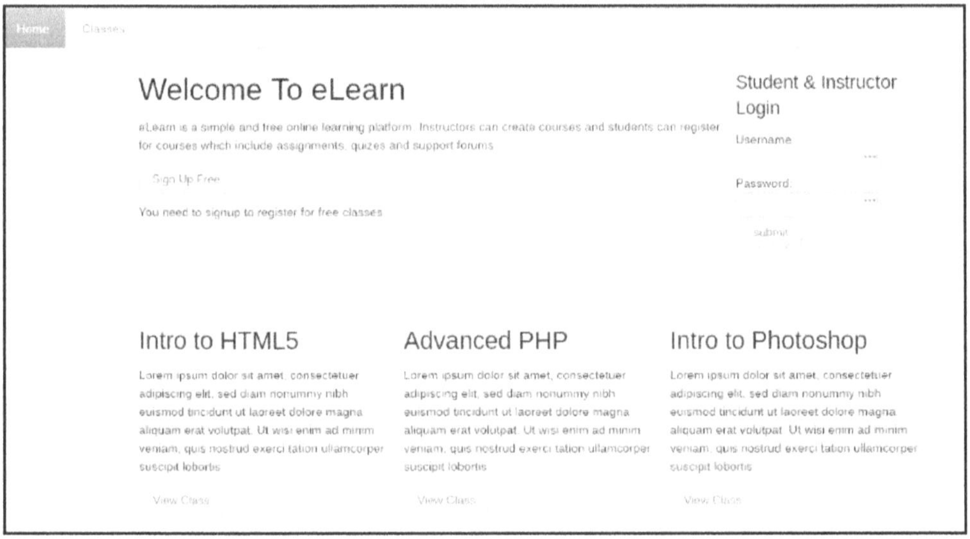

Our updated eLearn page

Now to check on this, I'm going to go back to our database here, so make sure we're in the correct database, that is `elearn`:

```
> db
elearn
>
```

And then we'll say `db.users.find` and there's the user:

User

Now we'll say `db.instructors.find` and that's good:

Output

You'll see we have classes in this case, which is just an empty array, and that is what we want. Also, we should not have any db students:

```
> db.students.find()
>
```

Good, so there are no students. Awesome! So that's working perfectly.

Running the app for the student

Now let's create an account and register as a student. We'll add all the required fields and click on Sign Up:

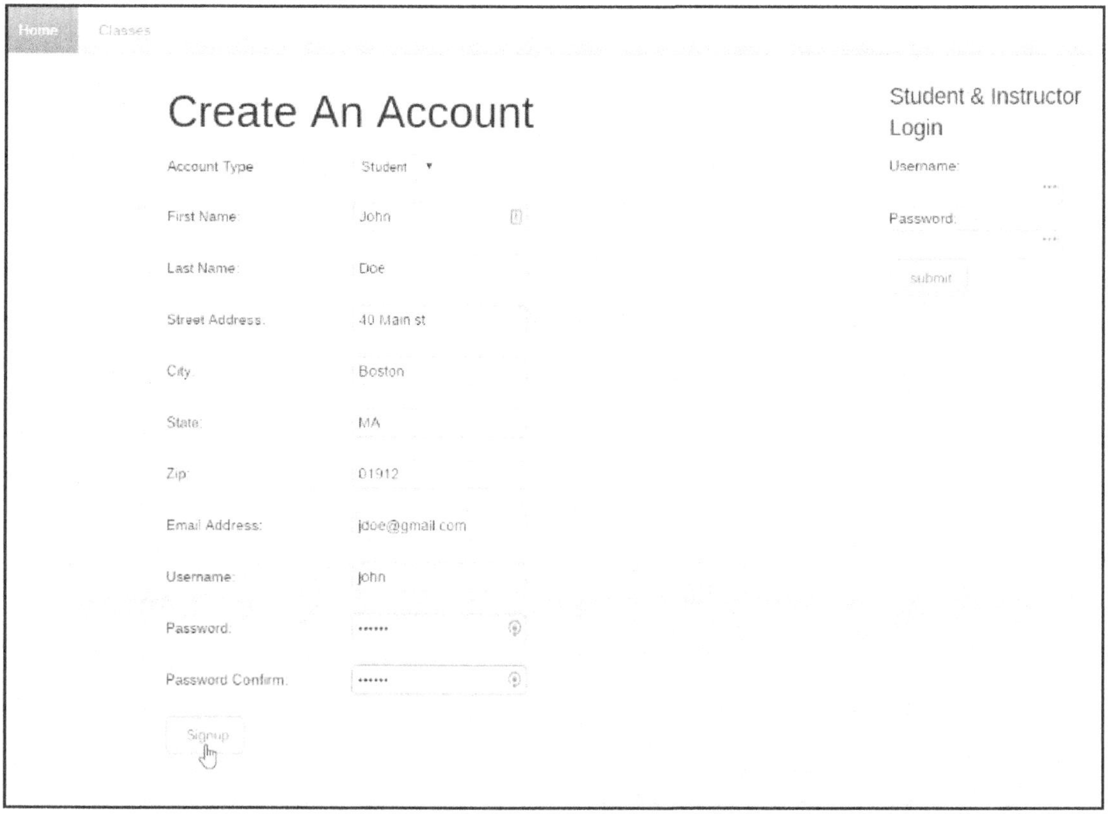

Account details

This will again redirect us to the main eLearn page. Now, if we go to the database and look for the `db.student.find()`, we'll get the object:

```
> db.students.find()
{ "_id" : ObjectId("56eacb212d46654067b1913a"), "first_name" : "John", "last_name" : "Doe", "email" : "jdoe@gmail.com",
"username" : "john", "classes" : [ ], "address" : [ { "street_address" : "40 Main st", "city" : "Boston", "state" : "MA"
, "zip" : "01912", "_id" : ObjectId("56eacb212d46654067b1913b") } ], "__v" : 0 }
```

Output

We'll also see the `db.users.find()`, as shown here:

```
> db.users.find();
{ "_id" : ObjectId("56eacab8?d46654067b19136"), "email" : "brad@techguywebsolutions.com", "username" : "brad", "password
" : "$2a$10$711olGDaXSLt9nLzpYSl3.kB7rUAoW0dwd5g2MC5416CTNRPU2Oly", "type" : "instructor", "__v" : 0 }
{ "_id" : ObjectId("56eacb212d46654067b19139"), "email" : "jdoe@gmail.com", "username" : "john", "password" : "$2a$10$oC
F09V0kuuFdWFLcgyXgg.o.MyduW3Kb6wLHDgrPfPSRbuIFpMkbq", "type" : "student", "__v" : 0 }
>
```

Find user output

So, the registration is done. In the next section, we'll take care of log in.

Logging in users

In this section, we're going to take care of the user login. Before we get to that, I want to address something. When we registered, in the last section, everything went well. The user got inserted, but we didn't get our message here, and we need to fix that. So, we're going to change `app.js` content just a little bit.

We go down to the `app.use` area and we're actually not even going to use `express-messages`. So, we can just get rid of the `res.local.messages`. Then we're going to just create two global variables: one for success messages and one for error messages. So, we're going to say `res.locals.success_msg` is going to equal `req.flash`, and then we are going to pass `success_msg`. We'll do the same thing for the error message. We'll change `success` to `error`. So, that's the `app.js` part:

```
// Global Vars
app.use(function (req, res, next) {
  res.locals.success_msg = req.flash('success_msg');
  res.locals.error_msg = req.flash('error_msg');
  next();
});
```

And remember, you have to have Connect-Flash and you have to have the middle layer initialized right above the app.use function:

```
// Connect-Flash
app.use(flash());
```

Now we go back into our users route in the users.js file, and go to our register post. Down at the bottom of our register post, we put this req.flash line. Now here I think it's just success. So, what you want to do is change it to success_msg:

```
req.flash('success_msg', 'User Added');
```

That should actually work, so let's save that.

Now we want to go to our main layout view, layout.handlebars. Right now, we just have messages and that's not what we want. What we want to do is check for the success message. So, I'm going to grab the code out of registers.handlebars where we have the div tag with the notice error. I'm going to grab the whole thing from the beginning div to the end div:

```
<div class="notice error"><i class="icon-remove-sign icon-large"></i>
{{msg}}
<a href="close" class="icon-remove"></a></div>
```

Before I paste that in, we're going to do an if statement. So, we're going to say if success_msg, and then down we'll end the if, and then in between we'll paste the above code:

```
{{#if success_msg}}
    <div class="notice error"><i class="icon-remove-sign icon-large"></i>
{{msg}}
        <a href="#close" class="icon-remove"></a>
    </div>
{{/if}}
```

Now, what we want to do is change the above msg to success_msg. And since this is a success, we want to change error to success. That'll make it green instead of red. Now if we want an error message, let's copy the above success message and then we're going to test for error_msg. We'll change this. We also want to change the class back to error:

```
{{#if error_msg}}
    <div class="notice error"><i class="icon-remove-sign icon-large"></i>
{{msg}}
        <a href="#close" class="icon-remove"></a>
```

```
        </div>
    {{/if}}
```

So, that'll test for both success and error messages. If there is any, it's going to output it as an alert. So, save that and just to test everything out, just to test the whole message system out, let's go ahead and register another user.

So, we'll say **Tom Williams, 5 barker st.**, **Salem**, **New Hampshire**. **Zip**. What else? **Email address**. **Username, password** And **Signup**.

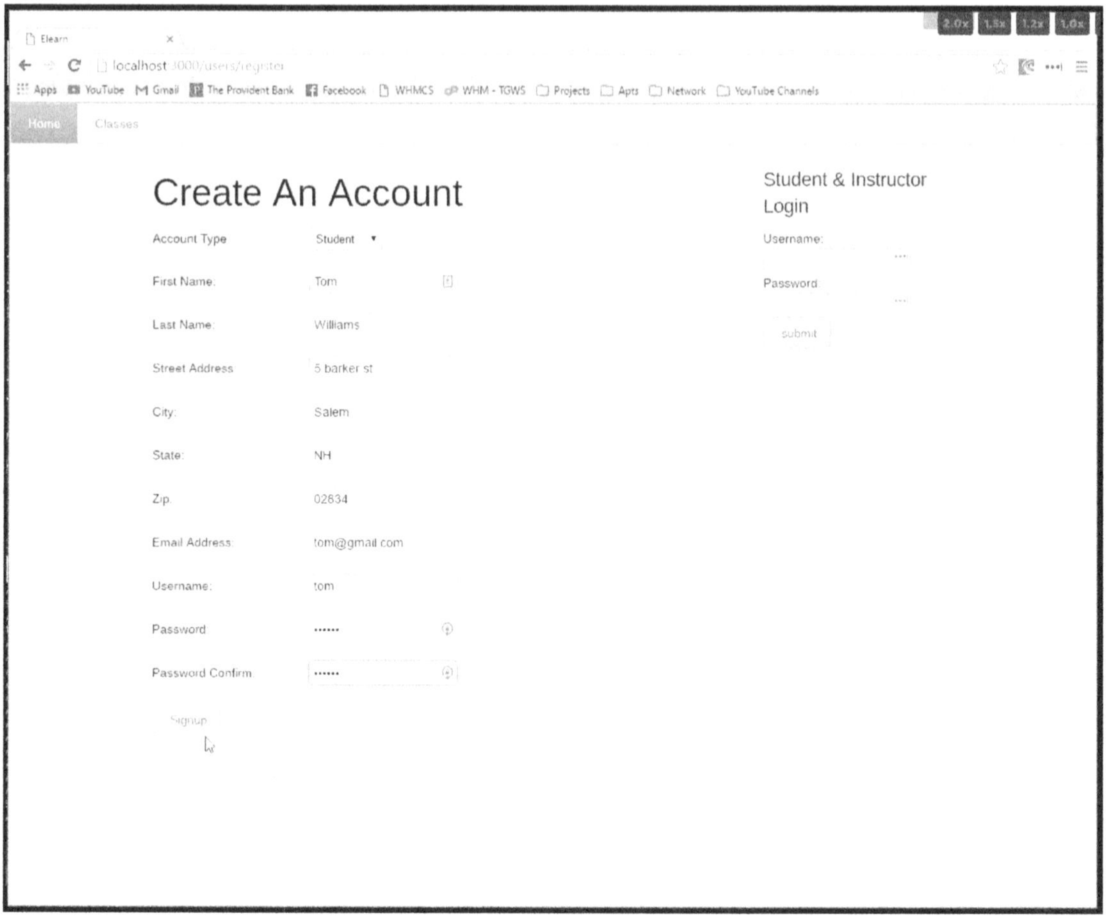

User addition

And there we go, **User Added**.

So, now we can use messages wherever we want. Now let's move on to the login.

Setting up the Login page

If we look at the code for the login, which is in a partial, our form isn't going to have anything. So, we want to say `method= post` and the `action` will be `/users/login`. Let's go to our users route file, we'll go right under the register, and I'm just going to copy the `router.get` method. We'll then say `router.post` and change `/register` to go to `/login`. Let's get rid of the `res.render`. Now, since we're using `passport`, we need to squeeze another parameter in the middle. We're going to say `passport.authenticate` and we want to pass in `failureRedirect`. We want it to go just to the **Home** page because that's where the login is.

Then we also want `failureFlash` and we're going to set that to `true`. Then when we're logged in, we'll set a flash message. So, let's say `req.flash` and pass in a `success_msg`, `You are now logged in`. Then we'll set the user type. We'll say `var usertype = req.user.type`. Then we'll say `res.redirect`. We want this to go to `/` and then we'll concatenate on `usertype`. We then say `usertype` and then we're going to concatenate an `s`. We'll make it plural and then `/classes`. You'll see why in a little bit:

```
router.post('/login', passport.authenticate({failureRedirect:'/',
failureFlash:
  true}), function(req, res, next){
    req.flash('success_msg','You are now logged in');
    var usertype = req.user.type;
res.redirect('/'+usertype+'s/classes');
});
```

Now what we need to do is we need to provide our local strategy. If you did this in the Node project, then this is pretty much the same thing. So, I'm going to paste it in:

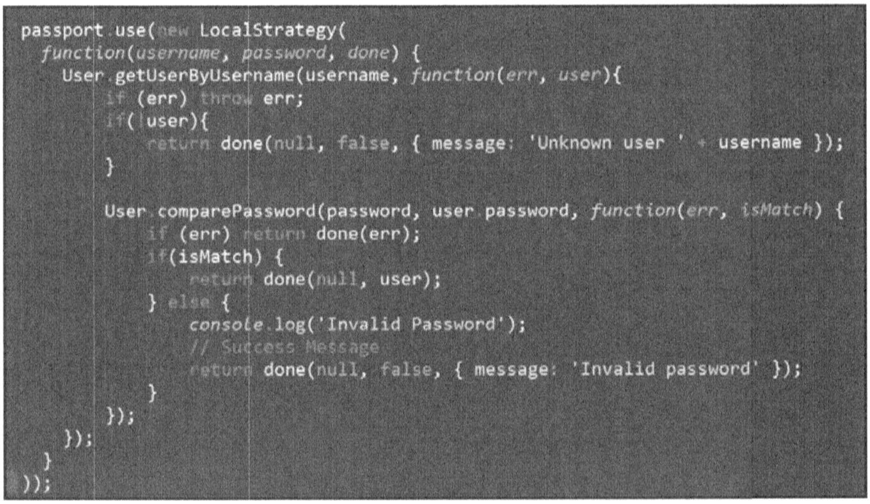

```
passport.use(new LocalStrategy(
  function(username, password, done) {
    User.getUserByUsername(username, function(err, user){
      if (err) throw err;
      if(!user){
        return done(null, false, { message: 'Unknown user ' + username });
      }

      User.comparePassword(password, user.password, function(err, isMatch) {
        if (err) return done(err);
        if(isMatch) {
          return done(null, user);
        } else {
          console.log('Invalid Password');
          // Success Message
          return done(null, false, { message: 'Invalid password' });
        }
      });
    });
  }
));
```

So, we're saying `passport.use` and then we're saying `new LocalStrategy`. In the code, we have a function, which is going to call one of the user model functions, `getUserByUsername`. We're going to pass in the `username` and it's going to let us know. If there's no user, we're going to return `done` with `false` as the second parameter. If there is a user, it'll keep going and we'll call `comparePassword`. We're going to pass in the candidate password and then the actual password and it's going to see if there's a match. If there is, we'll return `done` and pass in `user`. If there's not, then we're going to return `done` and pass in `false`. So, that's essentially what the code does.

Now, another thing we have to include here is the `serializeUser` and `deserializeUser` functions. So, `passport.serializeUser` is just returning `done` with the `id`. For `Deserialize`, we're going to call `getUserById`, which is in the user model. We already created these files `UserById` and `UserByUsername`:

```
passport.serializerUser(function(user, done) {
  done(null, user._id);
});

passport.deserializeUser(function(id, done) {
  User.getUserById(id, function (err,user) {
    done(err, user);
  });
});
```

> Make sure you have passport and local strategy present in the `users.js` file.

I'm pretty sure that's it for the actual login functionality. Let's save that and let's go to our application.

Now, the last thing we need to do with the login is handle the messaging. Because if we try to log in and we don't have the right password or username, we want it to tell us. So, what we need to do is go back to `app.js` and it's going to come at us in `req.flash` I'll copy the `res.locals.error` line and we're just going to take off the `_msg` so it's just error. That'll put whatever comes back to us in a global variable. So, we'll save that:

```
app.use(function (req, res, next) {
  res.locals.success_msg = req.flash('success_msg');
  res.locals.error_msg = req.flash('error_msg');
  res.locals.error = req.flash('error');
  next();
});
```

We'll go over to the layout and then we're going to test for that `error` global variable:

```
{{#if error_msg}}
    <div class="notice error"><i class="icon-remove-sign icon-large"></i>
    {{error_msg}}
        <a href="#close" class="icon-remove"></a>
    </div>
{{/if}}

{{#if error_msg}}
    <div class="notice error"><i class="icon-remove-sign icon-large"></i>
      {{error}}
        <a href="#close" class="icon-remove"></a>
    </div>
{{/if}}
```

We'll save that. Let's restart the server. And now if we go back and I try to just click on **Submit**, we get missing credentials. If I put in my username but the wrong password, we get **invalid password**. Then if we put in the correct info and click on **Submit**, we get **You are now logged in**:

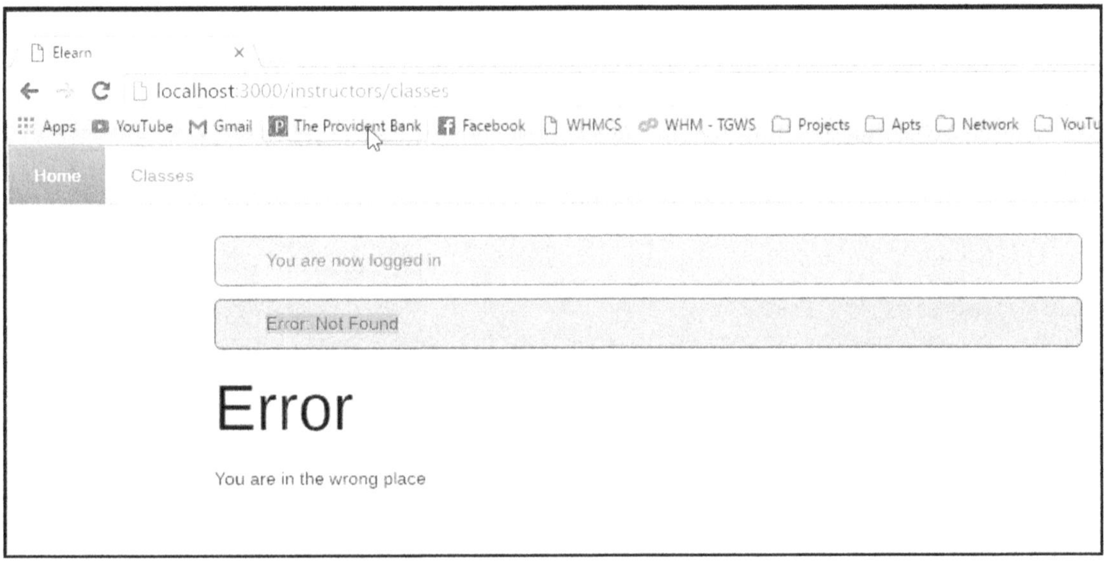

Error page on login

This **Error : Not Found** above has to do with the page not being in the route. You can look up in the `instructors/classes` URL and the reason we go to that error is because back in our `users.js` file and in the `res.redirect` route, we get into the user type. So, Brad is an instructor so he's going to `instructors/classes`. Now what we need to do is create this classes route within instructors and students.

Now, loading that page will take care of it a little bit, but for now, we want to finish our authentication functionality. We need a way to see if we're logged in or not, because now that we're logged in, we don't want the login form to show. We're also going to want other stuff to show or not to show. So, let's go to `app.js` and create something that's going to let us check to see if we're logged in or not. And we want to access this from anywhere, from everywhere. So, we're going to put it in `app.js`:

```
app.get('*', function(req, res, next) {
  // put user into res.locals for easy access from templates
  res.locals.user = req.user || null;
  if(req.user){
     res.locals.type = req.user.type;
  }
  next();
});
```

So, I'll paste it in and say `app.get` and then any page, or any route. So, this is going to work in any route. We're going to create a global variable called user. We're going to set it to `req.user` or `null`, if they're not logged in. If we're logged in, then we're going to get the type and we're going to put it in a global variable called `type`. So, we can check for this user value to see if they're logged in or not. Let's save that. And then we're going to go back to the `login.handlebars`, which is the partial:

```
{{#if user}}
    <h5>Welcome Back {{user.username}}</h5>
    <ul class="alt">
    <li><a href="/{{type}}s/classes">My Classes</a></li>
    <li><a href="/users/logout">Logout</a></li>
    </ul>
{{else}}
<h4>Student & Instructor Login</h4>
    <form method="post" action="/users/login">
        <label> Username: </label>
        <input type="text" name="username">
        <label> Password: </label>
        <input type="password" name="password">
        <input type="submit" class="button" value="Login">
    </form>
{{/if}}
```

The above code is checking for the user variable. So, if user, that means that they're logged in. If they are, then we want to just say **Welcome Back** and then their **username**. Then here we're going to have two links. One goes to `My Classes`. This has that type `s/classes` and then also a logout link. And since we restart the server, we have to log back in:

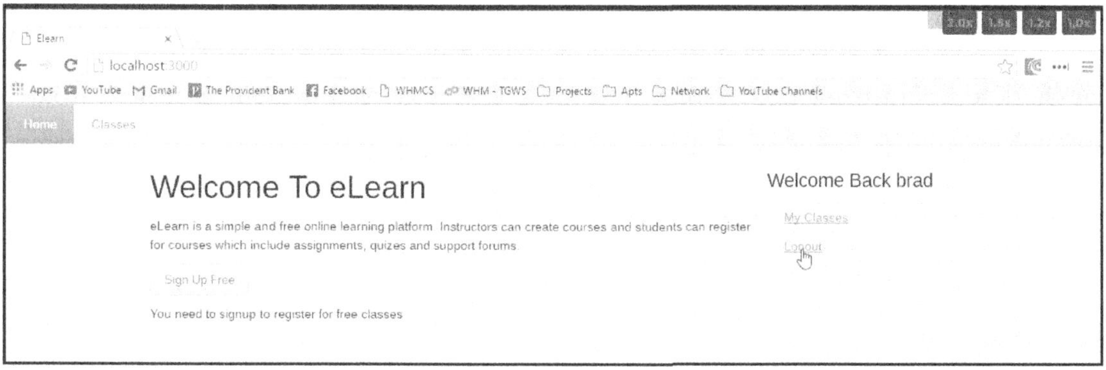

Welcome Back

Now you'll notice we get a **Welcome Back brad** and we have a link to **My Classes** and **Logout**. So, let's do the logout.

If we look at the following code, it's going to `/users/logout`:

```
{{#if user}}
    <h5>Welcome Back {{user.username}}</h5>
    <ul class="alt">
    <li><a href="/{{type}}s/classes">My Classes</a></li>
    <li><a href="/users/logout">Logout</a></li>
    </ul>
{{else}}
<h4>Student & Instructor Login</h4>
    <form method="post" action="/users/login">
        <label> Username: </label>
        <input type="text" name="username">
        <label> Password: </label>
        <input type="password" name="password">
        <input type="submit" class="button" value="Login">
    </form>
{{/if}}
```

So, let's go to our `users.js` route and we're just going to paste that in. We're using a GET request to `/logout` and all we need to do is call this `req.logout` and that'll do everything for us. And then we want to set a message, except this should be `success_msg` and then that should be fine. So, let's save that and we're going to have to restart:

```
// Log User Out
router.get('/logout', function(req, res){
    req.logout();
    //Success Message
    req.flash('success_msg', "You have logged out");
    res.redirect('/');
});
```

Let's go back and log in. Now if I click on **Logout**, it brings us back. It tells us we've logged out.

In the next section, we're going to start to take care of the classes, the students registering classes, and so on and so forth.

The Instructor and Student classes

In the last section, we made it so that we could log in and log out. So, what I want to do now is work on **Classes**; displaying them, displaying the currently logged in users classes, as well as being able to register for them. So, right now I can go to the app and log in by typing my credentials. This page created yet so we're going to get an error:

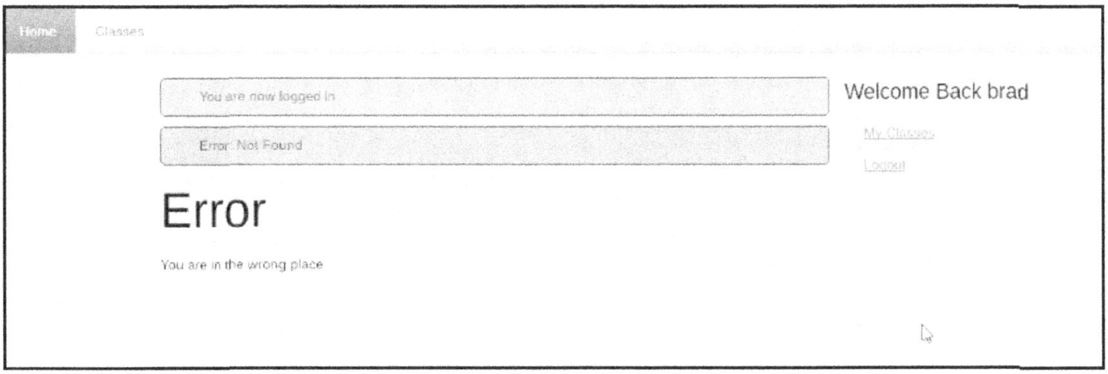

Error page 3

The same is the case if I click on **My Classes**:

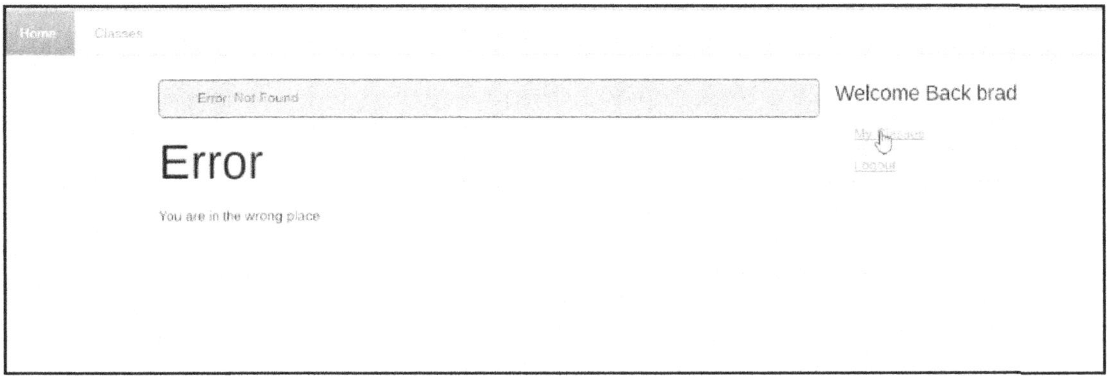

Error page 4

It's going to go to instructors/classes again. So, what we'll do is create two more routes: one for students and another for instructors. But before we do that, let's add it to our `app.js`. We want to go where we have the rest of our routes and just add those in for students and instructors, right below the `classes` route:

```
var classes = require('./routes/classes');
var students = require('./routes/students');
var instructors = require('./routes/instructors');
```

Then we also need to include them in the `app.use` statements.

```
app.use('/students', students);
app.use('/instructors', instructors);
```

Now let's go to routes and create those two new files. One is `students.js` and the other is `instructors.js`.

Configuring the student and instructor route

Let's open up instructors and students files. So, in students, I'm going to paste in code bit by bit. First of all, we'll include `express` and the `Router`. We'll also include all the other models:

```
var express = require('express');
var router = express.Router();

Class = require('../models/class');
Student = require('../models/student');
User = require('../models/user');
```

We're going to handle the students `/classes` route. So, let's add `router.get` and say `/classes` as the first argument and then a `function` as the second argument. In the `function`, we'll add the `req`, `res`, and `next` arguments like this:

```
router.get('/classes', function(req, res, next){

});
```

```
        {{#each student.classes}}
          <tr>
              <td>{{class_id}}</td>
              <td>{{class_title}}</td>
              <td><a href="/classes/{{class_id}}/lessons">View
Lessons</a></td>
          </tr>
        {{/each}}
    </tbody>
</table>
```

Basically, we just have the user's first name, then classes, and then a table with a list of each class and a link to view the lessons. So, let's save that and then we'll go to our instructors one:

```
<h2>{{instructor.first_name}}'s Classes</h2>
<table cellspacing="0" cellpadding="0">
    <thead>
    <tr>
          <th>Class ID</th>
          <th>Class Name</th>
          <th></th>
    </tr>
    </thead>
    <tbody>
        {{#each instructor.classes}}
          <tr>
              <td>{{class_id}}</td>
              <td>{{class_title}}</td>
              <td><a href="/classes/{{class_id}}/lessons">View
Lessons</a></td>
          </tr>
        {{/each}}
    </tbody>
</table>
```

And this is pretty much the same exact thing except for instructors. So, we'll save that.

So, let's see what happens if we reset the server. So, now you see we get **Brad's Classes**:

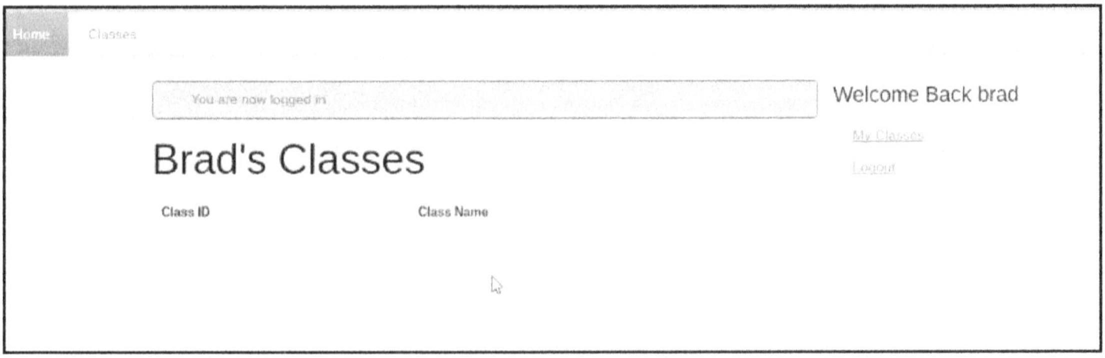

Brad's classes

If I click on **My Classes**, we see almost the same page:

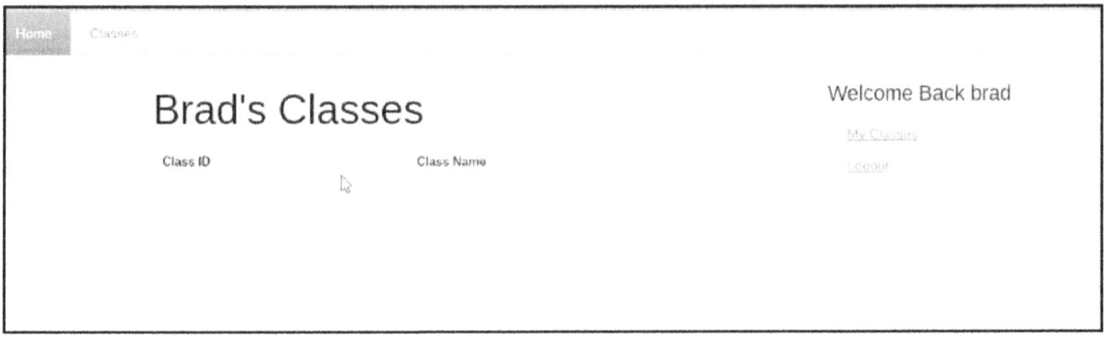

Updated classes page

We obviously don't have any classes yet. We haven't registered for any. Or actually, no, we're instructors. So, instructors are going to register just like students will. So, if we go to register for this class, instructors will be able to do that too:

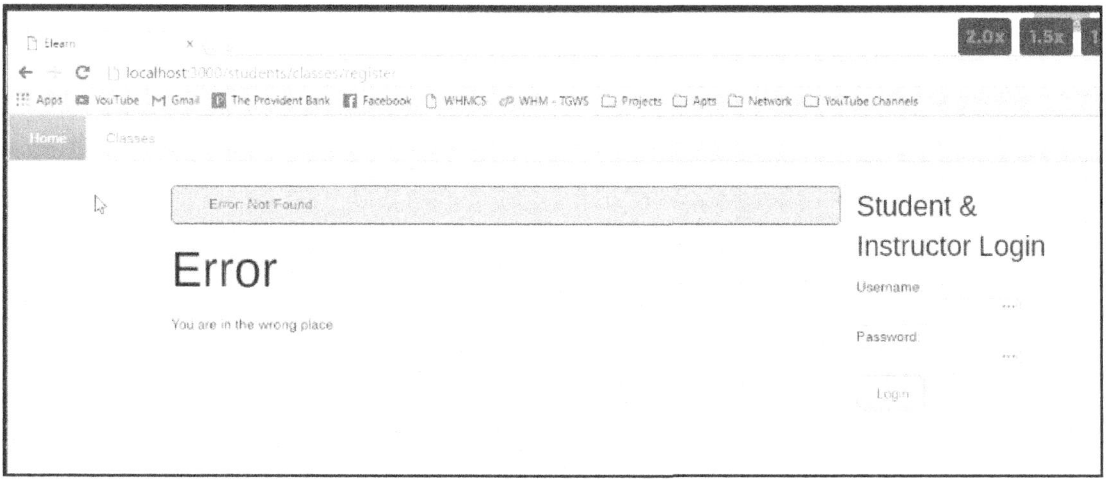

Error page 5

Now, you see when I click on **Register** for this class, it goes to **students/classes/register**. And we want to make that dynamic depending on who's logged in.

Making the link to register dynamic

If we look in `app.js`, in the `app.get` request, we're setting the type as a global variable. So, we can use that in the actual in the link to register. So, let's go to `views | classes` and then the details file. in this file, in the `if` user form, we have `students`. We can get rid of that and put in `{{type}}` and then just an `s`. So, let's save that file.

Now if we go back to the server and we go view class, now you'll see it goes to `instructors/classes/register`:

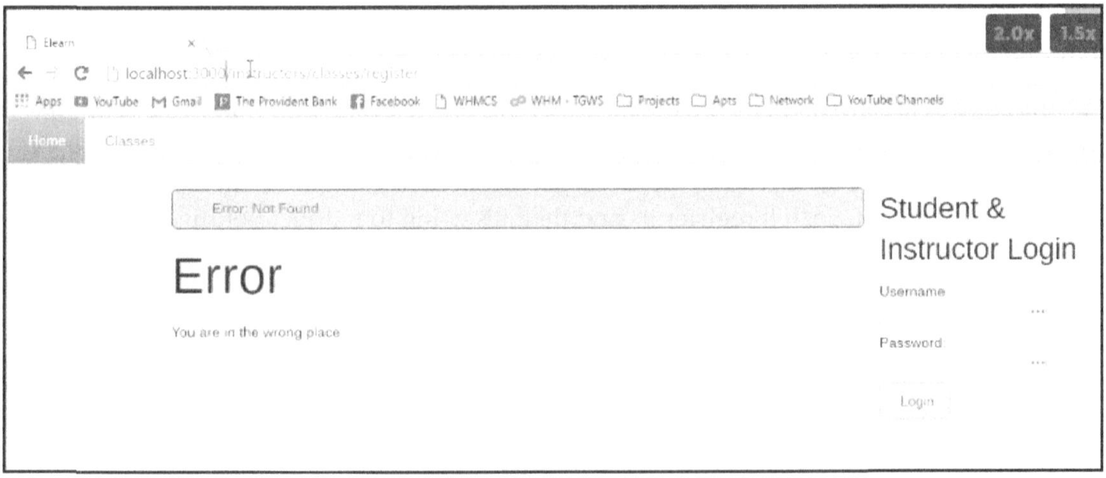

Error page 6

Making the instructor to able to register

Now, let's go back to our `instructors` route. Here, we want the instructor to be able to register. So, I'm going to paste the code in:

```
router.post('/classes/register', function(req, res){
    info = [];
    info['instructor_username'] = req.user.username;
    info['class_id'] = req.body.class_id;
    info['class_title'] = req.body.class_title;

    Instructor.register(info, function(err, instructor){
        if(err) throw err;
        console.log(instructor);
    });

    req.flash('success_msg', 'You are now registered to teach this class');
    res.redirect('/instructors/classes');
});
```

So, what we're doing here is `router.post classes/register`. Then we're going to initialize an array called `info`. In that array we're going to put the username, which comes from the currently logged in user. We're going to put in the class ID, which comes from the form. Now, when I say form I just mean the button, the **Register For The Class** button. This button is actually a form that we created if we look into our details.

So, the class id is actually in the `details.handlebars` as a hidden input, along with the student ID and the class title. So, back to the instructor route. We get the class title in there as well. And then we'll call `instructor.register`. We're going to create this register in the instructor model. So, it'll register us and then it's going to redirect, setting out a flash message. And then we're going to redirect to our **Classes** page, `instructors/classes`. So, let's save that and let's go to the instructor model. Here at the bottom, we're going to paste in this register function like this:

```
// Register Instructor for Class
module.exports.register = function(info, callback) {
    instructor_username = info['instructor_username'];
    class_id = info['class_id'];
    class_title = info['class_title'];

    var query = {username: instructor_username};
    Instructor.findOneAndUpdate(
      query,
      {$push: {"classes": {class_id: class_id, class_title: class_title}}},
      {safe: true, upsert: true},
      callback
    );
}
```

So, what we're doing is, remember, we passed in the info array. We're just setting those values to variables. Then we're creating a query variable. We're going to look for the username of the user that's logged in. Then we're going to call `instructor.findOneAndUpdate`, and we're going to pass in the query here. We're pushing the class that the instructor is registering with. We're pushing it on to the `classes` value inside the instructors collection. So, that's what that does. So, let's save the file and let's see what happens.

Testing the instructor registration to the classes

Let's go to the server and login. Then let's go to **Classes** and register for the class:

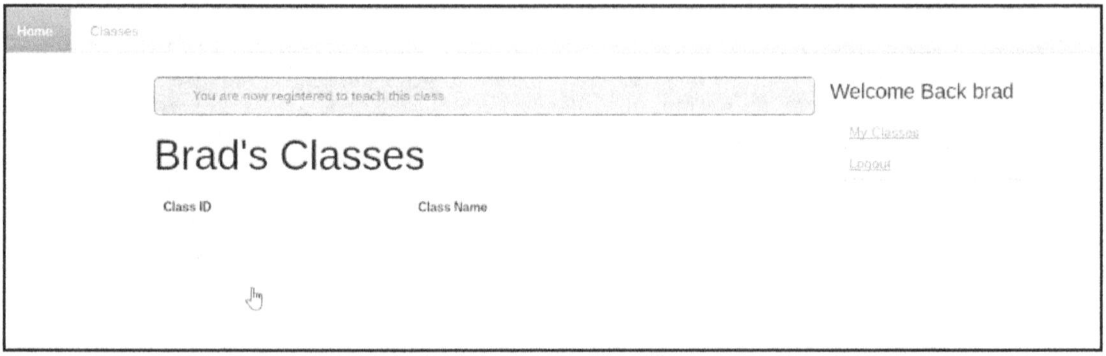

Class registration

You are now registered for this class, to teach this class. It's also showing up in the **My Classes** link:

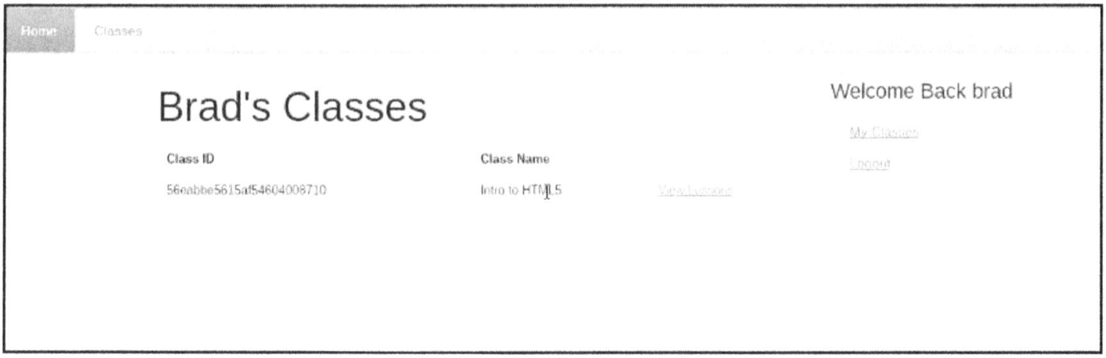

Instructor registration

Now, if we look at the instructor record in the collection, we should have a `classes` value. So, let's just check that out. So, let's say `db.instructors.find.pretty`:

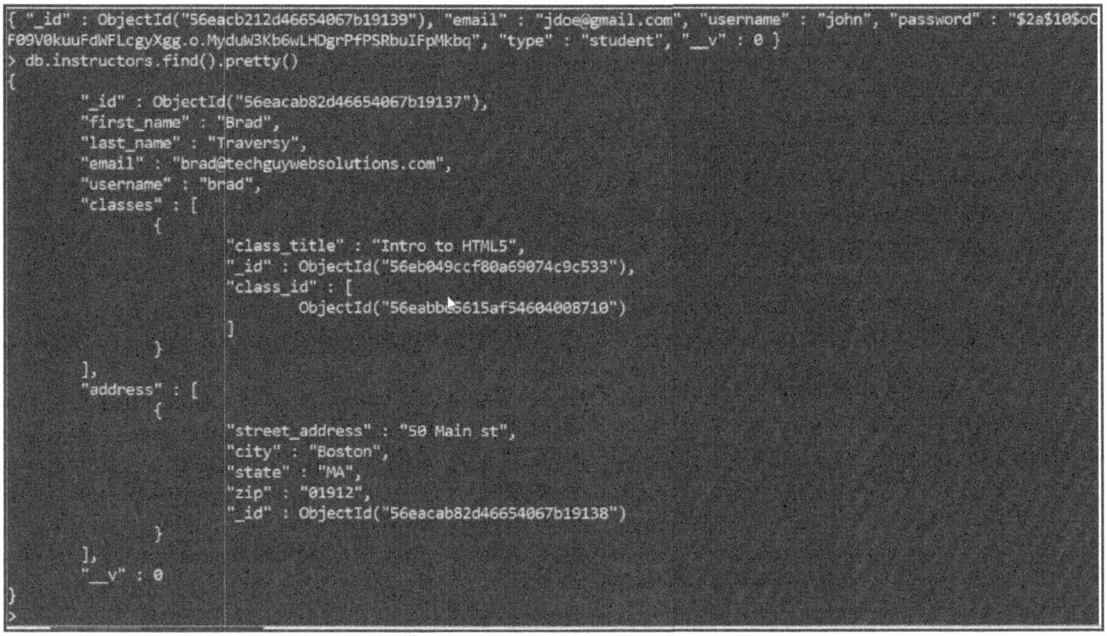

Code for the user

And then let's look at Brad. Now, you can see in `classes` I now have `Intro to HTML5`. This has an `id`, it also has the `class id`.

In the next section, we'll do this same kind of thing for students so that students can register for classes.

Class lessons – the last section

We're almost there! There's one last piece of functionality that we need and that is for lessons. We need to be able to add them and show them. I'm logged in the classes as an instructor:

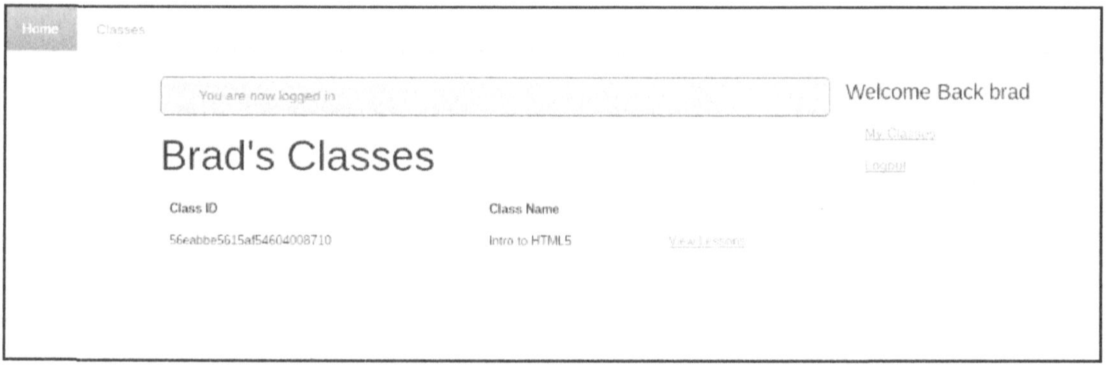

The classes page for Brad

Now, I want to have a link beside **View Lesson** page that says **Add Lesson**.

Setting up the Add Lesson link in the Classes tab

We're going to go to the views | instructors | classes.handlebars file. In this file, I'm going to create another <th> in the <thead>, and then we want another td <tbody>, like this:

```
<thead>
     <tr>
       <th>Class ID</th>
       <th>Class Name</th>
       <th></th>
       <th></th>
     </tr>
</thead>
<tbody>
     {{#each instructor.classes}}
     <tr>
        <td>{{class_id}}</td>
        <td>{{class_title}}</td>
        <td><a href="/classes/{{class_id}}/lessons">View Lessons</a></td>
        <td><a href="/classes/{{class_id}}/lessons">View Lessons</a></td>
     </tr>
     {{/each}}
</tbody>
```

Now, in `<td>`, I am going to add `Add Lesson` in place of `View Lesson`. We want this to go is `instructors/classes/` and then whatever the `id` and `/lessons/new`:

```
<td><a href="/instructors/classes/{{class_id}}/lessons/new">Add
Lesson</a></td>
```

Let's save this file, and reload the app:

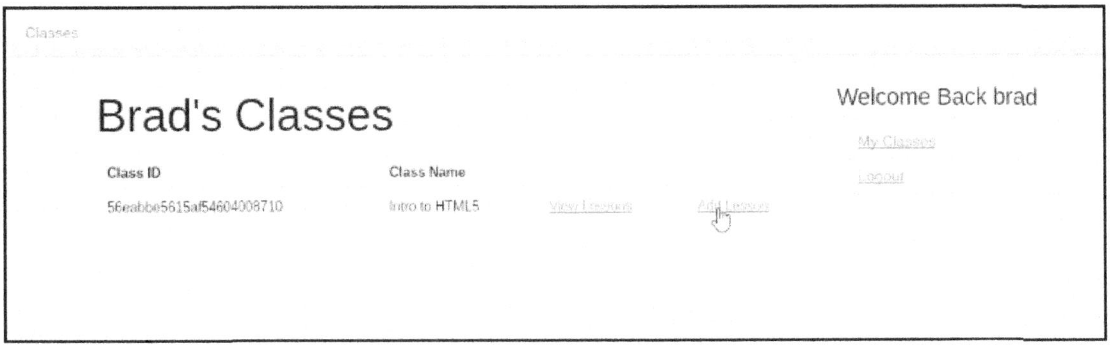

The Add Lesson option

So, now we have **Add Lesson**. If I click on the **Add Lesson** link, we're going to get an error:

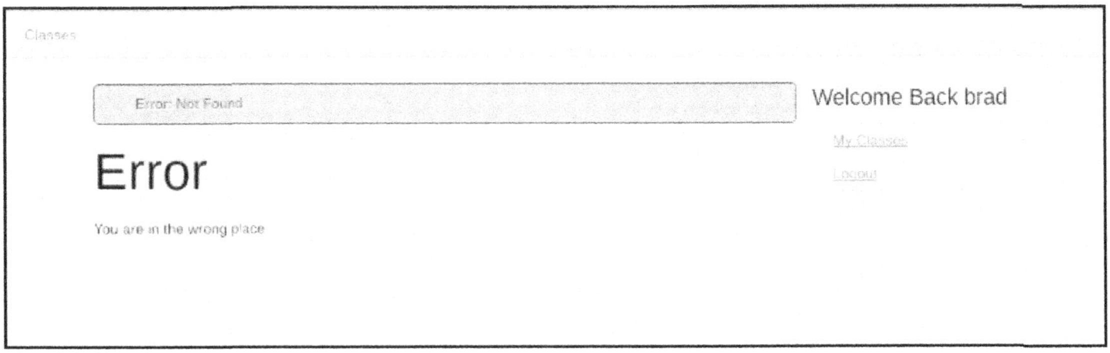

Error page 7

We need to create this route.

Creating route for the Add Lesson link

We'll go into routes and then `instructors.js`. And we'll go down to the bottom in this file. I'm actually just going to copy the `router.get` function and add it to the bottom:

```
router.get('/classes', function(req, res, next){
   Instructor.getInstructorByUsername(req.user.username, function(err,
     instructor){
       if(err) throw err;
       res.render('instructors/classes', {instructor: instructor});
   });
});
```

This will be `router.get`. Then, we go to `classes/:id/lessons/new`. Now, we're going to do is render the form, so I'm going to the `render` statement and then cut the remaining lines like this:

```
router.get('/classes/:id/lessons/new', function(req, res, next){
    res.render('instructors/classes', {instructor: instructor});
});
```

And we want to render `instructors/newlesson` and we can say `class_id` and set that to request, `req.params.id` like this:

```
router.get('/classes/:id/lessons/new', function(req, res, next){
    res.render('instructors/newlesson', {class_id:req.params.id});
});
```

Let's save the file.

Configuring newlesson.handlebars

We'll go to the `views`, `instructors`, and then we want to create a new file. We'll save it as `newlesson.handlebars`. And let's copy the register form and paste it in this file:

```
<h2>Create An Account</h2>
{{#if errors}}
            {{#each errors}}
                <div class="notice error"><i class="icon-remove-sign icon-
large">
                  </i> {{msg}}
             <a href="#close" class="icon-remove"></a></div>
             {{/each}}
     {{/if}}
<form id="regForm" method="post" action="/users/register">
     <div>
```

```
            <label>Account Type</label>
            <select name="type">
                <option value="student">Student</option>
                <option value="instructor">Instructor</option>
            </select>
        </div>
        <br />
        <div>
```

It's going to be a lot smaller, so let's edit it. This will just say `Add Lesson` as the heading. We'll just get rid of error code snippet. Then the action is going to be `/instructors/classes/{{class_id}}/lessons/new`:

```
<h2>Add Lesson</h2>
<form id="regForm" method="post"
  action="/instructors/classes/{{class_id}}/lessons/new">
```

Noe, let's get rid of `Account Type` div and we're going to have `Lesson Number` in the first name div. So, that's going to be a text field and then the name is going to be `lesson_number` and you can get rid of the value:

```
<h2>Add Lesson</h2>
<form id="regForm" method="post"
  action="/instructors/classes/{{class_id}}/lessons/new">
    <div>
        <label>Lesson Number: </label>
        <input type="text name="lesson_number">
    <div><br />
```

Then what I'm going to do is just copy that and then get rid of the rest of the divs in the file except for the **Submit** button at the bottom. Then we'll just paste in the code two more times. The second div will be the `Lesson Title`, and the last one will be the `Lesson Body`. In the `Lesson Body`, we're going to be have text area so we can get rid of the input type:

```
<h2>Add Lesson</h2>
<form id="regForm" method="post"
  action="/instructors/classes/{{class_id}}/lessons/new">
    <div>
        <label>Lesson Number: </label>
        <input type="text name="lesson_number">
    <div><br />
    <div>
        <label>Lesson Number: </label>
        <input type="text name="lesson_number">
    <div><br />
    <div>
```

```
        <label>Lesson Number: </label>
        <input type="text name="lesson_number">
    <div><br />
    <div>
        <label>Lesson Number: </label>
        <input type="text name="lesson_number">
    <div><br />
    <div>
        <input type="submit" value="Add Lesson">
    </div>
```

So, let's save that and make sure that the form actually shows up. So, we'll go to the app and we want to be logged in as an instructor and click on the **Add Lesson** button:

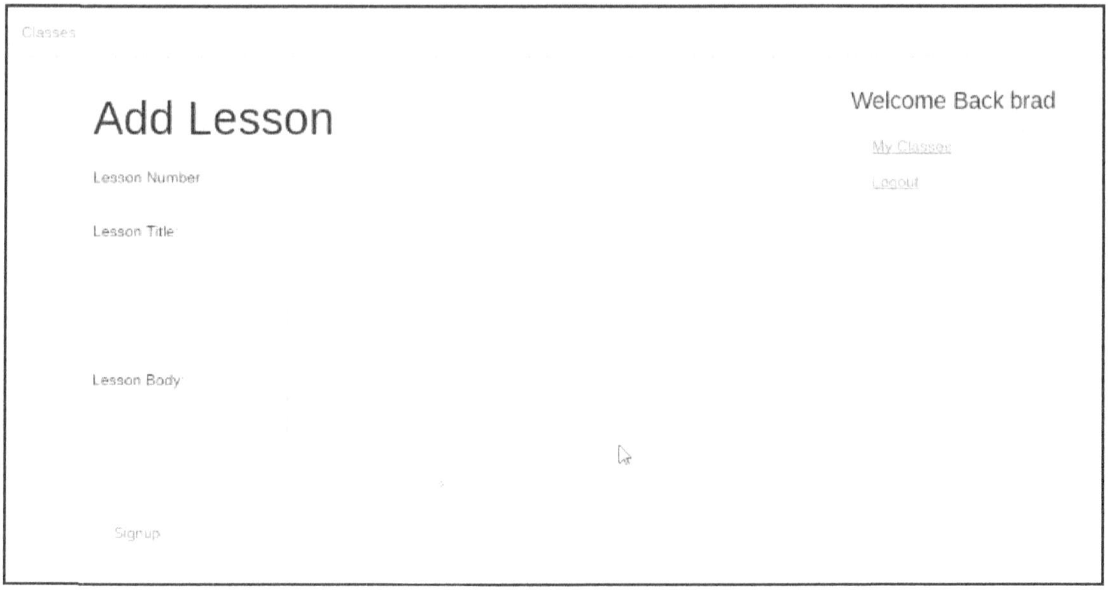

The Add Lesson form

So, there's our form. Now, if we look at the source code, you can see the `id` is in the action:

```
            <h2>Add Lesson</h2>
    <form id="regForm" method="post"
      action="/instructors/class/56eabbe5616af54604008710/lessons/new">
```

So, now what we need to do is we need to take care of the POST request.

Configuring the POST request

We'll go back to routes, `instructors.js`. Then, we'll go down the GET request and I'm just going to copy and paste this. This is going to be a POST request:

```
router.get('/classes/:id/lessons/new', function(req, res, next){
    res.render('instructors/newlesson', {class_id:req.params.id});
});

router.get('/classes/:id/lessons/new', function(req, res, next){
    res.render('instructors/newlesson', {class_id:req.params.id});
});
```

Then, that's going to go to `classes/:id/lessons/new` and we can get rid of the `render` statement:

```
router.get('/classes/:id/lessons/new', function(req, res, next){

});
```

Now, we want to get our values.

Getting our Add Lesson values

We'll create a variable called `class_id` and I'm going to set that to `req.params.id`, which gets it from the URL. Then we'll have `lesson_number`, and that's going to come from the form. So, `req.body.lesson_number`. Then we need the title in the body as well, which comes from the form. This will be body:

```
//Get Values
var class_id = req.params.id;
var lesson_number = req.body.lesson_number;
var lesson_title = req.body.lesson_title;
var lesson_body = req.body.lesson_body;
```

What we want to do is let's put these all inside an array. So, we'll create an array called info. And then we'll just go for multiple infos. We'll just do that like this:

```
router.post('classes/:id/lesson/new', function(req, res, next){
  //Get Values
  var info = [];
  info['class_id'] = req.params.id;
  info['lesson_number'] = req.body.lesson_number;
  info['class_id'] = req.body.lesson_title;
  info['class_id'] = req.body.lesson_body;
});
```

Then we're going to have a Class function in the model called addLesson. That'll take in the info array and then a callback function. The function is going to take an error and lesson. Inside the function, we'll just say console.log and say Lesson Added:

```
Class.addLesson(info, function(err, Lesson){
    console.log('Lesson Added..');
});
```

Then we'll do a success message. So, we'll say req.flash('success_msg'), and the actual message will say Lesson Added. We'll then just redirect to instructors/classes:

```
    req.flash('success_msg','Lesson Added');
    res.redirect('/instructor/classes');
});
```

So, now let's go to our class.js to add the Add Lesson model.

Configuring the class model for the Add Lesson model

In class.js, we're going to go to down at the bottom and put in the Add Lesson model. It's going to take in the info array and then a callback. Then, we're going to say class_id = info ['class_id']:

```
// Add Lesson
module.exports.addLesson = function(info, callback){
   class_id = info['class_id'];
```

Now, we are going to copy the `class_id` and paste it three times. The second one's going to be `lesson_number`. Then, we'll have `lesson_title` and `lesson_body`:

```
// Add Lesson
module.exports.addLesson = function(info, callback){
   class_id = info['class_id'];
   lesson_number = info['lesson_number'];
   lesson_title = info['lesson_title'];
   lesson_body = info['lesson_body'];
}
```

Under the `lesson_body`, we're going to add `Class.findByIdAndUpdate`. We're going to pass in a couple of things. We need the `class_id` first, and then we're going to `$push:{"lessons":{lesson_number}}`. Next, we'll have `lesson_title` and `lesson_body`. We'll put a comma at the end, like this:

```
Class.findByIdAndUpdate(
    class_id
    {$push:{"lessons":{lesson_number: lesson_number, lesson_title:

    );
```

Now, we're going to open up another set of curly braces. This is just options where we're going to say `safe: true` and `upsert: true`. So, if it's not there, it's going to insert anyway. Then we just say `callback` and we should be good:

```
  Class.findByIdAndUpdate(
    class_id
    {$push:{"lessons":{lesson_number: lesson_number, lesson_title:
      lesson_title,...}
    {safe: true, upsert: true},
    callback
    );
}
```

Changing the button text

So, now let's change the text of the button to `Add Lesson`. So, we'll go to the `newlesson.handlebars` file and in the `button` div, we'll say `Add Lesson` in place of `sign up`:

```
<div>
    <input type="submit" value="Add Lesson">
</div>
```

Now, we can restart our app and see **Add Lesson**.

Testing the Add Lesson link

We'll go to the app and log in as an instructor. Then, click on the **Add Lesson** link and add the credentials. We'll add the **Lesson Number** as `1`, **Lesson Title** as `Sample Lesson`, and **Lesson Body** as `This is sample lesson 1`. We'll then click on the **Add Lesson** button:

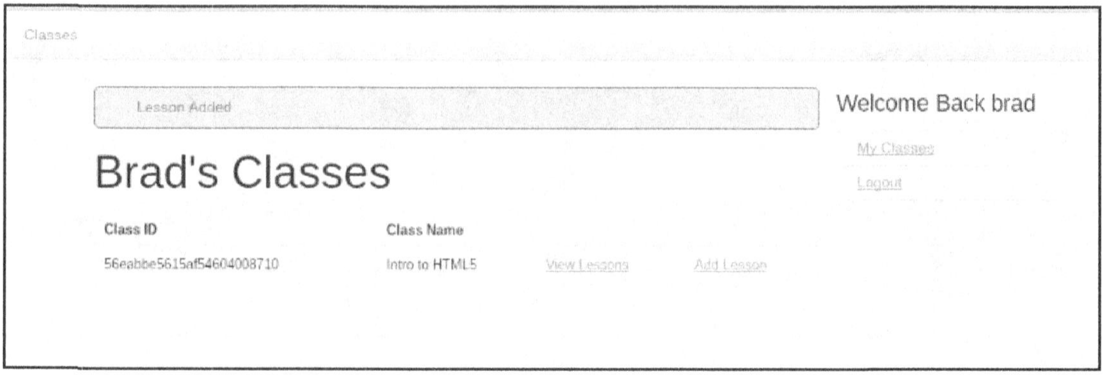

The final page

There we go, the lesson has been added. Let's check it out in the Mongo shell.

Checking the added lesson in the Mongo shell

So, we'll go inside the Mongo shell and let's make sure we're using the right database:

```
> use elearn
switched to db elearn
```

Then, I'm going to add `db.classes.find.pretty`:

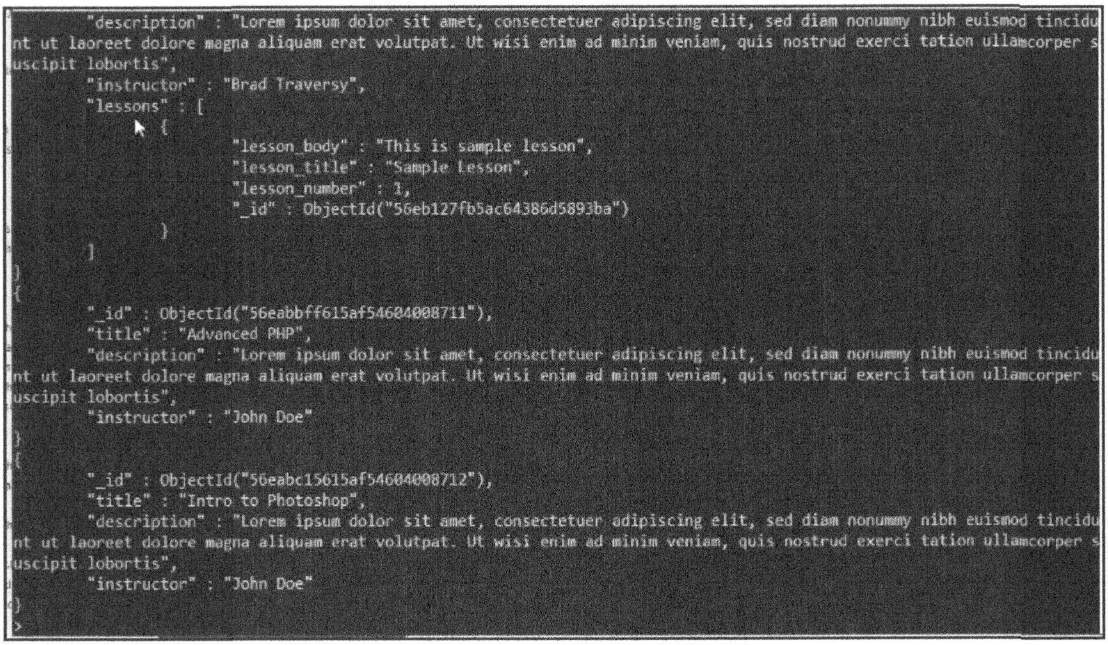

```
        "description" : "Lorem ipsum dolor sit amet, consectetuer adipiscing elit, sed diam nonummy nibh euismod tincidu
nt ut laoreet dolore magna aliquam erat volutpat. Ut wisi enim ad minim veniam, quis nostrud exerci tation ullamcorper s
uscipit lobortis",
        "instructor" : "Brad Traversy",
        "lessons" : [
                {
                        "lesson_body" : "This is sample lesson",
                        "lesson_title" : "Sample Lesson",
                        "lesson_number" : 1,
                        "_id" : ObjectId("56eb127fb5ac64386d5893ba")
                }
        ]
}
{
        "_id" : ObjectId("56eabbff615af54604008711"),
        "title" : "Advanced PHP",
        "description" : "Lorem ipsum dolor sit amet, consectetuer adipiscing elit, sed diam nonummy nibh euismod tincidu
nt ut laoreet dolore magna aliquam erat volutpat. Ut wisi enim ad minim veniam, quis nostrud exerci tation ullamcorper s
uscipit lobortis",
        "instructor" : "John Doe"
}
{
        "_id" : ObjectId("56eabc15615af54604008712"),
        "title" : "Intro to Photoshop",
        "description" : "Lorem ipsum dolor sit amet, consectetuer adipiscing elit, sed diam nonummy nibh euismod tincidu
nt ut laoreet dolore magna aliquam erat volutpat. Ut wisi enim ad minim veniam, quis nostrud exerci tation ullamcorper s
uscipit lobortis",
        "instructor" : "John Doe"
}
>
```

User code

There it is - we can see the lesson, lesson body, title, number, and also has an object ID. The next thing, and the last thing, we need to do is make it so that we can view the lessons in the class.

Setting up the View Lesson link in the class

To do that, let's go to the `classes` route, `classes.js`. I'm going to just paste in the `Get Lesson` model just below the `Class Details` model. It's very similar to the details:

```
router.get('/:id/lessons', function(req, res, next) {
   Class.getClassById([req.params.id],function(err, classname){
     if(err) throw err;
     res.render('classes/lessons', { class: classname });
   });
});
```

It's going to be / whatever and `id /lessons`. Then, we're going to get the class by its ID and we'll render `classes/lessons`. We'll save that.

Configuring the lessons.handlebars file

In our `views | classes` folder, we're going to create a new file called `lessons.handlebars`. I'm going to just paste the code in:

```
<h2>{{class.title}}'s Classes</h2>
<table cellspacing="0" cellpadding="0">
   <thead>
       <tr>
         <th>Lesson Number</th>
         <th>Lesson Title</th>
         <th></th>
       </tr>
   </thead>
   <tbody>
       {{#each class.lessons}}
       <tr>
         <td>{{lesson_number}}</td>
         <td>{{lesson_title}}</td>
         <td><a
href="/classes/{{../class._id}}/lessons/{{lesson_number}}">View
           Lesson</a></td>
       </tr>
       {{/each}}
   </tbody>
</table>
```

It's just going to be a table. We have the `class.title` at the top of the code here. Then, we're going to have the lesson number and title. We're going to loop through `class.lessons`. And then we're going to have a link that goes to classes, and finally the `{{../class._id}} /lessons/{{lesson_number}}`. Let's save that. Restart our app and then log in as the instructor. We'll go to the **View Lessons** button and click it:

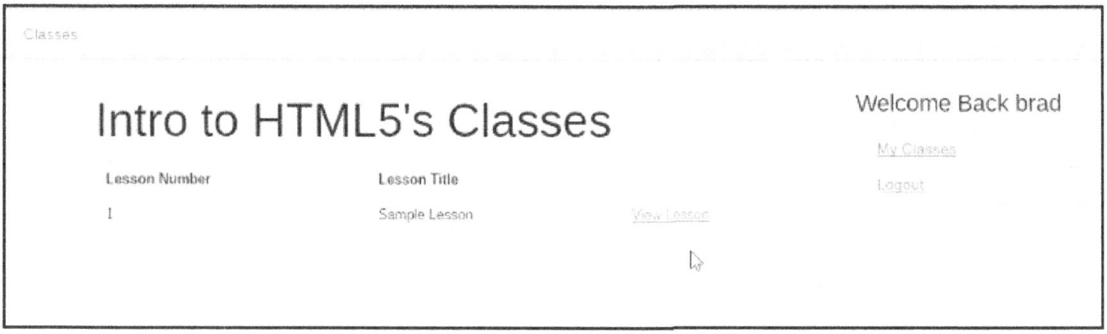

The Sample Lesson page

There it is - **Sample Lesson**.

Now, if I click on the **View Lesson** in **Classes**, we're going to get an error because we need to add that:

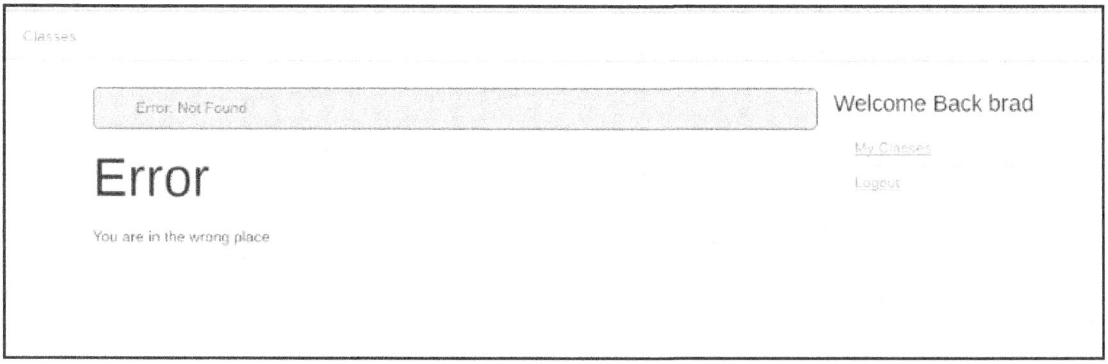

Error page 8

Viewing lessons in the class

For this, we'll go back to the `classes` route and let's paste the `Get Lesson` code:

```
//Get Lesson
router.get('/:id/lessons/:less_id', function(req, res, next) {
    Class.getClassById([req.params.id],function(err,classname){
      var lesson;
      if(err) throw err;
      for(i=0;i<classname.lessons.length;i++){
        if(classname.lessons[i].lesson_number == req.parms.lesson_id)}
          lesson = classname.lessons[i];
        }
      }
      res.render('classes/lesson', { class: classname,lesson: lesson });
    });
});
```

So, we're going to go to the `id/lessons` and then the `lesson_id`. Then we'll say `Class.getClassById`, we're getting the class. And then we'll loop through the lessons and we're going to get the specific lesson that matches the ID. Actually, you know what, this should actually be `req.params.lesson_id`. Let's save that. Then create, inside the `classes` (`views` folder), we're going to create a file and save it as `lesson.handlebars`. I'm going to paste the code in:

```
<a href=/classes/{{class._id}}/lessons">Back to lessons</a>
<h2>{{lesson.lesson_title}}</h2>
{{lesson.lesson_body}}
```

We have a back button to go back to the lessons, an `h2` with the title, and the body. So, let's save that and let's try it out. Now, let's log in to our app as an instructor. Go to **View Lessons** and click on the **View Lesson** button:

A working Sample Lesson page

There we go! Now we can read the lesson and we can also go back. So, that's it for this project. I think we have our application.

Summary

In this chapter, we created a project based on e-learning system. We worked on HTML Kickstart setup, setting an HTML-based web application.

We configured the layout of the app and then added classes to it. Then we looked into fetching classes, setting up partials, creating class models, and setting up routes for the models. Then, we looked into the user registration page. We created the user model and configured the user for both students and instructor. After this, we worked on the logging in system, setting up the log in page for users. Then, we looked into creating classes for both instructors and students. We also looked into configuring the student and instructor routes. Last, we set the **Classes** page and the detailed page for the classes. We set the **View Lesson** and **Add Lesson** links and routes for the classes.

Now, obviously this wouldn't be a production app for an online learning system, but it is a start and we have a nice ability to scale this application.

With this in place, we have now reached the end of the book. I hope you enjoyed the different projects we discussed throughout the book.

Other Books You May Enjoy

If you enjoyed this book, you may be interested in these other books by Packt:

The Node Craftsman Book
Manuel Kiessling

ISBN: 978-1-78712-814-9

- How to connect to databases like MongoDB and MySQL from your Node.js application
- How to unit tests and end-to-end tests for your code
- When and how to leverage migrations for setting up a continuous deployment workflow
- Detailed insight into how the Node Package Manager, NPM works
- How object-orientation actually works in JavaScript
- Ways to keep your code fast and efficient using asynchronous and non-blocking operations
- How to use and create event emitters
- How to use REST frameworks to write full-fledged web applications
- How to integrate Node.js with Angular

Web Development with MongoDB and Node - Third Edition
Bruno Joseph D'mello, Mithun Satheesh, Jason Krol

ISBN: 978-1-78839-508-3

- Work with Node.js building blocks
- Write and configure a web server using Node.js powered by the Express.js framework
- Build dynamic HTML pages using the Handlebars template engine
- Persist application data using MongoDB and Mongoose ODM
- Test your code using automated testing tools such as the Mocha framework
- Automate test cases using Gulp
- Reduce your web development time by integrating third-party tools for web interaction.
- Deploy a development environment to the cloud using services such as Heroku, Amazon Web Services, and Microsoft Azure
- Explore single-page application frameworks to take your web applications to the next level

Leave a review - let other readers know what you think

Please share your thoughts on this book with others by leaving a review on the site that you bought it from. If you purchased the book from Amazon, please leave us an honest review on this book's Amazon page. This is vital so that other potential readers can see and use your unbiased opinion to make purchasing decisions, we can understand what our customers think about our products, and our authors can see your feedback on the title that they have worked with Packt to create. It will only take a few minutes of your time, but is valuable to other potential customers, our authors, and Packt. Thank you!

Index

V

W

Made in the USA
Las Vegas, NV
18 September 2025

28162811R00171